PRAISE FOR *ICE W*

In 1972, Canada's birthright, our gam   o
inspection. Gary J. Smith wasn't asked   ey
series between the Soviet Union and Canada, he was asked to referee
something greater. He was handed the Cold War. He was twenty-
eight years old. With suspicion aroused on both sides, each whisper,
every secret, kept feeding into the question, "What is hidden in their
hearts?" Such a question bears discussion and publicity. One man had
the necessary skill set. Finally, the incredible story of the glue in '72. The
Ice War Diplomat.
Ron MacLean, host of Hockey Night in Canada

The Canada–Russia series was a truly iconic moment in hockey history.
But it was more—a fascinating time in Canadian diplomatic history.
Gary J. Smith was a young, Russian-speaking diplomat with a ringside
seat. His story is engaging and brilliantly told.
Bob Rae, ambassador and permanent representative of Canada
to the United Nations

They were just supposed to be exhibition games, but the Summit Series
turned out to be bigger than the Stanley Cup, and a highlight of my
career. I enjoyed Gary J. Smith's accurate and excellent account. *Ice War
Diplomat* brought back very good memories.
Frank Mahovlich, hockey legend and Team Canada member

This vivid portrayal of the characters who made the Series happen is a
thriller! Smith renders brilliantly the diplomatic skills and sharp minds
displayed off-ice and in backrooms that delivered not just a unique
hockey faceoff, but a top foreign policy priority of the Canadian PM. His
own backstory as a first-time diplomat makes us relate even more.
Anne Leahy, ambassador of Canada to Russia 1996-1999;
first secretary, Canadian embassy to the USSR 1980-1982

An engaging and colourful eye-witness account, *Ice War Diplomat* greatly increases our understanding of the 1972 Summit Series between Canada and the USSR, by focusing on its little-known but crucial diplomatic history. As Smith shows, staging the series that led to one of Canada's most iconic sports moments was first and foremost a triumph of diplomacy.

Brendan Kelly, head of the Historical Section at Global Affairs Canada and author of *The Good Fight: Marcel Cadieux and Canadian Diplomacy*, winner of the 2020 J.W. Dafoe Book Prize

Gary J. Smith is the original hockey "Insider." His *Ice War Diplomat* contains sweeping history, sharp analysis, keen new insights, and enough action to stand with the best of hockey books. But there is so much more here, much of it unknown before. He was the only one with full access to both sides during the 1972 Summit Series and, believe me, the games off the ice were often as challenging as those on. It's like seeing the series all over again, with sharper eyes.

Roy MacGregor, author, columnist and feature writer for *The Globe & Mail*

Canadian hockey fans remember Canada's breathtakingly narrow victory in the fabled 1972 eight-game series against the Soviet Union. Now Gary J. Smith, then a young diplomat at the Canadian embassy in Moscow assigned to be Canada's link with the Soviet hockey authorities, offers the definitive account of how the Soviets viewed, prepared for and reacted to the series. A tour de force of reportage, history and analysis.

Jeffrey Simpson, national columnist for *The Globe & Mail*

A rare side of the Summit Series story that has never been told. A fascinating insider view of how Canada/Russia '72 was much bigger than the game.

James Duthie, TSN hockey host

ICE WAR DIPLOMAT

HOCKEY MEETS COLD WAR POLITICS AT THE 1972 SUMMIT SERIES

GARY J. SMITH

Douglas & McIntyre

For Laurielle (RIP), who shared the
extraordinary diplomatic adventure

DOUGLAS AND MCINTYRE (2013) LTD.
P.O. Box 219, Madeira Park, BC, VON 2HO
www.douglas-mcintyre.com

Cover photograph credit to Frank Lennon /
        Library and Archives Canada / e008440339
All photographs from the collection of Gary J. Smith, unless otherwise noted.
Edited by Derek Fairbridge
Indexed by Chandan Singh
Cover design by Anna Comfort O'Keeffe
Text design by Libris Simas Ferraz / Onça Publishing
Printed and bound in Canada

DOUGLAS AND MCINTYRE acknowledges the support of the Canada Council for the
Arts, the Government of Canada, and the Province of British Columbia through the
BC Arts Council.

LIBRARY AND ARCHIVES CANADA CATALOGUING IN PUBLICATION
Title: Ice war diplomat : hockey meets cold war politics at the 1972 Summit Series /
        Gary J. Smith.
Names: Smith, Gary J. (Diplomat), author.
Description: Includes index.
Identifiers: Canadiana (print) 2022015063x | Canadiana (ebook) 20220152640 |
        ISBN 9781771623179 (softcover) | ISBN 9781771623186 (EPUB)
Subjects: LCSH: Smith, Gary J. (Diplomat)—Anecdotes. | CSH: Canada-U.S.S.R.
        Hockey Series, 1972.
Classification: LCC GV847.7 .S65 2022 | DDC 796.962/66—dc23

TABLE OF CONTENTS

FACEOFF

THE FIRST CANADIANS known to lace up their skates and play ice hockey in Russia, it would seem, were rugged soldiers of the Canadian Siberian Expeditionary Force during the winter of 1918–19, in Vladivostok, in the Russian Far East, abutting the Pacific Ocean. The Force, comprised of close to forty-two hundred men and one nursing matron marshalled from across Canada, had set sail from Vancouver and Victoria and arrived in the Siberian city just as the First World War was winding down in Western Europe. Britain had asked the Canadian government for their deployment as part of a large international force led by a Japanese lieutenant-general. Their mission was to stabilize the Eastern front against Germany after the new Bolshevik government led by Vladimir Lenin had signed an agreement to withdraw Russia from the war. There were hundreds of thousands of tons of residual military equipment to protect; a desire to ensure Germany did not gain access to Siberia's vast natural resources; and the goal of keeping the Pacific port open to those fleeing the revolution and the fighting. Most of Siberia was still under the control of anti-Bolshevik "White" forces.

The Canadian commander, Major General James H. Elmsley, had a problem on his hands. He had dispatched the North West Mounted Police squadron westward by rail to Omsk, over four thousand kilometres away, but the bulk of his troops were assigned to protection and police duties in the Vladivostok area, far from any fighting. They were bored and there had been a mutiny in Victoria by some of the Quebec members of one battalion of the Canadian Rifles, who felt this was an ill-advised operation for King and Country and who had no desire to be involved in a revolutionary civil war in a distant land.

Reportedly, Elmsley's main concern was with a "Battalion of Death."[1] Not members of the Red Army but blond, red-cheeked wayward women shipped east by the Bolsheviks from Moscow and Petrograd (St. Petersburg) with the promise of fast and easy money. The general knew social diseases could run rampant through his troops and so ordered extra drills and exercise and stepped-up sports, prime among them being ice-hockey. Rinks were created, and with the assistance of YMCA personnel assigned to his staff, enough hockey equipment was brought over from Canada to suit up an eight-team league. It was said to have been one of the "main amusements" right through the winter.[2]

By the time the snow and ice melted in the spring of 1919, the Canadians were on their way back home. The hockey in Siberia had been a one-season wonder.[3]

Russia's winter sport at that time and for decades before and after was not Canadian ice-hockey, but bandy, unofficially known as "Russian hockey," a somewhat similar game but played on a frozen soccer-sized field, with eight to eleven players per side on the ice at any one time, short side borders of fifteen centimetres (often made of snow), and shorter sticks which had a bow. A ball was used instead of a puck. The goalie, occupying a wider net,[4] wore two catching gloves but had no stick. The emphasis was on skating, passing and use of the feet as well as the stick in moving the ball forward. The Russians played the game in Scandinavia in the initial years of the twentieth century, but it never became an Olympic sport, which hindered its development internationally.

Canadian "ice-hockey" was introduced into the Soviet Union in the 1930s by visiting Canadians, but the first organized game in the USSR would have to wait to be played until 1946, in the recovery period after the Second World War. When the Soviet Union first entered international play at the World Championships in Stockholm, Sweden, in 1954, it did so with a bang—immediately displacing Canada and winning the gold medal.

This intersection of hockey and history, hockey and diplomacy, is the subject of this book—as well as the personal story of a young Canadian diplomat and his wife on their first assignment, who found themselves in Cold War Moscow, landing in the middle of a historic sporting event between the best hockey players of both countries. To help navigate the road, a few cursory passages, however inadequate, might be in order about the history and interaction of our two protagonists: Russia and Canada.

Russia is the only country which makes Canada appear small. It is almost twice as wide as Canada, with a land mass 1.7 times larger, encompassing eleven time zones compared to six in Canada. Russia's estimated population in 1970, at one hundred and thirty million, was over six times greater than Canada's at that time, and if one counted the USSR as a whole, then there were ten Soviet citizens for every Canadian.[5] If Canada is said by some historians to suffer from too much geography and not enough history, then Russia suffers from too much of both.

Russian history is long, tumultuous and bloody, featuring multiple foreign invasions over the centuries from the east, south, west and north—the Mongul descendants of Genghis Khan, Tamerlane, the Teutonic Knights, the Turks, the Swedes, the Poles, the Grand French Army under Napoleon, the German army led by Kaiser Wilhelm II in the First World War, and then the Germans again in a more vicious and destructive assault under Adolf Hitler in the Second World War.

Russia and the Soviet Union, of course, were not always on the receiving end of death and mayhem. Both state incarnations[6] were expansionist powers in their own right. The Finns, Poles, Estonians, Latvians, Lithuanians, Ukrainians, and peoples in other parts of Eastern Europe, the Caucasus and Central Asia knew this only too well, as did those further afield.

There were home-grown purges, pogroms, starvation policies associated with agricultural collectivization, a mass of wealth and privilege at the top and little to nothing at the bottom. Political repression of one kind or another, aided by various secret police agencies, has been passed down through the ages from the tsars to the communists and beyond. Evocative names like Ivan the Terrible, Peter the Great, and Catherine the Great are sprinkled throughout their history, with periods of darkness and of light.

The Russian people, perhaps quite naturally given the circumstances, are ever suspicious of both foreigners and of each other. Russia is a patient and long-suffering nation. At the same time, Russians will often describe themselves in terms of "exceptionalism"—a people neither from the East nor the West—using the same self-proclaimed language as Americans. There is much talk of the distinctive "Russian soul," plus references to the "Third Rome," the doctrine dating from the fifteenth and sixteenth centuries that Russia and Moscow replaced Rome and Byzantium Rome (Constantinople) as the ultimate centre of true Christianity and of the Roman Empire. They are a patriotic people, as Stalin found during the darkest days of the Second World War when he appealed to them to rise up, not to save communism, but to protect "Mother Russia." (It is to this sense of Russian nationalism that President Vladimir Putin appeals today.)

Winston Churchill famously defined Russia in a 1939 BBC broadcast as "a riddle, wrapped in a mystery inside an enigma." For him, Russia was an inscrutable and menacing land, but his quotation continued, "perhaps there is a key: Russian national interest." Churchill was trying to come to grips with why Stalin would sign a Non-Aggression Pact with his archenemy, Hitler, and agree to divide up Poland between them. Over eighty years after Churchill's remarks, a Russian social activist would tell a *New York Times* correspondent: "We have our own historical path, and you will never understand it. You will never understand Russia because it still doesn't understand itself."[7]

Canada's history has followed a much different and decidedly more straightforward course. There is the indelible stain of colonialization and the treatment of Indigenous peoples, but since then foreign invasions of this nation have been relatively minor compared to those over the course of Russian history.

The personal experiences of the average Canadian and Russian citizen are worlds apart. Is it even possible for Canadians to put themselves "in their shoes" in an attempt to understand their thinking? Maybe not—but a diplomat has to try. To at least know some dates, places and the course of events. To try to understand. To avoid putting everything into black and white.

Studying the history of Canada's relations with Russia is akin to a roller-coaster ride: up, down and sideways, sometimes with long climbs or precipitous drops. Despite the similarities of being continental in size and located across the North Pole from one another, there was little direct engagement during Canada's early years after Confederation in 1867.

Many thousands of Doukhobors settled in remote areas of Western Canada after being expelled from Russia in the late 1890s due to their opposition to both tsarist government policies and the Russian Orthodox Church. Their memories of Russia were uniformly negative. Canadian business interests, on the other hand, saw great commercial opportunities in the Russian Far East and in the vast lands of Siberia. The Canadian timber industry brought technology to Russian forests, and there was a brisk market for Canadian farm implements manufactured by Massey Ferguson/Massey Harris, whose tractors and harvesters were regarded as the best in the world at the time. Canadian Pacific, another global company, sold rolling stock and rails and provided technical and managerial advisors to aid in the construction of the Trans-Siberian Railway, leading to its completion in 1905.

The first class of Canadian trade commissioners, hired entirely from university graduates in 1914, included Leolyn "Dana" Wilgress, from McGill, on the strong recommendation of a famous Professor Stephen Leacock.[8] Trade commissioners were billed as "Canada's Salesmen to the World," and Wilgress's first foreign assignment, in 1916, was not to the USA, the UK or France, but to Omsk, the leading city in Siberia. He moved on to Vladivostok in 1918 and became an integral part of a Canadian Economic Commission intended to spur further commercial opportunities in the region. He was there when the Canadian military arrived, but after their departure, business began to dry up.

While Canadian soldiers and the Bolshevik Red Army did not draw blood in the Vladivostok area, there was fatal combat in northwestern Russia, near Archangel and Murmansk. British and Canadian units initially had been deployed there to prevent the Germans from taking over the two strategic naval ports. When the Bolsheviks demanded that all foreign soldiers leave, there were several clashes, resulting in deaths on both sides, including Canadian members of the Artillery regiment. They remain buried in the area.

In the 1920s, twenty thousand or so Mennonites left Russia for Canada. In the same time frame, and into the 1930s, there was support in Canada, largely among the working class and intellectual circles, for the ideals of communism. This was particularly the case during the Great Depression, which caused concern in Canadian business and political circles.

In September of 1939, when Canada entered the Second World War with Britain and France against Germany, the Allies were not at war with the Soviet Union, despite Stalin's pact with Hitler. The situation changed dramatically on June 22, 1941, when Hitler invaded the USSR. Suddenly we were allies with the communists and with Stalin.

Not long passed before Canadian military units stationed in Britain came to the rescue of Soviet mine workers stranded on a remote Norwegian island. Nine hundred miners were evacuated to Murmansk, and in return the Canadians picked up French soldiers who had been interned in the USSR. Large shipments of Canadian goods and military equipment began to flow across the Atlantic and Pacific to Murmansk and Vladivostok, two Russian cities which Canada knew well by this time.

Dana Wilgress, who had risen through the ranks to occupy the senior-most position in the Department of Industry and Commerce, re-emerged on the scene in early 1942 when Canada established formal diplomatic relations with the Soviet Union. He was named Canada's first

Head of Mission with the rank of minister and then, in 1944, became Canada's first ambassador.

Before departing for the temporary wartime capital of Kuibyshev, on the southern Volga River, Wilgress found himself in Toronto attending what would become the first of many large-scale public rallies in Canada to collect and send food, clothing and medical equipment via the Red Cross to our new ally. Many leading elements of Canadian society and industry became heavily involved, including Prime Minister Mackenzie King. The brutal battle at Stalingrad and ultimate Soviet victory over the German Sixth Army had captured the imagination of Canadians and spurred on Canadian public support.

The solidarity with the USSR would not survive the war's end. In Churchill's 1946 words marking the beginning of the Cold War, a totalitarian Soviet "Iron Curtain" had fallen over Eastern Europe. Closer to home, in Ottawa, a cipher clerk in the USSR embassy, Igor Gouzenko, defected with details of a Soviet spy ring in Canada and in the United States.

Ideological conflict returned to the top of the Canadian-Soviet bilateral agenda. Relations plummeted. Canada was to play a leading role in the creation of the North Atlantic Treaty Organization (NATO) in 1949 to bind North America and Western Europe together in collective defence. In 1951, to back up its words, Canada deployed an Air Force division as well as an infantry brigade, totalling some ten thousand men, to Europe to help deter any possible Soviet military aggression. More than a million solders from NATO and the Soviet Union led Warsaw Pact of Eastern European satellite countries would face off across the West and East German border, backed by tanks, missiles and nuclear weapons.

This was the political background faced by Pierre Elliott Trudeau in 1968 when he assumed the office of prime minister, and by those fans in Canada who dreamed of a hockey series between the best of the best of the capitalist and communist worlds. This, then, is that story.

CHAPTER ONE

THE REFEREE ULTIMATUM

T HE TWO SENIOR KGB OFFICERS masquerading as Soviet hockey officials flinched as shattered glass and ice hit the walls and floor of the cramped, colourless ante-room of Moscow's otherwise stately Palace of Sports. It was late morning of Thursday, September 28, 1972. The decisive Game Eight of the Canada–USSR Summit Series was due to be played later that evening. Team Canada's assistant coach, John Ferguson, had sent the side table and its pitcher of water flying as he leapt to his feet from his hard wooden chair, launching a verbal broadside against the two Russians: "You sons of bitches—you suckered us."

Fergie was not a person you wanted to anger. He had been a very productive NHL scorer during his eight seasons with the Montreal Canadiens before retiring the previous year, in 1971. He was better known however as Jean Beliveau's left wing protector and someone who let his fists do the talking.

The small room fell silent. The tension thickened.

There was no need for me to translate what Ferguson had said. There was no mistaking the force and intent behind his words, and any-way the two Russians spoke perfect English. I knew them both.

Alexander Gresko had appeared unexpectedly on the Moscow scene as deputy head of the International Department of the Soviet Ministry of Physical Culture and Sports in April of 1972, when I first encountered him. A basic background check had shown that he had been kicked out of the United Kingdom in October of 1971 as part of an extensive expulsion of one hundred and five Soviet diplomats and other officials for "activities incompatible with their diplomatic status." In plain talk: "spying." Gresko was said to have been engaged in attempting to recruit well-placed British citizens to betray their country by working for the Soviet Union. The dark-haired and youngish-looking Gresko had a surface affability that covered a combative nature, and his clothing displayed a smattering of London tailoring.

The second KGB officer, older and greyer, with a long face, aristocratic nose and a perpetually sly grin, had a semi-sophisticated air, aided by a more fashionable suit. Kiril Romesky, who always seemed to have a different title as part of his duties at the Physical Culture and Sports Ministry, was senior to Gresko but normally let his junior countryman do the talking. When he did pipe up, almost always in Russian, you paid attention.

Romesky had been a late addition to the small Soviet delegation travelling with the USSR team to Canada for the first four games in early September 1972 for what had initially been billed as an eight-game home-and-home "Friendship Series." As second secretary at the Canadian embassy, I had been involved from the beginning in negotiations for the series, and due to my Russian-language capability and position as a defenceman on the "Moscow Maple Leafs" beer-league hockey team, I had been tasked to be the Canadian government's "Liaison Officer and Interpreter." Thus, I had flown from the Soviet capital to Montreal, Toronto, Winnipeg and Vancouver with Romesky, other officials and the Soviet team. His principal job was to ensure the Soviet players remained disciplined off the ice and to deter any potential embarrassing situations for the USSR, such as a possible defection.

Another person shoehorned into the ante-room was Team Canada's head coach and general manager, Harry Sinden. He and Ferguson had just finished running the morning on-ice practice with Team Canada at the Sports Palace, and this was a convenient location for the continuation of the extremely heated argument over who would be the two referees for the final game. The series was now deadlocked at three victories apiece, with one tie, after consecutive and stunning one-goal victories by Canada in Games Six and Seven, both winning goals scored by Paul Henderson. Everything was now on the line.

Sinden often appeared harried, preferring to keep the top button of his shirt undone and his tie askew, even when wearing his official blue Team Canada blazer and chequered grey pants. He was a contrast to the more dapper Ferguson and to Team Canada leader Robert Alan Eagleson. The "Eagle," or "Big Bird" as he was nicknamed in some quarters, was also present in the ante-room. Eagleson was a dynamic force of his own—the founding executive director of the National Hockey League Players Association was a hard-driving Toronto lawyer and consummate networker with political ambitions.

Like Eagleson, Sinden ran hot, as if he had jet fuel in his veins. In describing his own actions, he was fond of using the converse expression "losing my cool"—which he did often. But then Harry had the weight of the entire nation of Canada on his shoulders. Team Canada, with its roster of all-star NHL professionals, was expected to sweep the ice clean against the so-called "amateurs" of the Soviet Union. Sinden had won a Stanley Cup with the Boston Bruins in 1970 and, perhaps of more significance in his current context, had played and beaten the USSR team at the 1958 World Championships in Oslo, Norway, as part of the Allen Cup champion Whitby Dunlops. Harry Sinden was fully expected to deliver victory for Canada and Canadians in this monumental series as well.

When Team Canada stumbled badly out of the gate in the first game in Montreal on September 2 and went on to lose the Canadian portion of the series with two losses, one win and a tie, the blame game began in earnest, and the wrath of the country and the media fell on the players—but particularly on Sinden. His reputation took an awful beating. Now he had much to prove in the communist capital, with wall-to-wall media coverage, including over one hundred Canadian journalists desperately seeking photos and juicy copy, and under the close attention of nearly three thousand frenetic Canadian fans who had come to Russia to watch the games. No pressure, eh?

From the moment Sinden had been named head coach, in mid-June of 1972, he had expressed his dissatisfaction with the arrangements for referees and the use of the international rules that had been negotiated and signed in April in Prague as part of the overall series agreement between the Canadian Amateur Hockey Association (CAHA) and the Soviet Ice Hockey Federation. Sinden believed the deal favoured the Soviets, as they were familiar with this system, and that two referees with no linesmen would miss a lot of infractions, or they would compete with each other to see who could call the most penalties. During follow-up negotiations in Moscow in July he attempted to change these arrangements, but the Soviet side would not budge from the agreed position that these were international, and not NHL, matches.

For the first four games, in Canada, the April agreement called for a pool of four American referees with international experience: Gord Lee, Len Gagnon, Frank Larsen and Steve Dowling. They would split the first two games. Both sides would then agree on which two refs to choose for Games Three and Four based on their initial performance. If there was no agreement, then Canada would pick the referees for Game Three and the USSR for Game Four. Lee and Gagnon started out fairly well, largely staying out of the spotlight. Team Canada's opening game 7–3 loss was not laid at their doorstep. On the other hand, Larsen and Dowling were said to have been subjected to a strong scolding in their dressing room by the general secretary of the Soviet Ice Hockey Federation, Andrei Starovoitov, following the USSR's 4–1 defeat in Game Two in Toronto. A wastebasket and chair or two had apparently been kicked over and the word "barbarians" used to describe Team Canada's "excessive and illegal physical play." Starovoitov would call Sinden late that night arguing that Lee and Gagnon be used exclusively for the final two games in Canada. Sinden obliged him, but later would say he noticed the refs had tightened up in Games Three and Four, to the detriment of Team Canada. It convinced him more than ever that, from the beginning, NHL rules should have been in place—enforced by NHL referees. However, he did readily admit that Team Canada had displayed poor play and a lack of stamina in these two games, which was beyond the scope of the referees.

The fat hit the fire in Stockholm during the two exhibition games there, on September 16 and 17, against Team Sweden, which were intended as a warm-up for Team Canada on the wider Olympic-sized ice, as would be used in Moscow. These games turned into a nasty bloodbath, with spearing, cross-checking and slashing galore. Team Canada's Wayne Cashman, for one, endured fifty stitches to sew up his tongue, which was split severely by a Swedish butt-end. Sinden blamed the referees for letting the games get out of hand, in particular the two West Germans, Franz Baader and Josef Kompalla (whom he later would call "Badder" and "Wurst"). Both were part of the four-person European pool to be employed in Moscow (Sweden's Ove Dahlberg and Czechoslovakia's Rudolf (Rudy) Bata being the other two). Sinden said the two West Germans were "absolutely terrible; they couldn't even skate," adding that "they were miles behind the play all night and don't know the damn rules." He blamed their "incompetence" for making the game very bitter by not calling penalties on the Swedes for "backstabbing" and other dirty stickwork.[9]

According to Sinden, at the end of the second period of the second game, a donnybrook broke out in the joint corridor that led from the ice when he continued to berate the German officials while players from both sides shouted insults at each other. A shoving match ensued, which drew a crowd of Swedish photojournalists and eventually Swedish police, apparently with dogs. Sinden later described the scene as "ugly." Canada's ambassador to Sweden, Margaret Meagher, controversially called Team Canada's actions a "disgrace" and issued an apology. It is a matter of debate if she did the right thing in calling out her fellow countrymen publicly, but it was certainly not Canada's finest hour in this Scandinavian country.

Sinden had left Sweden with three conclusions: one, refereeing would be the biggest problem in Moscow; two, if the team did not start playing better it would lose; three, no matter how bad the Swedish experience had been it might help bring the players closer together as a team.

Game Six (on September 24, the second of the four games in Moscow) reinforced Harry's first concern. Baader and Kompalla were back on the ice. Team Canada won a 3–2 squeaker to get back into the series, but Sinden was apoplectic about the refereeing, saying the two Germans were the most incompetent officials he had ever seen. They had called eight penalties on Team Canada for a total of thiry-one minutes, including a questionable infraction in the last two minutes, against only four minutes (two minors) for the USSR team. Mind you, twelve of those minutes involved Canada's Bobby Clarke, for his ankle slash of the leading Soviet scorer, Valeri Kharlamov, but still the distribution of penalties was disproportionate. Sinden said the Germans had done everything they could to help the Russians and was insistent that this was the last game for the two officials.

Sinden however had gone far beyond just yelling and shouting at the referees from behind the boards. He and Ferguson threw towels and a fold-up chair onto the ice in an effort to create a scene for the crowd and television audience and draw attention to their disdain for the officiating. They hoped the Germans would be shamed into altering their behaviour. Ferguson was given a bench penalty for his actions. At the end of the second period, as had happened in Stockholm, Sinden, at close quarters, chased the two referees up a common corridor while screaming at them. He was accompanied by Bobby Orr, who was in the vicinity and in street clothes, still recovering from off-season knee surgery that had prevented him from playing. This time it was Soviet officials and the Soviet police who intervened. By the time the game came to an end, the militia were lined up shoulder to shoulder in the runway to the dressing rooms.

The pressure continued to build.

Romesky put in an appearance the following morning, September 25, his first direct encounter with Sinden and Ferguson. He came to deliver a series of official protests against the conduct of Team Canada coaches and players, both on and off the ice. Sinden countered that the root cause of the incidents was the incompetence of the German referees. With them gone, he promised, everything would settle down. He thought he had made his point with Romesky. Dahlberg and Bata were assigned to referee Game Seven on Tuesday, September 26. Afterward, Sinden had complaints about them as well but acknowledged that the penalties they called on Team Canada were deserved. Winning helps with magnanimity. A new problem with another official however raised its head. This time with the goal judge, who was quite late in putting the light on to signal Paul Henderson's winning goal in the 4–3 victory. Ferguson flooded the ice with players to congratulate Henderson so there would be no doubt that he scored. It was a portent of things to come.

There had been more than enough on my plate with other diplomatic issues, such as accompanying NHL president Clarence Campbell and two NHL owners on their meetings with Soviet officials to explore a new European professional league and an NHL–Soviet club-vs-club series, so I had stayed out of the current fray about the referees—at least until I saw Gresko on the morning of September 27 after Game Seven. He told me without batting an eye that they had decided Baader and Kompalla would be on the ice for Game Eight and requested I inform Sinden, Ferguson and Eagleson. Gresko's flimsy rationale was that the Soviet authorities did not wish to discriminate against the West Germans, which was a view he claimed was put forward and shared by the Swedish and Czechoslovakian referees.

I knew instantly this was a Molotov cocktail that would create a fiery explosion. Harry, of course, was livid when I drove over to the rink to pass along this "good news." Gresko, in the interim, went to Eagleson's hotel room and walked into a firestorm, as was to be expected. Much steam was generated, but Gresko held his ground ultimately, saying it was a decision taken by higher-ups, even though he acknowledged he had agreed the day before that the West Germans were out. It seemed clear that the Soviets were trying to stack the deck in their favour now the series was tied up and they were no longer assured of winning.

At a follow-up session at the rink with Gresko, the coaches of both teams went over and over the terms of agreement for the referees, with plenty of invective spread around, but there was no movement. The Soviet coaches, Vsevolod Bobrov and Boris Kulagin, didn't want anything to do with this or any other meeting of this kind—not with the KGB involved. Their business, they would say, was limited to coaching.

And then Eagleson dropped the ultimate bomb. If the Soviets tried to use the Germans, there would be no Game Eight. Team Canada would simply pack up and go home.

My head spun. This had not been part of any scenario nor any pre-planned negotiating strategy. Had we even thought through the consequences of going home or was this just a spontaneous gut reaction and outburst of bravado?

In hockey terms, the series would end in a tie, or would it? International rules state that in the event of a series tie, the winner is the team that scores the most total goals—the USSR at this point. Also, teams that leave the field of competition, for whatever reason, are usually looked upon in an unfavourable light.

Then there were the thousands of Canadian fans to consider. They had come on special charter flights and were scheduled to depart the same way two to three days later. They couldn't leave early, and many had already reached the limits of their endurance with Moscow. They had come for the games, not the joys of Soviet tourism. If Game Eight was cancelled, they would become highly emotional, and with time on their hands this pressure cooker would likely boil over. A bugle-playing Canadian fan already had been thrown in jail for busting up a hotel bar and knocking into an undercover Soviet policeman. The bugler faced a possible sentence of one to five years' hard labour. The pre-series assessment put together by Hockey Canada and embassy officials predicted that thirty-five Canadians would be arrested. But if the lid blew off because of a cancelled game, the Soviet police would not be looking the other way or going easy on us, as they had been so far. We would quickly blow through that estimate.

THE GLUE THAT WAS HOLDING this whole series together was the fact that the political leadership of both countries wanted it to happen. Prime Minister Pierre Elliott Trudeau had visited the USSR in May of 1971 as part of an engagement policy with the Soviet Union to reduce the risk of military confrontation. Soviet Premier Alexei Kosygin visited Canada five months later, and he and the prime minister had signed plans for a General Exchanges Agreement (a sort of people-to-people exchange) that included Science, Education, Culture and Sports. The latter provided the high-level government-to-government framework in which the hockey series could be negotiated, after a decade or more of frustration that our best players could not play against their best. Trudeau was also personally engaged in the actual games, arguing for the inclusion of Bobby Hull on the roster, dropping the puck in Montreal, and also attending the second game, in Toronto, with wife Margaret. He and Kosygin had been exchanging telegrams as the series progressed, bantering about how the games would inspire friendship between the two countries.

The Soviet leadership had its own reasons to engage with Canada. It wanted to end its isolation and the sanctions placed upon it by Western nations after Red Army tanks had barged into Czechoslovakia in August of 1968 to quell the liberalization and mass protests there. Moscow was also worried about US President Richard Nixon's diplomatic overture toward China, which could leave the Soviet Union to face united enemies. If there could be ping-pong diplomacy between Washington and Beijing, why not hockey diplomacy between Moscow and Ottawa?

General Secretary of the Communist Party of the Soviet Union Leonid Brezhnev was a known hockey fan and attended Game Five, the first game in Moscow, with Premier Kosygin. Brezhnev apparently also took steps to head off an attempt by Mikhail Suslov, the so-called "Grey Cardinal" of the Politburo, the Soviet Union's executive policy-making committee, not to agree to the series. Suslov was the chief party ideologist and charged with maintaining the purity of the Communist Revolution, including the development of "Soviet Man" who, ideally, would stand above all others in his strength and achievement. Suslov, it is said, had heard that Canadian experts were predicting an eight-game sweep of the USSR team. So, when the chairman of the Sports Committee, Sergei Pavlov, came looking for the approval of the Politburo, Suslov objected. Russian sources said Suslov had berated Pavlov and told him that if the Soviet team was humiliated, Pavlov would not only lose his Communist Party card but also the large apartment, car, special clothes and food that came with it, and that the only job Pavlov would ever get was that of a toilet cleaner—if he was lucky. Kosygin, who was in charge of the administrative Council of Ministers, supported Pavlov, while Brezhnev reportedly replied that based on his own observations, he believed the team would acquit itself well. Suslov was overruled, and the series was approved from the Soviet side.

In keeping with his desire for high-level engagement with the USSR during the series, Trudeau had sent an official delegation to Moscow to be present for the four games played there and to pursue additional co-operation in other sectors. That delegation was led by Senator Arthur Laing and included Ed Ritchie, the Under Secretary of State for External Affairs (Canada's top diplomat at the level of officials). Ritchie had accompanied the prime minister during the May 1971 visit and was an avid hockey fan who had played for the Oxford University Blues. All of these connections and potential ramifications were turning in my mind following Eagleson's bombshell, and I told him we were moving beyond just hockey and into the realm of high-level politics and diplomacy. Senator Laing would have to be consulted. We would have to go later that evening to see Laing at the Bolshoi Theatre, where the Soviet government had invited the Canadian delegation to attend a ballet performance of *Anna Karenina* featuring the music of Tchaikovsky.

In the interim I had managed to pass a message along to my boss about what was happening, Canadian Ambassador Robert A.D. Ford, a masterful expert on the Soviet Union, having served there in his current capacity for eight years and on two previous occasions for over five years during Stalin's murderous time.

The historic Bolshoi, first opened in 1825, had a dazzling interior of red and gold. Senator Laing, Ritchie and the ambassador, with their Soviet hosts, were seated in a prestigious box closed off on the back side by a velvet curtain. Eagleson, Sinden and I approached the box during the first intermission and asked to speak privately with them. Laing had been briefed by the ambassador beforehand but heard Eagleson out. His answer was short and clear. There was no way Canada would cancel the series. There was too much at stake. We would have to go back to negotiating the referee issue with the Russians and do the best we could. I was to join the negotiations. The orchestra started tuning up for the second act and that was it. Eagleson was agitated, but we withdrew, with him grousing all the way about having been undercut by Laing. Sinden later referred to it in more colourful poker terms as having "our hole card turned over."

Laing was right, though—cancellation was not an option.

When the discussions about officiating resumed at the Palace of Sports mid-morning on Thursday, September 28, Sinden and Eagleson kept on pushing. Ferguson remained silent. Time marched on in heated argument—thirty, forty and then fifty minutes went by. Romesky kept grinning, while Gresko continued to stonewall, ultimately shouting that we were now in Russia and therefore Russian rules applied.

My new-found experience in Moscow had taught me firsthand that the communist state was not a bottom-up society reflecting the views of its citizens but a top-down one carrying out the will of the Soviet leadership. Those who challenged party rule or embarrassed the Politburo would quickly find themselves with a one-way ticket to Siberia. KGB officers were not exempt. Even they did not want to be on the wrong side of their big bosses.

After invoking the names of Brezhnev and Kosygin, I posed the question of whether the two Soviet leaders would want to explain this unscrupulous altercation to Senator Laing and through him to Prime Minister Trudeau. Letting this thought simmer with Romesky and Gresko, I then suggested that maybe a way out of this impasse was to have each side choose one referee. After a moment's reflection, perhaps with that eastbound train ticket on their minds, they agreed.

Sinden was quick to jump at the apparent opening. We will take the Swede, Dahlberg, he proclaimed enthusiastically.

And we will take Kompalla, Romesky retorted, opting, as might be expected from him, for the ref who had called the most penalties on Team Canada.

The pressure in the room released for a minute or two as this seeming compromise took hold. It didn't last long. Romesky went back to grinning. Dahlberg, he said slowly, unfortunately had fallen ill in his hotel room and would not be available for tonight's match. We would have to choose somebody else.

Ferguson erupted.

Starting a physical fight might have seemed like a satisfying course of action at this point but would have solved nothing. Fergie could be arrested for assault. With some effort we calmed him down, though Sinden and Eagleson were seething as well. I was chagrined that my ploy had not worked exactly as planned. Dahlberg had seemed fine when last seen at breakfast, and if he was now ill it was a "political illness." The KGB were masters at gaining leverage on people. They had pulled a fast one on us, but there was nothing further we could do at this late stage with the game just hours away, and Sinden and Ferguson and their players were required to return to their hotel. Harry went ahead and selected Bata from Czechoslovakia. Far from ideal, but at least one of the West Germans would remain on the sidelines.

The ugly bickering, bad feelings and raw emotion of the past few days only took a few hours off and would return quickly enough, even before Game Eight began. The off-ice saga would soon merge with the saga occurring on the ice.

And here I was, in the middle of this storm enveloping a sports contest that was being watched religiously by virtually all twenty-two million Canadians across our vast country and by a television audience of over one hundred fifty million in the even larger Soviet Union. I had just turned twenty-eight a few weeks earlier, slightly older than the average age of players on Team Canada, with four years of diplomatic service under my belt, including nineteen months in the heart of communism.

How had I landed in this predicament?

CHAPTER TWO

THE WORLD BECKONS

"You will never be a diplomat. You are from the wrong class and you have no money."

Mr. Eric Chabeaux was not pulling any punches. Of French Huguenot heritage, he was born in Liverpool in 1904 and tough conditions at home had led him, at sixteen, to cross the Atlantic in steerage class to seek new opportunity in Canada, where he became a well-regarded bookbinder and active union member. Diplomats, in his experience, were "toffs" with titles from wealthy families who had attended the right schools and had the right connections. Those from the working class need not apply.

I was enamoured of his only daughter, Laurielle, someone a young man could only dream about: an elementary school teacher with a thousand-watt smile, who loved fast cars and who was as beautiful on the inside as out. It was understandable that her dad wanted the best for her and her future. He and his wife, Mabel, had their fingers crossed that a few previous dates with the conservative medical student down the street might lead to marriage. I had the inside track, however, through a summer romance at Camp Manitouwabing, near Parry Sound, Ontario, where she taught tennis and I taught horseback riding.

"Times had changed," I countered. This was Canada. The government was reaching out to a broader demographic to staff an expanding foreign service, and it was my understanding it would be covering the costs normally associated with the conduct of diplomacy. Canada was being democratized. You no longer had to have your own money to represent your country.

Still, he was right about my background. I was certainly no toff—far from it. Life early on was a struggle. My mother was one of thirteen children born in the small francophone town of Lafontaine, on the southern end of Georgian Bay, in Ontario. Her mother had pressed twenty-five cents into her hand in the Depression-era 1930s as her brother harnessed up the horse and cutter to take her to the bus terminal in nearby Penetanguishene and onward to a nanny's job in Toronto.

My father, of English and Dutch origin, was a fast-talking door-to-door salesman pitching Hoover vacuum cleaners when he rang the bell at the house in Toronto where my mother worked. They took a shine to each other and soon married, in 1942, while he had become a member of the Militia's Canadian Forestry Corps, operating on the home front during the Second World War.

The marriage foundered early on, and my younger sister, Carol, and I would spend years on end with one parent or another. In the late 1940s we ended up with my mother, living in modest but adequate wartime housing back in Penetanguishene.

It is difficult to say why and how a youngster becomes interested in events beyond one's own backyard. Perhaps it has most to do with one's own circumstances and the questions surrounding them. Little things piqued my curiosity, like the small, colourful metal license plates that came as cereal-box prizes. Each new plate of a different American state or Canadian province sent me scurrying to a map at school to find out where Arkansas, New Mexico and Saskatchewan were located.

Certainly, a sterling elementary teacher like Mrs. Switzer played a role in making history dance in a way that ignited youthful imagination. In my memory bank is a class contest in which each student had to select a historical event from the Encyclopaedia Britannica, research it, then deliver a presentation before the class. Italy's changing role in the First World War caught my attention, starting with alliance of the Central Powers of the German Empire and Austria-Hungary and then a year later the signing of the secret Treaty of London, thereby changing sides to join the Triple Entente of Britain, France and Russia. The presentation was deemed the best and was foreshadowing, no doubt, an interest in international political and military affairs.

Penetanguishene had a lot more winter than summer. When the westerly winds from Lake Huron and Georgian Bay picked up, they would pummel the area with heavy driving snow, which could start as early as October and last through April. Hockey weather. Organized hockey required equipment and often transportation at early hours. I found myself limited to street hockey, pick-up games and small in-house contests on the school's makeshift rink. While many of the francophones in town rooted for the Montreal Canadiens, I, like most Ontario kids my age, was a Toronto Maple Leafs fan. I filled a scrapbook with newspaper photos of guys like Ted "Teeder" Kennedy, Turk Broda and Eric Nesterenko, though he never seemed to live up to his promised billing as the next Leafs star. There was a picture of goalie Al Rollins being escorted from the ice with an injury and the game being delayed for a long period of time in the era of one dressed goalie per team.

My clippings were facilitated for a while by extra copies of the *Toronto Star*, which I delivered until I was overcome by my inability to manoeuvre my sleigh over the hilly snow-covered streets of the town in winter, the mounting size of the *Saturday Star*, and the recurring reluctance of some customers to pay their bill. The best *Star* headline for me was when I opened the parcel of papers and read: Canada 5, USSR 0, following the victory of the Penticton Vees at the 1955 World Hockey Championships in Krefeld, West Germany. We were back on top after the surprise first-ever victory in 1954 of an upstart team from some country called the Soviet Union.

We had no radio and were the last on the street to get a television, in 1956—a small rented Crosley perched on four long legs, with rabbit ears for reception. There was only one station, CKVR from Barrie, which provided largely snowy transmission and signed off mid-evening during the week with the playing of "God Save the Queen" followed by a test pattern.

Saturday night was different. That was hockey night. The station stayed on until eleven p.m., which permitted Esso's Murray Westgate to sign off with his famous "Happy Motoring," following the Hot Stove League discussion of the game. It was a thrill to listen to Foster Hewitt describe the action, but often you could not see the players through the grainy transmission, or they would be mere ghostly figures.

My last thought of Penetang Protestant Separate School, at Christmas 1956, when we moved to Toronto with my father to live in his mother's house, was of my name appearing outside of the principal's office indicating I was leading the school's hockey scoring race. It wasn't a big deal given the small number of students, but it was something of which to be proud.

Goodbye small town. Hello Jones Avenue, south of the Danforth, Earl Grey Senior Public School and then Riverdale Collegiate. There were lots of ways to get into trouble in the hurly-burly of the city, but equally plenty of positive opportunities. The Danforth and Toronto offered both.

Riverdale, like other Toronto high schools at the time, had a cadet corps, which was mandatory to join for all grade nine and ten boys. There was also a rifle range in the school basement—with live ammunition. The residue of the Second World War.

While at school we were introduced to the nuclear age. There were the odd drills to evacuate to the basement or "duck and cover" under your desk. Air-raid sirens were installed around the city, and some people built bomb shelters in their basements or backyards.

Riverdale was associated with the Third Battalion of the Queen's Own Rifles, and so when you turned sixteen you could join that militia unit for training and some adventure in the evenings or on weekends at the impressive University Avenue armoury. It paid a few dollars but not enough for a seat at Maple Leaf Gardens to watch the Leafs. Corporations and law offices corralled many of the best seats and others were passed down through family estates and personal wills. Once the Leafs started making the playoffs and actually winning Stanley Cups in the late fifties and early sixties, those additional tickets that did come on sale at the box office were quickly scooped up. Scalpers on the street commanded premium prices.

With no connections and limited funds, the best a teenager could do was to purchase standing-room-only tickets behind the blue or grey seats. There were no reservations for standing room; space was allocated on a first-come basis. Here, agile teenagers had an advantage, as we could burst ahead once clearing the ticket-takers when the doors opened and run flat out up the escalators to the second level (blues) or up the stairs to the cheapest area at the fourth level (greys) at the top of the Gardens. Once you secured a spot, however, it was wise to stay there and protect it throughout the game. Drifting off to the washroom or refreshment stand could find your place filled in by others.

There was a military band in an enclosed space on the south side of the Gardens, with an enormous picture of the Queen above the musicians, and they would keep us entertained before the game and between periods. Four groups of two men each pulled barrels of hot water on wheels to flood the ice. It was thrilling when the crowd roared as the Leafs hit the ice. Here were boyhood dreams transformed from newspapers, radio and television, even if it was at a good distance: guys like captain George Armstrong and Dave Keon up front, Carl Brewer and Tim Horton on defence, Johnny Bower in net.

My friends and I had much greater luck obtaining an actual seat and at a much better price by going to the Gardens on Sunday afternoon to watch the double headers involving the Toronto Marlies and Saint Michael's Majors versus various Ontario Hockey League (OHL) teams from outside the city. The games were fast and competitive and many future NHL stars passed through their ranks. Indeed, a number of these players would later lace up for Team Canada: Phil Esposito, Pat Stapleton, Stan Mikita, and Dennis Hull of the St. Catharines Teepees; Rod Gilbert and Jean Ratelle of the Guelph Biltmore Mad Hatters/ Royals; Don Awrey of the Barrie Flyers; Rod Seiling from St. Mike's; Bill

White and Ron Ellis of the Marlies; Paul Henderson of the Hamilton Red Wings.

My own hockey career didn't amount to much. Despite four competent years on the offensive and defensive lines of the Riverdale Raiders junior and senior football teams and being able to smoke home runs at house-league baseball games, my sole attempt to make the school hockey team came to an abrupt end when my name was not posted on the team board after an initial practice. It seemed I was unable to skate fast enough and to shoot hard enough, though there never was an explanation.

Acquiring diplomatic skills wasn't a consideration or even a blip on the distant horizon in those days, but some part-time and summer jobs provided possible lessons. Selling hot dogs on commission in the stands at Exhibition Stadium during Toronto Argonauts football games without blocking anyone's view might be considered adroit public marketing.

The art of compromise was enhanced when discussing whether closing time on Saturday nights at an IGA grocery store meant you could start cleaning up the produce section beforehand and leave at six p.m. sharp, or whether the brooms and pails only came out at that point, delaying the evening's activities until at least seven and with no extra pay. Or selling a suit, a sports jacket and several ties when the customer was just looking for a shirt at Studio 267 on lower Yonge Street might have had something to do with the attributes of friendly persuasion. Certainly, discretion and patience came into play when selling women's shoes and discussing the actual size of one's feet as well as colour and style preferences at Robert Simpson's flagship store at the corner of Queen and Yonge.

A summer spent as a forest ranger with Ontario's Department of Lands and Forests in Parry Sound brought exposure to brawling trappers and other people experienced in the bush who would often go off-kilter at nights with excessive drinking and threats to knife each other. Whether to intervene and mediate or to simply let matters play out might have been a precursor to some form of diplomacy.

SOMETIMES HARD WORK and ambition are not enough to get you to where you are going in life. Often you need a fortunate break or two. The fortuitous inauguration of the federal government's student loan program in the autumn of 1964 enabled me to supplement my earned income to pay for tuition, books and other costs for first-year university. Without it I would have had to have gone in another direction.

As the school year ended, the head of the campus World University Services (WUS) club was due to join a group of international students who were studying in Canada on a three-week all-expenses-paid familiarization tour of Western Canada. At the last minute she had to drop out and, for no apparent reason other than I was standing around in the politics class with her, she asked if I could take her place.

The thirty-plus-hour train trip from Toronto to Winnipeg went by rocks, lakes and trees and then trees, lakes and rocks in a seemingly infinite procession. The international students, mainly from small Caribbean islands and African countries, were amazed at the enormity of the wilderness and small communities along the way and kept asking when they would be leaving Ontario, knowing it was only one province of Canada. "Ontario never ends" was the constant refrain. From Winnipeg, we then took a fascinating bus tour across the three Prairie provinces. The journey whetted my appetite for the broader world and Canada's role in it.

My first encounter with a real live Canadian diplomat occurred at the Glendon campus of York University in Toronto. Escott Reid had been chosen, as of January 1, 1966, to be the first principal of a new bilingual liberal arts college devoted to public policy, public administration and international affairs. He had been a star in Canada's "golden age of diplomacy" after the Second World War and had been deeply involved in the creation of the United Nations and NATO, and Canada's outreach to Asia, Africa and Latin America, followed by time at the World Bank. When he arrived, I was engaged with the campus newspaper, *Pro Tem*, and with the student power movement—in other words challenging the existing norms. His offer to me and others to discuss it over a glass of sherry seemed out of place and out of time, but he was a good listener and his accounts of the world were fascinating, even if delivered in a rather stiff manner. One of his books, *Radical Mandarin*, suggested he too could challenge convention.

THE REAL DOOR opener occurred one evening in the autumn of 1966 when taking a break from my studies in the university library. I noticed a sizeable crowd had formed in the corridor and asked someone what it was all for. It turned out that the Ontario government was hiring a limited number of university students from across the province to act as hosts and hostesses for Ontario's pavilion at the World's Fair in Montreal the following summer. Though pressed for time and assessing my chances as limited, it was another opportunity staring me in the face.

Whether it was due to my mother's francophone background, my course of studies in political science and economics, my personality, or having worked previously for Ontario's Department of Lands and Forests was not clear, but to my great surprise a position was offered to me, together with three other York students. We became part of a contingent of twenty-four young men and twenty-four young women.

EXPO 67 was tremendously exciting and to actually work there was wonderful. Sixty-two countries participated: the largest number ever at a World's Fair to that point. A record fifty million people passed through the gates during the six-month duration. The Queen attended, as did American President Lyndon Johnson. France's President Charles de Gaulle was dis-invited following his unacceptable shout of "Vive le Québec libre" from the balcony of Montreal City Hall on July 24. We hosts and hostesses spent much of our time controlling the crowds and answering the most popular question (about the location of the washrooms), but we had privileged access to every pavilion and parties with our counterparts from other countries. Representing your province to the world was a privilege, and it provided an unparalleled learning experience as well as being great fun.

THAT AUTUMN THE Canadian government held its annual exams for entrance to the Public Service and to the Foreign Service. Approximately six thousand persons applied at various sites across Canada and at a number of Canadian embassies around the world for students studying abroad. One such location was a crowded gymnasium at Malvern Collegiate in east Toronto. Participants were obliged to complete a lengthy multiple-choice questionnaire about Canada and its history, current events and international issues. A second test posed a hypothetical situation and asked you to write a short essay about how you would deal with it. The whole process took about two hours.

My results must have been satisfactory because several weeks later an invitation arrived requesting my presence at an oral interview in downtown Toronto with representatives of the Public Service Commission, the Department of External Affairs, as well as the Department of Industry, Trade and Commerce (ITC). I was hyped and strode through the interview door in confidence, with a large smile on my face, only to be greeted with the first question, asking if I had ever travelled abroad. I had not—aside from a quick student visit to Washington. But I pulled my wits together to say, "No, but the world came to Canada at Expo, and I met it there." That response appeared to work, and I was able to carry on answering other questions and listing my extracurricular activities and various part-time jobs. Good grades in third year didn't hurt.

The competition was exceedingly stiff, and time passed with no word. In January 1968, the Ontario government offered me a position in the recently created Intergovernmental Affairs Secretariat at the impressive annual salary of seven thousand two hundred dollars a year. Jobs were numerous that year with various companies, including multinationals like Ford, IBM and Shell, setting up recruitment offices on university campuses and competing with each with offers of generous salaries and assorted benefits.

Then, returning to my apartment from campus one snowy February day, I turned the key to the mailbox to find a letter from Ottawa. There were two offers, to become either a Probationary Foreign Service Officer with External Affairs or a Junior Trade Commissioner with ITC. Starting annual salary: $6,660. Starting date: May, three months away. All this was conditional on graduation from my four-year Honours BA in Political Science as well as obtaining a security clearance from the RCMP.

I sought the advice of an Expo colleague who had previously taken a position with Ontario's Intergovernmental Affairs. She did not hesitate in recommending the "broader tableau" of Ottawa and international affairs, which she said more than made up for the salary difference. I opted for External Affairs, preferring its political and international security portfolios rather than the commercial nature of the Trade Commissioner Service.

I wasted no time in showing the letter to Mr. Chabeaux. He acknowledged my achievement but was still not totally convinced his initial assessment was wrong about me and diplomacy. However, and more importantly, he graciously gave his consent to marry Laurielle, even if it meant his only child would be leaving for Ottawa and unknown foreign lands.

CHAPTER THREE

COLD WAR BAPTISM

T HE NATION'S CAPITAL became magnetic in the spring of 1968. Business was expanding, as was government, but Ottawa had the added drawing card for graduating students and others in the form of the hip new philosopher prime minister, Pierre Elliott Trudeau, a leader who attracted adoring crowds. Expo 67 had created the euphoria of a new era in a staid country, and Trudeau was seen as Canada's version of America's John F. Kennedy. JFK's clarion call in his 1961 inaugural address to civic action and public service, "Ask not what your country can do for you—ask what you can do for your country," continued to echo across the northern border.

I pitched up in Ottawa on May 13, 1968, eleven days following my last exam. It was three weeks after the new PM assumed the reins of office and before he turned Lester Pearson's previous Liberal minority into a majority government in the June 25 election.

Securing accommodation was my first order of business, but it posed a dilemma. My significant student loan, which now had to be repaid, suggested modest lodgings. But I wanted something nice for Laurielle upon her move to Ottawa following the end of her elementary teaching job in Toronto and after our planned wedding in July. Financially risky perhaps, but I rented a one-bedroom apartment in a new building in Ottawa's Centretown.

External Affairs was created as a government department in 1909, a first step in a process that would last until 1931, to assume responsibility from Britain for the full conduct of Canada's own international relations. Initially "The Department" was housed in a small second-floor office over a downtown barber-shop on Bank Street. Nearly sixty years later, it continued to be scattered around Ottawa in a dozen or so buildings. There were, however, two prestigious locations. The first was the East Block on Parliament Hill, where the prime minister, the secretary of state for External Affairs, and the department's top six officials were situated. The second was across the street in the olive-coloured Langevin Block, at the corner of Wellington and Elgin streets. This contained External's geographic units responsible for bilateral relations with the United States, Europe, Asia, Africa and the Middle East, as well as Latin America, Mexico and the Caribbean.[10]

External Affairs hired twenty-two recruits in its class of 1968 (twenty-one male and only one female).[11] A francophone colleague and I were the first to report for duty. We were given sheaves of personnel and financial papers to sign, as well as the Official Secrets Act, which obligated us not to share classified material or information with anyone without a similar clearance. There also was the matter of ethical behaviour and the reminder that we were about to become professional civil servants required to serve all political parties in an equal manner and not to publicly demonstrate any personal political preferences we might have.

One unexpected document caused me to gulp. If I intended to get married, there was a requirement to seek the written permission of the under secretary of state for External Affairs, the department's senior bureaucrat. This necessitated another RCMP background check; this time of Laurielle and her family. I knew there would be no question of character, but realized investigators would be looking into her family connections to determine whether there was any evidence or possibility that she, and therefore I, could be blackmailed by hostile forces. It was noted that more than one aspiring officer had to choose between a diplomatic career or his future bride.

Like our predecessors, all members of the class of '68 were designated as "probationary foreign service officers" for a period of one year.

If during that time we did not measure up to the expected standards, our employment could be terminated without cause.

Putting those weighty matters to the side, I waited for the big news. What would be my first assignment? The answer: assistant on the Soviet desk located in the Langevin building. Great.

In fourth year at York, my classmates largely focused their attention on the Vietnam War and the domestic social unrest in the United States. Many Canadians took to the streets themselves to protest and to welcome American draft dodgers. Thousands of others of a different persuasion signed up to fight with the US military. There was wall-to-wall television coverage, and Canada had many real and pseudo experts on America.

What we didn't have were many experts on the Soviet Union, the other half of the Cold War equation and the other half of the nuclear weapons faceoff, plus a country which was providing military assistance to North Vietnam. Being somewhat of a contrarian, I signed up for a course about Soviet government. Unfortunately, the assistant professor was dreary and the textbook was heavy on the theory of communism and bureaucracy. It lacked any clear insights into what was really happening in the USSR and how the system and its personalities actually functioned—not that the Soviet leaders wanted foreigners to know. What I did find fascinating and followed assiduously in the media while at York were developments in Czechoslovakia and the efforts of its president, Alexander Dubček, to create "socialism with a human face" by easing rigid social and authoritarian conditions. This so-called "Prague Spring" challenged Moscow's communist orthodoxy and that of the other East European countries it controlled. Months passed with the threat of a Soviet military intervention.

The European division of External Affairs, divided between Western and Eastern Europe, was located on the Langevin's main floor near the impressive principal entrance with its polished granite columns and central staircase. The wide corridors, large offices and sixteen-foot ceilings provided an air of solemnity that suited the practice of speaking only in hushed tones. Foreign diplomats were frequent visitors, wishing to obtain or provide information. The conveyed message to all inhabitants of the building was that this was a place of serious business—the nation's business.

In its early to middle years, External Affairs had heavily recruited Canadian graduate students studying at Oxford and Cambridge, in the UK, and to a lesser extent from the Sorbonne, in France, and Harvard, in the US. One would encounter them in the corridors wearing tweeds and brogues and speaking with clipped British accents, or those with the cosmopolitan dress and language of Paris—Mr. Chabeaux's vision. They were salted though by a good number of battle-hardened veterans who had completed their degrees after the war at Canadian universities and then in the 1950s and '60s by increasing volumes of lawyers, postgraduates and undergraduates, like myself, who had studied exclusively in Canada.

Under Secretary Marcel Cadieux (the very person who had the ultimate authority to sign or not sign the permission to marry) had the practice of calling in the new probationary officers, in small groups of five or six, for an "introductory chat." His office was in a prestigious location at the end of the second floor of the East Block, facing Wellington Street. To reach it you had you pass what was said to be "Killer's Row," where the assistant under secretaries were located. I initially thought it derived its name because the occupants died an early death from overwork and pressure but was corrected: it was a sarcastic reference to this being the place where good ideas from more junior officers often met their demise.

When we were ushered into his office, Cadieux was working in shirt sleeves behind his ornate desk with his broad pants braces, very much in evidence, assisting his stout figure. Quickly putting on his jacket, he beckoned us to stand beside him next to his unlit fireplace. He was known to be a stern taskmaster but also a brilliant international lawyer who had battled the French and Quebec governments over the province's legal role abroad.[12] Cadieux asked us to look around the room at each other and to recognize that we had not only come from different parts of Canada but that each of us had passed through a highly selective process. We were among the best the country had to offer. It would take fifteen years, in his view, to make out of us good diplomats who could well serve the country:

five years to forget the various academic theories about the world that we had learned at university, and ten years of hard work in the trenches at headquarters and abroad. We left his office rather chuffed but knowing we were only starting down the diplomatic road and many potential pitfalls lay ahead. The initial challenge was to get through the probationary year.

It didn't take long to realize that diplomacy is a life-consuming profession. World events, big and small, that may require your attention can occur at any time of the day or night, on weekends or during holidays. One Friday shortly thereafter I was planning to leave for Toronto after work at five p.m. to assist Laurielle with the wedding plans. At noon I was told to see the head of the European division, John Halstead, a tall, ramrod-straight former wartime officer in the Royal Canadian Navy. He informed me that two Soviet Bear bombers had crossed into Canadian airspace over the North Atlantic, where they had been challenged by Canadian fighter jets.[13] He had called in the Soviet ambassador to lodge a formal protest and he wanted me present to take notes and prepare telegraphic reports of the meeting for the Canadian military, our embassies in Moscow, Washington and London, and our NATO delegation. The meeting was set for six p.m.

The Soviet ambassador, with an assistant of his own, showed up promptly. He claimed to have no knowledge of the incident but suggested that it must have been accidental if it had happened. Perhaps the aircraft were on their way to Cuba and had drifted off course. Halstead set him straight with the details of where and when and stressed such action must stop; it could lead to a dangerous military incident. After the meeting ended, I escorted the ambassador and his aide to the front door and returned to my office to write a draft summary of the conversation. Halstead waited to see the results for accuracy purposes, made a few corrections, and orally signed off on it. He instructed me to prepare the final report and then ensure the communications people sent it out immediately. I finished up around nine p.m. and staggered into Toronto after two a.m. Saturday morning, somewhat the worse for wear. It was all part of the job.[14]

One perk of being in the Langevin Block was that you could take a moment or two to watch the military honour guard and band march past each morning at ten a.m. en route to and from the waiting crowds on Parliament Hill.[15] On occasion I would catch a distant glimpse of the prime minister, but no close encounters.

Embassies almost always celebrate their National Day by hosting a reception at noon or in the early evening, and they invite local dignitaries as well as contacts from government, business, the media and the academic world, along with fellow diplomats and their own nationals. In Hungary's case, it shares July 1 with Canada, but in Ottawa their embassy selects another close date due to it being a Canadian holiday.

On this occasion the director of East European division was invited but begged off at the last minute due to work pressure. I was too junior to be on the guest list but was instructed to attend in his stead, with the admonition to ensure the Hungarian ambassador knew I was there as the division's representative. This was my first outing at such an event and so showed up at twelve noon sharp, only to be greeted by a wall-to-wall crowd and a reverberating noise level that made any serious conversation almost impossible. No one wanted to see me, let alone talk with me, a total unknown. If I attempted to lean into someone for a chat, they would look over my shoulder for more interesting guests and move on. There was a crowd forming near someone who looked like he might be the ambassador so, not to be intimidated, I joined the line. The din continued as suddenly I found myself in front of the gentleman, who indeed was the Hungarian ambassador. I shook his hand and yelled, "East European division," before being pushed further along. The ambassador might have been insulted by the low level of our representation, but at least he knew someone had shown up. Mission accomplished.

The arcane ways of diplomatic protocol and the art of making your presence known were becoming clearer. As the weeks in July moved on, I spent most of my time studying reports coming in from our embassies and the "five eyes" intelligence community,[16] analysing whether the USSR was going to take military action against Dubček's liberalizing measures.

Yes, No or Maybe seemed to be the options. There also was time to become acquainted with the "Visits Panel," which examined requests from Soviet Bloc officials and individuals wishing to visit Canada. Were these people a security threat or not? Even if they were, there might be a diplomatic, political or business reason to grant them entry. It often took time to decide and required the assistance of the RCMP.

THE WEDDING DATE of Saturday, July 27, was fast approaching but still no letter of permission. Laurielle knew the RCMP had interviewed some of her neighbours and friends a few weeks previously, but we became very worried. All the plans for the ceremony, reception and dinner, as well as guest lists, were set. I kept calling the people in personnel division, who tried to assure me everything would be all right, but they reiterated that nothing was official until it was official. Then two days before the big day, a cream-coloured envelope was delivered to my office with "by hand" typed on the front and on the back the embossed letterhead, in French only, "Ministère Des Affaires Exterieures, Canada." My heart skipped a beat. Inside was a letter in English from the office of the under secretary of state for External Affairs, dated the same day, which read:

> Dear Mister Smith
>
> I am pleased to give my consent to your proposed marriage to Laurielle Marie Chabeaux. I would suggest that shortly after the marriage has taken place you send a memorandum to Personnel Operations Division in Ottawa to inform them of the date of the ceremony.
>
> May I take this opportunity to extend to you and your fiancé my very best wishes for your future happiness and success.
>
> Under Secretary

Another hurdle overcome. We henceforth would be a couple and a diplomatic team.

After a one-week honeymoon in Quebec City, it was back to monitoring Soviet intentions toward Czechoslovakia. NATO analysts and the authors of other official reports were still unclear about what would happen. Some predicted the USSR would use military force, as had happened in East Berlin in 1953 and Hungary in 1956. These analysts also cited the Berlin Blockade of 1948–49, when the Soviet Union shut off all land transport to West Berlin and the Western allies led by the US were forced to mount a round-the-clock airlift of food and other supplies to the citizens in the western part of the beleaguered city. The erection of the Berlin Wall in 1961 was a further example of the measures Moscow would take to maintain its influence and to control dissent in Eastern Europe. Others made the point that there was a new leadership team in Moscow, with divided power between Brezhnev, Kosygin and Nikolai Podgorny, and they were not keen to replicate the brinkmanship of former premier and party boss Nikita Khrushchev, who had brought the world to the precipice of major conflict during the 1962 Cuban missile crisis. There also seemed to be Soviet buy-in to the concept of easing tensions—"detente"—between East and West.

Normally Soviet military preparations would be monitored by an array of personnel and equipment from NATO countries, but nothing had happened for months. Also, this was August, holiday time in Europe and North America, and many key officials were not at their posts. The same applied to Western political leaders, including Prime Minister Trudeau, who was holidaying in Spain after his gruelling leadership contest and election campaign.

Then, in the late night and early morning of August 20 and 21, the military and diplomatic telexes came alive and External's operations centre called with the news that troops and tanks were moving into Czechoslovakia. Within twenty-four hours the country was overrun by approximately two hundred and fifty thousand soldiers and roughly two thousand tanks from Hungary, Poland and Bulgaria, led by the Soviet Army and the special forces of its military intelligence unit, the GRU.[17] The most pressing concern for NATO members was whether this military assault was limited to Czechoslovakia or might be part of a much broader operation, including an attack on neighbouring West Germany. Canada had thousands of troops and considerable fighter aircraft stationed near the Czechoslovak border, and they, like other NATO forces, were on high alert.

Ottawa immediately set up a high-level task force to monitor and analyse the situation on a twenty-four-hour basis and to consider what if anything should be done beyond calling for an urgent meeting of the United Nations Security Council. Assessment reports were prepared and recommendations were debated. It was my first involvement with the concept of "carrots and sticks." Which policies should be adopted to encourage good behaviour by an adversary and which policies employed to discourage bad behaviour? Several tense days passed before a clearer picture emerged of what was happening. On Saturday, August 24, the secretary of state for External Affairs and acting PM in Trudeau's absence, Mitchell Sharp, called the task force together in his office in the East Block. I was asked to attend as secretary of the task force and to take notes. It was exciting stuff. Here it was only three months on the job and I was in the middle of a major international crisis.

As we assembled, the minister asked about coffee and sandwiches. The cafeteria in the East Block was closed on Saturdays and no support staff were available. Somebody would have to go out onto the streets of Ottawa to find an open restaurant. Being last in the pecking order meant that someone was me. So instead of recording options and decisions, I ended up taking orders for egg salad and ham and cheese. Peace or war for me at that moment had become a question of mayonnaise or mustard.

By the time of my return with the goodies, the broad outlines of our response were already becoming clear. The Soviet-led invasion was limited to Czechoslovakia and was not a direct threat to NATO nor to Canadian forces. Dubček and his closest advisers had been arrested and taken to Moscow by KGB units but returned shortly thereafter under strict supervision and with a firm mandate to reduce and dismantle the spring reforms. Hard-line communists completely loyal to Moscow would be given more power and the Iron Curtain would be reinforced.

Canada and other NATO countries would protest the smothering of human rights and fundamental freedoms, but we would not go to war over these transgressions. High-level visits would be curtailed and cultural contacts diminished, but there would be little action in cutting off mutually advantageous trade. The basic rationale was that Czechoslovakia was within the Soviet sphere of influence as laid out at the Yalta Conference toward the end of the Second World War. We would not challenge that. Where we did take decisive action was to accept some fourteen thousand persons in what was one of Canada's largest co-ordinated post-war refugee movements. Many were skilled labourers and professionals who made a significant contribution to Canadian society and our economy, as did those Hungarians who had fled their country for Canada a decade before.

The USSR would lay out a justification for its action, claiming it had the right to intervene in any socialist country in which socialism or the fundamental interests of other socialist countries were threatened. This approach would become known as the "Brezhnev Doctrine."

BY THE TIME Remembrance Day rolled around, my six-month period in the East European division had come to an end. My next assignment was a functional division, Arms Control and Disarmament. The offices in the Daly Building, at the northwest corner of Rideau Street and Sussex Drive, were decidedly less grand than those in the Langevin Block, and the former department store had markedly deteriorated since its heyday decades before. It was slated to be torn down. Few foreign diplomats came to visit.

As it turned out, my new director was our former ambassador in Czechoslovakia. He was one of those on leave when the tanks began to roll and had not wanted to return to Prague to witness the round up and confinement of those he knew and admired personally as leaders of the liberalization movement. We had a brief discussion about what had happened, but he did not want to dwell on what some observers had said was his "missed call," even though he was far from being alone. Quickly changing the subject, he told me I was to work on measures to prevent Chemical and Biological Warfare (CBW). Together with nuclear weapons, they make up the category of "Weapons of Mass Destruction" due to their ability to create large-scale death and devastation.

Canadian soldiers in the front lines at the Ypres salient in Belgium, during the First World War, had been among the first to suffer the horrors of a chlorine attack by the Germans. The low-lying gas filled the trenches and men collapsed to their death grabbing their throats. Defensive measures were quickly sought, including using bandannas soaked in water or urine, and then masks of varying quality were developed, but the only way to attempt to deter the attacks was for the Allied forces, including Canada, to develop and use retaliatory gas weapons of their own. Lethal mustard gas and phosgenes were increasingly used.

After hostilities ended, all nations set to work to deal with the scourge of chemical weapons and in 1925 were successful in negotiating the Geneva Protocol to prohibit their further use. However, the prohibition of the production and stockpiling of such weapons could not be agreed upon and remained a key priority for the Canadian government for decades to come, as did banning biological weapons.

My assignment was to assist in the marshalling of arguments Canada could use to persuade other countries to become signatories to such international treaties. Down the hall were External's United Nations experts and an array of brilliant lawyers who specialized in international law. Months and months were spent consulting with them about the right approaches for Canada to adopt. It was extremely challenging for all concerned, but a Biological Weapons Convention was signed in 1972 and entered into force in 1975. It took two more decades of hard work though before a similar Chemical Weapons Convention (prohibiting their large-scale use,[18] development, stockpiling and transfer and their precursors) was finalized in 1997 with the signatures of a hundred and ninety-three nations.

RELATIONS BETWEEN THE USSR and Czechoslovakia hadn't completely fallen off my radar, and in March 1969, international hockey became a surrogate for the bad blood between the two countries. There were two highly emotional games between them at the IIHF World Tournament in Stockholm, and for the first time ever the Czechoslovaks beat the Soviets in both matches (2–0 and 4–3). The latter victory in particular set off large-scale celebrations at home, with an estimated five hundred thousand persons in the streets. The excitement quickly turned into demonstrations against the Soviet military stationed in their country. Placards were seen with messages like "Czechoslovakia 4–Occupation forces 3" and "No tanks were there so they lost." The Prague office of the Soviet airline, Aeroflot, was burned, and there were other incidents of violence. The authorities in Moscow then used what would be called the "Czechoslovak Hockey Riots" as a pretext to remove Dubček and his supporters for good and drive a final stake through the remnants of the Prague Spring.

As May 1969 approached, my probationary period was coming to an end, successfully it seemed, and a foreign posting was in the cards. Many of my contemporaries, who remained single, were sent to Indochina to be part of the Canadian delegation to the International Control Commission in Vietnam, Laos and Cambodia, where they often found themselves in close proximity to ground and aerial bombardments and military action of one kind or another.

Then my call came. I was to be assigned to the Canadian embassy in Moscow. Before any bags could be packed, though, I had to spend a full academic year learning Russian in Ottawa.

CHAPTER FOUR

RUSSIAN SCHOOL

"GRANNY" TANCHIK GREETED Laurielle and me at the door of the former elementary school in the Ottawa suburb of Vanier. Located on a nondescript side street, the shabby two-storey brick building had seen better days when new and full of children. Now it housed the Canadian Forces Foreign Language School; the student body was decidedly older and much more limited in number.

Laurielle had decided to take a leave of absence from her elementary teaching job to join me on the course. Moscow was designated a "hardship" posting and nothing would have made it harder than if one of us could speak the language and the other could not. This would have created an unneeded and unwanted dependency of one upon the other and restricted Laurielle's independence and engagement with the local culture. The foreign service was littered with broken marriages due in part to unequal treatment, lack of spousal employment, and difficult circumstances such as a language barrier. The loss of Laurielle's teaching salary put a crimp in our budget, as we were still encumbered with my student loan payments. And so, we moved into a less desirable apartment down the street, accustomed ourselves to a less expensive diet, and became full-time students of the Russian language.

The Canadian military had been providing foreign language training to selected personnel going back to wartime.[19] There were individual instructors in Chinese, Japanese, Polish and Serbo-Croatian for the military attachés and their spouses being assigned to embassies in Beijing,

Tokyo, Warsaw and Belgrade. The prime focus of the school though was Russian, with its staff of three instructors.

Granny Tanchik was one of those three Russian instructors. She looked like a grandmother, with rimless spectacles and grey hair pulled back in a bun, but she was the one who insisted on the name. Made her more personal, she said. And who wouldn't want to learn a foreign language from their grandmother? She had sparkle to her as well as a reputation for discipline. But we weren't included in her new brood. Too bad, I thought; she looked like she could be fun and help Laurielle and me get through what was to be a gruelling one thousand or more hours of language training.

Gaspodin Dudarev was the second Russian teacher. A tall, charming, elegant gentleman with a ready, engaging smile who waved his long cigarette holder in the air to punctuate conversation. There was some mystery about him—he was reputably of noble stock, whose family had fled to Belgrade during the Russian Revolution. When Tito and the Communist Party took over Yugoslavia in 1945, Dudarev and his family decamped again, this time for Canada.

Jan Drent and his wife, Janice, were assigned to Mr. Dudarev. The Drents were several years older than us, with a daughter, and we quickly found them to be a lovely, beguiling couple who were being launched, like us, toward a common destination. As a naval commander, he was to be a military attaché at the embassy.[20] We became fast friends.

Our own instructor, Gaspodin Galko, was of a different nature. Heavyset with a round face, he lacked personality and any form of humour. He looked as if his limited wardrobe had never met an iron. Born in Belarus, he found himself, like millions of others, caught between the destructive juggernauts of Stalin's Red Army and Hitler's *Wehrmacht*.[21] As both forces and their accompanying secret police units and execution squads swept back and forth and back again, ordinary citizens struggled mightily to stay alive; their homes and towns were pulverized. At war's end, Galko found himself as a "DP" (displaced person) in the ruins of Central Europe before finding a new opportunity in Canada to apply his teaching skills. It was a past he didn't wish to discuss.

We got down to the business of learning Russian. There were just three portable desks in the large classroom. Laurielle and I sat side by side facing Galko, whose desk was directly in front of us. No hiding in the back of the classroom or having time to look absently out of the window. It was either my turn or Laurielle's to speak, and we settled into a routine of "your turn, your turn, your turn" for eight hours a day— day after day and then week after week. Two hours of homework were assigned each evening for good measure.

Russian is a soft, pleasant language to speak but is complicated by its Cyrillic alphabet, with thirty-three letters instead of the twenty-six in the English alphabet. We learned that six letters sound and look alike (A, E, K, M, O, T). Eight Russian letters look like their English counterparts but are pronounced differently (for instance, the Russian P is pronounced like the English R). Then there are sixteen Russian letters which do not exist in English but have similar pronunciations. There was much to learn. Top of the list was that CCCP in Cyrillic script is transliterated as SSSR in Latin script and in English means Union of Soviet Socialist Republics (USSR).

There are two grammatical numbers (singular and plural), six grammatical cases (nominative, genitive, dative, accusative, instrumental and prepositional) and three grammatical genders (masculine, feminine and neuter) all of which can result in one word having many different spelling combinations. The result is that Russian resembles older languages like Latin and Ancient Greek more than most modern languages. I kicked myself more than once for not paying more attention in my high-school Latin class, where my marks were rock bottom. Back then I saw no purpose in it; now there was. Grind, grind, grind. Your turn, your turn, your turn.

But there was much more to being assigned to Russia than learning the language.

AS THE LEAVES turned colour and fell to the ground, the CBC radio program we listened to in the car en route to school began to feature the phenomenal voice of Ivan Rebroff, one of those rare singers with the gift of a four and a half octave vocal range, from soprano to bass, who beautifully performed classic Russian folk songs like the "Song of the Volga Boatmen," "Kalinka" and "Cossack Patrol." Many of his recordings featured the classic Russian instrument, the balalaika, including his haunting rendition of "Lara's Theme" from the 1965 movie *Dr. Zhivago*. Watching that movie and reading the original novel by Boris Pasternak was in itself an introduction to the history of the Russian Revolution, the vastness of the country and the struggle of individualism. The marvellous winter scenes, with horse-drawn sleighs and the ice-covered house at Varykino, all fired up your imagination—even if it turned out that much of the movie was filmed in Spain and Finland, with a few snippets of Alberta's foothills (as seen from a Canadian Pacific Railway train) to add a slice of Canadian content.

During our limited free time on weekends, we would dip into the vast treasure trove of Russian literature. From the sprawling historical novels of Leo Tolstoy to Anton Chekhov's classic short stories of frustrated dreams and unfulfilled expectations to the idealized prose and poetry of Alexander Pushkin. And after putting down a book, there were always LPs to place on the record player, with the evocative symphonies, ballets and operas of Tchaikovsky or the stirring piano concertos of Rachmaninoff, to name just a few. Or we could envision the numerous ballet stars performing at the Bolshoi and Kirov theatres. Russia had such a rich tapestry of culture to choose from.

We realized though that having cultural icons with international reputations was no guarantee against a country producing dictatorial or authoritarian governments and murderous leaders. Pasternak, as well as Alexandr Solzhenitsyn's searing works about the Soviet gulag prison system, had made that clear in the case of Russia. Just as Beethoven and Goethe being part of German history did not prevent the rise of Nazism.

Laurielle and I came to the end of our Russian language training in June of 1970. It had been tough sledding for both of us, but here we now stood, in front of the school director as he handed us a Royal Canadian Air Force Certificate of Completion. More than a thousand hours of instruction.

A night and day of celebration might have been called for, but we had received news a few weeks earlier that our posting had been cancelled. The position I was to occupy in Moscow had been eliminated as part of Trudeau's budgetary cuts to External Affairs and National Defence.

Personnel division suggested we be sent to Yugoslavia instead, but the ambassador there rightly said it "made no sense," as it would be a waste of our Russian language skills. Instead, we moved for a third time within Ottawa. Laurielle went back to teaching in September, and I was sent to New York for three months to the United Nations General Assembly meetings as an "advisor" to the First (Political) Committee.

As it turned out, the prime minister's own visit to the USSR, scheduled for the autumn, was postponed due to the "October Crisis," involving the kidnapping of a British trade official in Montreal and the murder of the deputy premier of Quebec by a militant separatist group, the Front de libération du Québec. Suddenly Ottawa, of all places, was part of a state of "apprehended insurrection" and armed Canadian troops filled the downtown streets. Laurielle described to me on the phone how she had to pass through military checkpoints as she went back and forth to school and to shop for groceries.

Upon returning to Ottawa in mid-December, the much-awaited call finally occurred.

"Moscow is on." The prime minister had rescheduled his visit for May, and they wanted me to be there by the end of February to help prepare for it. There would be a period of overlap with another officer, and the new plan was to fill his position come the summer. Easy to say. Harder to prepare for with only two months' notice.

Laurielle submitted her resignation at her elementary school as of the end of the calendar year. We gave notice for our apartment. Plans were made for a trip to Toronto for a farewell with family and long-standing friends. Medical shots, including for typhoid and tetanus, were received and recorded in our yellow-and-black international health certificates. Medicines and items of personal hygiene, said to be in short supply in Moscow, were purchased in bulk. Needed dental work was completed. Diplomatic visas for the USSR were processed. Paperwork for a "posting loan" was submitted to permit us to purchase some "representational" dishware and cutlery, as well as a "black tie" and the appropriate dresses for formal occasions. Arrangements were put in place with a specialized kennel outside of Ottawa to ship Sabu, our Samoyed dog, direct to Moscow. And because we had so few possessions, beyond Sabu and various clothing items, we were able to largely avoid the time-consuming and frustrating experience of the government's strict and complicated inventory requirements. By mid-February we were finally ready to depart for Moscow.

My official diplomatic title was to be "Second Secretary and Vice-Consul"—normally, a diplomat starts at the bottom of the ladder as "Third Secretary," but my time at the United Nations had moved me up a rung. The Vice-Consul designation, which was proclaimed in a formal scroll with the Queen's name on it, stated I had the shared consular responsibility, with a few of my Embassy colleagues, to "aid and protect those Canadian citizens who may trade or visit or reside within the Consular district of Moscow"—namely, the entire Soviet Union.

Ottawa was on course to record its highest seasonal snowfall ever (444.1 centimetres); far beyond anything ever experienced in Moscow. We figured this would provide us with a good bragging point upon our arrival. So would the fact that Ottawa was listed as the second-coldest capital in the world, behind Ulan Bator in Mongolia but ahead of Moscow. For a Canadian, the weather equalled, and sometimes even surpassed, hockey as a subject of conversation.

CHAPTER FIVE

TO MOSCOW...
WITH SKATES

I T WAS LATE afternoon on February 22, 1971, when our British
European Airways flight from London landed in light snow at
Moscow's Sheremetyevo airport. Laurielle and I let out a sigh of nervous
apprehension. This was it. No more book learning, analysing or cultural
interaction from the safety of home in one's own country. We would now
be directly experiencing life in the heart of communism. Were we ready?
We were both twenty-six years old.

Peering from the aircraft windows, we watched as several armed
guards surrounded the aircraft. Clad in belted grey heavy sheepskin
coats down to the knees, felted boots and the ubiquitous four-sided fur
hats, they were imposing and clearly well protected from the apparent
biting wind and cold. Metal badges depicting the hammer and sickle
were front and centre on their hats. Members of the Border Security
Forces, a unit of the Committee for State Security (KGB), the guards
presumably were doing double duty: ensuring no one left the aircraft
surreptitiously while also preventing any of their fellow citizens from
hitching an unauthorized ride to the West on the return flight.[22]

The BEA flight had been close to empty, carrying the odd Western
businessman or journalist and a smattering of foreign tourists—the latter
brave enough to face the Russian winter and Intourist, the USSR govern-
ment-run tourist organization, which was hard pressed to convince the
security-conscious bureaucracy about the merits of providing quality
accommodation, varied meals and reliable domestic travel arrangements

to foreigners. Soviet officials and those few others who were permitted to travel abroad were obliged to fly on Aeroflot, the state-run aircraft.

Our red diplomatic passports put us into a separate line at Passport Control. After much looking up and down, comparing our faces with the photos in the passports, and ensuring our diplomatic visas issued by the Soviet embassy in Ottawa were in order, the grim-faced official applied his stamps and waved us through to the arrivals area. No cheery welcome was offered. Our faces broke into smiles, though, when we caught sight of Jan and Janice Drent, our friends and colleagues from the Russian language school who had arrived the past summer and with six months under their belts were already experts in our untested eyes. There was much to catch up on and many questions to ask as we piled into a black embassy vehicle, an imported Ford, with its distinctive white licence plates and black letters and numbers (CD-03), which readily identified it to Soviet authorities and others as being a diplomatic vehicle belonging to Canada.

We had not driven very far from the airport under the darkening sky when we came upon three massive x-shaped steel tank traps on the right-hand side of the road. They had been erected in 1966 in the town of Khimki as a memorial to mark the farthest point of the German advance in December 1941. I had read descriptions of the battles in books, but it was startling to see how close the Wehrmacht had come to Moscow. The outskirts of the city were only a twenty-minute drive away.

There was little traffic. Snow removal was underway. Old women were sweeping the sidewalks with short three-foot-long brooms, which forced them to bend over to do their work. Russian women had to shoulder a heavy load in many functions throughout the country, given the massive loss of men during the war. Decrepit dump trucks lined the streets waiting their turn to be fed snow by a strange vehicle with two pinball-like flippers at the bottom of an upwards-moving conveyor belt. The streets were dimly lit. No garish neon lights proclaiming the products of this store or that one. The only advertising we could see consisted of billboards displaying Party messages, portraits of Lenin, Marx and

Engels, and the odd movie poster announcing a state-controlled film. Elevated display cases on the street contained each page of government and party newspapers. Most of the stucco-clad pastel-coloured buildings were badly faded or peeling. A general aura of shabbiness prevailed.

The embassy driver, a Russian, finally turned into a walled apartment complex on Kutuzovsky Prospect and past two guards manning a security box. They saluted as we went by. The eight-storey yellow-brick building was divided into five segments, each with its own entranceway from the parking lot. There was no access from the street. Each entry had a stairway surrounding an elevator, which you could watch going up and down, and an adjacent long, tubular garbage chute that emptied into the basement. There were no Soviet citizens in the building, only a motley assortment of foreign diplomats and their families from around the world, a sprinkling of resident businessmen, and various journalists assigned to newspaper "bureaus" to report firsthand on events in Moscow and the Soviet Union. The exterior of the Drents' building was a carbon copy of the other buildings that stood at attention along the broad boulevard named for General Mikhail Kutuzov, who had commanded the Imperial Russian Army when it repelled Napoleon's invasion in 1812. A carbon copy, that is, except for the walls and security guards.

The major difference in accommodation between locals and foreigners, beside the basic rule that they had to be separated, was the interior configuration of the apartments. The Drents and other foreigners had a modest living room with adjoining dining room, two bedrooms, a bathroom and a smallish kitchen, achieved by putting two standard Russian apartments together. Each Russian family had only one living/dining room and a bedroom, while the bathroom and kitchen were shared with another family. Space and privacy were at a minimum, but at least the apartments were heated, had running water, and were a physical improvement over run-down wooden housing. There was high demand for these apartments, however small, and the government decided who would be allotted one and, indeed, through residency permits, who might live in Moscow.

There was no doubt the Soviet government faced a major challenge regarding housing. Vast areas of the country had been decimated by the Nazi onslaught, and apparently the only way to deal with the shortage was the rapid construction of apartment blocks, no matter how small or poorly assembled. That it was now twenty-six years after the end of the war demonstrated both the magnitude of the challenge and the inefficiency of the response.

We had a pleasant evening with the Drents going over what to expect now we were on the ground. Janice had served a tasty pork roast and explained how she went about putting food on the table for Jan and their three-and-a-half-year-old daughter, as well as how to fete other military attachés and foreigners at diplomatic dinners. The pork and vegetables had come from a "special" store reserved for foreigners and privileged Russians, such as high Communist Party officials, senior military and security officers, and foreign currency earners such as musicians, ballerinas and hockey players who were permitted to travel abroad. Payment was by coupon only, controlled by the government.

Janice explained that one could also order wine, beer, cigarettes, tinned goods, electronics and other household items from two export firms in Copenhagen that trucked items in weekly. Fresh milk (on the recommendation of the British and American embassy doctors), fresh fruit and green vegetables came in once a week by train from Helsinki—the order being placed by the embassy Friday noon and delivered at a Moscow train station the following Tuesday. Both arrangements required payment in hard currency.[23]

The Russians had a terrible time bringing fresh fruit to Moscow for their own citizens. The collective farm system was inefficient. Vast bureaucracy throttled initiative, and there were poor road networks from the south of the country, where the majority of the fruit was grown, plus a lack of refrigerated trucks and trains. The government had higher priorities than fruit for the use of its limited supply of hard currency, therefore if it couldn't barter with another country, like Cuba; for whatever reason, importing fruit was not a viable option.

Janice described how their daughter, Margaret, was enrolled in the Russian "Detsky Sad" (kindergarten) across the street and like the other young girls wore a pinafore and large bow in her hair. Although the Russian staff was leery of Westerners, Janice was very pleased with the genuine care and affection shown their daughter, that was in keeping with the high esteem in which Russians as a whole hold children. Janice expressed her pleasant surprise with the speed at which Margaret was learning the Russian language.

Older Canadian children had a choice of attending either the Lycée school for francophones in Moscow, run by the French government as part of its international education system, or for anglophones the so-called "ABC" school organized by the American, British and Canadian governments. Both were small and lacked lab and sporting equipment but made up for it with the enthusiasm of the staff, hired from among the foreign community, and the quality of the students. Some families chose to leave their children behind in boarding schools. Laurielle, as a teacher herself, was warmly welcomed and took on an elementary class and helped out with art lessons throughout the ABC school.

Before leaving the Drents to spend the night in temporary embassy quarters, we were informed that Laurielle and I were invited to have lunch with the ambassador and his wife at noon the next day and to show up at the "official residence" a half hour early for separate meetings. These so-called "interviews" had for years sent chills up and down the spines of newly arrived Canadian diplomats and particularly their spouses, ever since Robert Arthur Douglas Ford had taken up his current ambassadorial position in 1964. The word was he and his Brazilian wife, Theresa, would take those thirty minutes, and the following luncheon, to make respective judgments on your appearance, manners, deportment, sociability, intelligence and Russian language capability, and then the two of them would compare notes as to whether you were deemed to be "presentable."

There was never any formal response as to whether you and your spouse made the grade as a team. If you received an invitation to the

Fords' special social events, then that was evidence of acceptance. If no invitation was forthcoming, you drew your own conclusions. Not only could the latter situation be dispiriting, it could impact your career. Representational skills were an important part of a diplomat's attributes, and in those days your spouse played a full supporting role. Indeed, a spouse's abilities to represent Canada were included on her husband's annual rating report even if she was not a government employee.

Ambassador Ford was a daunting figure. Tall, with slicked-back black hair and a moustache, he walked with a cane to assist his legs, which had never fully recovered from a childhood case of polio. Impeccably dressed at all times, he wore his suit pants high under his rib cage with suspenders and reinforced pockets, which you could grab to assist him getting into and out of vehicles. He looked like what you would expect an ambassador to look like. He had studied history and English at Western, then received an MA in history from Cornell University before being recruited into External Affairs in 1940 at the age of thirty-five. There were two early assignments in Moscow during Stalin's time, followed by a series of successive ambassadorial positions in Colombia, Yugoslavia, Egypt and then back to Moscow for the third time. By 1971, he had become the dean of the diplomatic corps as the longest continuously serving ambassador to the USSR from any country. As such, he represented the common interests of all embassies to the Soviet government on matters such as security, accommodation and travel restrictions. Soviet officials respected him for his language skills and knowledge of their country, while foreign governments around the world, including in Washington and London, sought his views and analysis.[24]

When you were summoned to the ambassador's office to discuss an issue, you wasted no time getting there and had to be prepared to defend the language and substance of any of your reports. He insisted on timeliness, that vocabulary be concise and at the same time descriptive, and, naturally, that you had your facts straight and opinions substantiated. Ford did not have to say that the embassy in Moscow had a reputation to maintain—you understood that from day one.

If the ambassador would hold his tongue with Soviets out of diplomatic necessity that was not the case with Theresa, to whom he was devoted. They had met and married while both served their respective countries in Colombia. She was sophisticated yet outspoken, temperamental but insightful. She would call you "darling" rather than your first name, and she knew how to entertain in an elegant way that would outdo most Parisian hostesses. People would come away dazzled by the effort she made on their behalf.

If she spotted you or your spouse talking to a fellow Canadian embassy colleague at one of her gatherings, it wouldn't take long for her to approach you with an order to "circulate." As she would make clear, it was your job to talk with the guests, not with each other. You could do that on your own time. Theresa was not everyone's cup of tea, but if you wanted to learn about setting a high standard in the art of diplomatic hospitality, there was no better teacher.

WITHIN A FEW days we were assigned an apartment of our own in a new building for foreigners in the far southwest area of the capital. It was more than double the height of the more centrally located buildings, but even though it had just been constructed it appeared to be falling apart. Windows and doors did not fit properly, plumbing pipes and electrical wiring were shoved through walls without any effort to fill in the resultant holes, bits and pieces were falling off or missing from external walls.

Our apartment was sparsely if adequately furnished as we awaited our shipment of personal goods. We were situated on the seventeenth floor with an excellent view over the neighbouring area, including a small housing complex nestled in a forest. It seemed out of place. A local Russian said it was where our "good British friends" resided. We gathered that he was referring cryptically to Donald Maclean and Guy Burgess, who had spied for the USSR and defected to Moscow in 1951, and the double agent Kim Philby, who followed suit in 1963. Philby's deception was one of the worst intelligence failures to hit the West during the Cold

War. Philby was believed to have been the British intelligence officer who outed many of his fellow colleagues, including possibly David Cornfield in the British embassy in Bonn, West Germany, who later went on to write spy novels under the pen name John le Carré.

Having secured accommodation, our next task turned to retrieving our dog, Sabu. She was due in on the weekly Air Canada flight from Montreal. Just hours before proceeding to the airport to pick her up, a telephone call came through from the assistant Air Canada station chief, Aggie Kukulowicz, who explained the dog had missed the flight. Something about her having eaten the vaccination and state-of-health papers that had been attached to the side of her kennel. No documents meant no shipment. Air Canada would have her vaccinated for a second time with the hope she would be on the next weekly flight. Sure enough, seven days later, Aggie called to confirm Sabu was on board. He would be busy dealing with incoming passengers but explained where to locate the dog. Somehow the Soviet baggage handlers decided on a different course of action and transported her directly to the unheated freight sheds in the woods on the opposite side of the airport. A half-hour later, with night setting in and a cold wind blowing across the snow-drifts, I tracked her kennel down under a mound of parcels. A smiling clerk explained they were just trying to keep her warm. Sabu went on to become a favourite on the streets of Moscow. Pedestrians, when learning she was a Samoyed, quickly referred to Laika, who was a similar breed. Laika was a kind of canine Russian folk hero since, in November 1957, she became the first animal to orbit the Earth. Soviet citizens had been conditioned not to talk to foreigners, but they loved dogs as much as they did children and would engage in some limited conversation. It was a case of canine diplomacy at work.

Next up: we needed to obtain personal transportation. The locally made Zhiguli[25] and larger Volga were in extremely short supply for individuals, and there were long waiting lists except for those Soviets in privileged positions or foreigners with hard currency. The squat Zhiguli might have been considered a muscle car because it required a lot of muscle to change gears with the floor stick-shift, but it would usually start in the winter and once rolling was serviceable. We purchased one as a second vehicle.

Maybe it was foolish youth, but after having owned a series of used vehicles, we also opted for a new Ford Mustang. The "pony car" had hit the North American market in 1964 to much fanfare and became extremely popular following its dramatic appearance in the Steve McQueen movie *Bullitt*. Ford had a reduced price for diplomats, which also excluded all taxes and duties, thereby putting it in our modest price range. The easiest shipping arrangement was for Ford of Canada to ship the car to a dealer in Helsinki and for us to take the train there and drive the car back to Moscow. All went well until we crossed the Finnish-Soviet border. The two countries had been at war; Finland had fought on the side of Germany, and in retribution the USSR had seized a portion of Finnish territory. As a result, maps and signage were not always accurate. At one point on our journey we reached an intersection and stopped, unsure which direction to follow. After a brief interlude we noticed an official-looking man step from the woods and signal with his arm that a right turn was in order. Sometimes a surveillance system works to your advantage.

We pulled into Leningrad to overnight and parked the car in front of a local hotel. In the morning, we discovered the windshield wipers had disappeared, the two side mirrors had been ripped off, and the large Mustang-emblemed gas cap on the back of the car was gone. A bad start and a learning experience, but the hotel administration helped us find serviceable replacement parts. My confusion about why someone would make away with side mirrors was cleared up a few weeks later at a ballet performance when I noticed a woman nearby had opened her purse and, instead of a compact mirror, took out a car mirror to check her image. Another case of demand and supply.

AGGIE WAS QUICK to recruit me for the Moscow Maple Leafs hockey team, of which he was the captain. The Canadian embassy had a modest recreational team in the early to mid-sixties, but it was limited to six or seven players and only had games against less skilled American embassy personnel. Peter Worthington, the resident correspondent for the *Toronto Telegram*, was dragooned into joining the team in the mid-sixties and revelled in wearing a jersey with James Bond's "007" emblazoned on it as a deliberate thumbed nose to any local Russians watching the outdoor games. As the Canadian embassy staff grew in size and those who could play hockey increased, there was a growing nucleus for a more organized endeavour, which occurred in 1966 when Aggie arrived with the opening of the Air Canada resident station.

Aggie had long since abandoned his given first name of Adolph. While it was once common and popular in Central Europe, where his parents were from and when he was born in 1933 in Winnipeg, it was no longer the case after 1939 when the Second World War began.

Aggie had that magic aura of having played in the NHL—even if his tenure in the league was limited to only four games with the New York Rangers spread over the 1952–53 and 1953–54 seasons. He scored one goal during his NHL career. We were impressed and so were the Russians. Here was a guy who had made a living playing hockey for fifteen years, moving hither and yon with teams like the Quebec Citadelles, Saskatoon Quakers and New Westminster Royals, as well as the Seattle Totems, St. Paul Saints and Minneapolis Millers in the US.

Aggie, his wife, Diane, and three children were no strangers to travel and airports, and therefore, with his language skills, it was no surprise that he ended up with Air Canada in Moscow after his hockey career ended. He had a natural affinity for people and easy-going manner, and everyone took to him without hesitation. Dealing with baggage, freight and passengers wasn't always glamorous, but it was vital in a place like Moscow, and he quickly became a reliable, go-to person for a variety of issues—including, of course, hockey. With his Canadian hockey connections and access to Air Canada facilities, he was able to secure a number of cast-off uniforms from the Toronto Maple Leafs following their Stanley Cup victory in 1967.[26] It didn't take long for the newly attired Canadian embassy team to be dubbed the Moscow Maple Leafs. The team was largely composed of Canadians, but several Finns and Swedes joined in, and after much searching for a competent goaltender, a Marine from the US embassy was found to be suitable.

Each Saturday afternoon the team would suit up and play a match at various outdoor rinks, including Lenin Park, primarily against the members of the Soviet Ministry of Foreign Trade or TASS, the Soviet news agency—both organizations' personnel were authorized to deal with foreigners. On a rare occasion a more exotic team, like Accordion Factory Number Thirteen, would be given permission to play against us. Embassy family members would attend, sitting in the limited stands and bundled up against the wind, cold and possible snow. There was always the traditional exchange of pins or small gift items at centre ice before each match, with one innovation on our part that the Russians always appreciated: a case of Canadian beer. It was the Russians' choice when to start drinking the contents.

Aggie played centre and, with his size (six foot three and a hundred and seventy-five pounds) and experience, it usually didn't take long before he was across the blue line putting the puck in the Russian net. My position was a shaky left defence, playing behind my stellar embassy colleague Peter Hancock, who through a combination of competence and mainly luck became known as "Goal-a-Game" Hancock. The skill level of all our players was many notches below that of Aggie.

Our team more than held its own in these outdoor games, but toward the end of the season, the TASS team challenged us to a match at the big indoor Palace of Sports, with the notice that they would publish the results around the world on their wire service. We should have known what was coming, but it became patently clear when two members of their team appeared on the ice with only skates and sticks and no other equipment. The ringers were both defencemen brought in from one of the Soviets' top clubs, Dynamo, and their purpose was to stop Aggie, which they did, plus blast shots from the point at our overwhelmed goalie. It was no contest. They claimed it was only fair, given Aggie's presence, while we protested, saying he was a regular player on our team, not ringers brought in for only one game. The lopsided score was published. It was a lesson about the importance to establishing agreed-upon rules with the Russians.

Once a year we had a game with the embassy of Czechoslovakia, followed by a banquet, which we took turns hosting. Although the Czechoslovaks were members of the Warsaw Pact, and we were from a NATO country, there was great affinity and fellowship at these events, and Czech beer was every bit as good as Canadian brews. A few of them spoke broken English, but those of us who could spoke with them mainly with Russian as our lingua franca. Both countries loved hockey, and it was amazing as the evening festivities wore on, after an evenly played match, how they began to quietly confide in us about their distaste for our host country. They were officially allies of the USSR, but the Soviet invasion of their country had clearly left them bitterly aggrieved.

When Canada dropped out of world competition in 1970 and sanctioned matches against international teams, the Moscow Maple Leafs became the only Canadian team engaged in playing the Russians. The team developed its own hockey crest and created a t-shirt which proudly stated, "Moscow Maple Leafs, Canada's Greatest Road Team."

While we all loved our hockey team, not everyone was a fan of the Toronto Maple Leafs and the colours blue and white. We set out to remedy this problem with the embassy broomball team, which needed sweaters for our matches on Sunday afternoons against the Swedish, Finnish and American embassies.

The Canadian Club in the basement of the embassy building was open on Friday nights for beer, snacks, darts and socializing, and it became a popular gathering spot for personnel from Western countries. As our beer supply was running low, we decided to write to John "David" Molson, the president of Molson brewery in Montreal with an order for fifteen hundred cases of Molson Ex and Molson Canadian. In the same letter we conveyed a request for sweaters from the Montreal Canadiens, which Molson's owned at the time, so that the Leafs wouldn't be the only team represented in Moscow. The task of writing the letter fell to me.

A couple of weeks passed, but then a telegram arrived. Our gambit of combining commerce with sports and pride had worked. The iconic *bleu, blanc et rouge* sweaters of the Habs would arrive shortly via Air Canada, while the beer would be shipped by sea to the ice-free port of Murmansk, where we would have to make arrangements for onward shipment to Moscow.

The information about the sweaters was great news—less so about the beer. Murmansk was about two thousand kilometres from Moscow, and it was winter. Our local administrative officer said the risk of pilferage with a cargo as precious as foreign beer was extremely high and recommended we hire armed guards to ride the train for protection. Even that didn't work, for when the beer finally arrived at the train station in Moscow, over half of it had disappeared and the other half was frozen solid and not drinkable. Molson repeated the order in the summer with better results, but we found it more reliable and cheaper, though less patriotic, to order Heineken beer via truck from the Danish export firms.

Beer aside, we were now equipped in our new Sunday best: Montreal uniforms. We dubbed ourselves "The Moscow Canadiens" or "Les Canadiens de Moscou."

The game of broomball itself was a modified version adapted to local circumstances. We played on the frozen tennis court of the British ambassador and not on a full-sized rink. The brooms were not the normal hockey-stick length, given the close quarters, but the three-foot switch brooms used by the old women on the streets. Dipped into a pail of water and then put outside to freeze solid before the game, they were a lethal weapon. The Finns and Swedes were friendly competitors but not so the Americans, who were represented by the Marine detachment at the US embassy. They didn't like to lose at anything and were in tremendous physical shape. Their upper body development though made them top heavy, and their lack of familiarity with maintaining their balance on ice made them vulnerable. Our tactic was to propel ourselves from the snow built up at the side of the tennis court and hit them low, often toppling them and retrieving the ball. The Marines didn't take it lightly, and a few years later two of them were sent back to the United States by their ambassador for cold-cocking Canadian players.

The weekend sporting outings often left you bruised and limping, but they were a great way to blow off steam in the pressure cooker of life in Moscow. Still, there was work to be done.

CANADA'S BRILLIANT FORMER ambassador to the US, Allan Gotlieb, once described the role of a diplomat as three professions in one: one-third journalist, reporting home on what was happening in the country where you were assigned and detailing its relevance to Canadian political, military, security, economic, trade, immigration, social and other interests; another third lawyer, negotiating a multitude of agreements and articulating the positions and opinions of the Canadian government on a variety of matters of national interest; and the other third innkeeper, responsible for organizing visits and meetings and providing food and drink to facilitate them, with the aim of securing successful outcomes for Canadian objectives. So it was for me and my colleagues in Moscow.

One of the key questions for the embassy to answer, as it was for all Western embassies, was the vital matter of who was really in charge in the Soviet Union. Where did power lie? Who was making the decisions, in what field, and what was the rationale behind the decision making? What were the leaders' short- and long-term intentions, and could they be subjected to influence or persuasion?

Given the pervasive secrecy in the USSR, this was no straightforward task. There was no public accountability. Soviet leaders would appear together just twice a year, atop the Kremlin walls: on May 1 for the colourful parade to honour workers; and on November 7 to mark the anniversary of the Communist Revolution with another parade, this one featuring marching soldiers, tanks and missiles to demonstrate Soviet military might. In each case, the Soviet leadership would line up in order of importance (precedence), or as it was called by some, "stroke order," and over time one could determine who might be moving up in authority, moving down, suddenly disappearing, or witness someone new emerging on the scene. What the implications were though was a different story. All this was part of what was described as "Kremlinology"—trying to figure out what was happening in the Kremlin.

One of my functions with the embassy was to read through the Soviet government newspaper *Izvestia* (News), which came out every afternoon. My closest colleague, Peter Hancock, who was also conversant in the Russian language, was responsible for the Communist Party daily, *Pravda* (Truth), which appeared every morning. Ordinary Russians often sarcastically said there was never any news in *Izvestia* and never any truth in *Pravda*.

One day a photograph appeared in *Izvestia* of some members of the Soviet leadership standing outside during the winter opening of a new factory. The leaders were not lined up in their customary order, which was puzzling, so I brought it to the attention of Hancock. We compared it to the picture of the same event that ran in *Pravda*. They were different. What did it mean? Was there a divergence in views about the leadership between the party and the government? We decided to send it to Ottawa for further study.

We had taken ourselves too seriously. The response from Ottawa stated there was nothing to our observations and then upbraided us for forgetting, as good Canadians, that people move around when standing in the snow.

A diplomat's life had not only a day shift and a night shift but was a twenty-four-hour shift. You had to be ready to be dragged from your bed to deal with some unexpected crisis or to work through the night or the weekend as circumstances dictated. You never knew what was coming next, but it almost always was interesting and challenging and could involve headline stories and prominent personalities. It is not a career for those who favour routine and stable hours. Not everything brought a smile to your face or gave you a sense of accomplishment. Nor was every encounter one of champagne and caviar. There also was a dark side to being a Western diplomat in Moscow.

CHAPTER SIX

SWALLOWS
AND RAVENS

O F COURSE LAURIELLE and I had been briefed in Ottawa about the
KGB and efforts to entrap us, but reality set in at my first meeting
with the embassy security officer when he put his fingers to his lips and
proceeded to play cocktail music from various speakers in his office. The
hubbub of voices at a cocktail party was supposed to mask our conversation, but he chose to whisper nevertheless and to use a writing pad on
which the words could be erased by lifting the cover sheet.

The walls had ears, he explained. So did the roof and the basement. The KGB played a never-ending game of installing listening
devices in the exterior walls of the Chancery[27] under the pretext that
they needed to be painted, plastered or repaired or that electrical wiring
or telephone lines needed to be replaced. The basement provided even
more excuses—plumbing or sewer line repairs. We were not allowed
to bring in personnel from Canada to do the maintenance work, but
Canadian "technicians" would arrive to "sweep" the building and remove
the installed devices. In no time the Russians would be back at it. We
had a Canadian mechanic on staff whose job was to service the official
embassy vehicles and our own personal cars—not only to keep them
running but to make sure there was no "extra wiring" installed while
they were left unattended. Conversation inside the Chancery, as a result,
was limited to general pleasantries. If there were important matters of
policy or significant personnel issues to discuss, we would retreat into
a cramped copper-shielded box suspended above the floor. As a result,

we stuck primarily to writing. Draft after draft was prepared on pink paper. Initially handwritten and then typed by our Canadian secretaries. Once we were happy with the content (diplomats love wordsmithing, so it took time) and it had been approved by the ambassador or a senior officer, it would be retyped and then taken to the communications room to be coded and sent by telex to Ottawa and, as appropriate, to other Canadian embassies around the world. If the subject matter was not urgent or was especially lengthy, such as a dispatch about the state of the Soviet economy, then it would go by red diplomatic bags, which were picked up and carried by hand aboard aircraft by special diplomatic couriers from Canada. The bags had their own seats and never left the sight of the couriers.

Members of the Canadian Corps of Commissionaires, who were retired military personnel, were assigned to the embassy to guard entrances to the Chancery and to buzz in Canadian personnel to the secure area. In the evenings they patrolled the inside of the building and ensured that all documents were locked up in the large safes each of us had in our offices. Typewriter ribbons were taken out and wastepaper baskets and phones checked.

The streets however belonged to the Soviet militia and KGB. One and often two guards stood on the sidewalk in front of the main Chancery door questioning anyone not recognized as embassy staff. There were often tussles on the street when they prevented entry "for security reasons," primarily to Russians but sometimes to visiting Canadians. On occasion someone would be bundled into a black car and driven away. There also was a sentry box—or "milibox," as we called it, shortening militia—at the entrance to the embassy parking lot beside the Chancery, and all vehicles and passengers coming and going were closely scrutinized. All our apartments and telephones were also bugged. Our technicians were not allowed to work on living quarters and all maintenance was undertaken by the Russian Diplomatic Service Board (UPDK). We simply had to put up with the "listening devices" at home, but it took some getting used to. We had been instructed by Ottawa not to discuss family matters, nor personal financial issues, and if we had an argument with a spouse, to "take it to the parking lot." But who knew in advance when some disagreement might erupt, necessitating a pause in order to get your hat, coat and boots on and to go outside? Then there was the question of bedroom activities. Not everyone was comfortable knowing that someone in the apartment complex basement was listening to your every tender moment. Laurielle laughed when I sloughed it off by saying the listeners might learn something new.

UPDK had another weapon in its arsenal: the crew of maids supplied to each diplomatic household. Officially, these staff members were hired to ensure that each apartment stayed clean (fighting off the copious and surprisingly large cockroaches was a major challenge, as was the garbage generated from the different food and sanitary habits of people from around the world). The second stated reason was "to make life easier for our foreign guests." We were assigned a forty-year-old woman, Marina, with a round face and a prominent gold tooth, who was kind and gentle in every respect. Marina adored our dog, Sabu, from the beginning, and two years later, when our daughter was born, we could not have asked for a more caring and loving person to watch over her. Trouble was that toward the end of each month Marina would start to become nervous. After some time and following growing rapport with Laurielle, Marina revealed that she had a monthly obligation to report on us to the Soviet authorities. There were questions to answer about our state of mind, whether we were getting along with each other, whether we worried about money, and whether she was aware of any incriminating information or items around the apartment which could be used against us.

Another part of the KGB playbook, to unsettle you when you were out of the apartment, was to rifle through your belongings to check for themselves. Nothing was ever thrown on the floor or wildly left out of place—just enough movement of things so you knew they were there and could enter at any time. Once in a while something would go missing. Our Air Force attaché was ordered to leave the country on forty-eight hours' notice for what the Russians called "activities incompatible with his official status." The night before he and his wife were to leave Moscow, they attended a farewell dinner hosted by colleagues in the Military Attaché Corps. When they returned afterward to their apartment, an expensive ring he had given his wife a few days earlier was gone. A farewell of a different kind, with a boot from the KGB.

Eavesdropping, electronic intelligence, and information from the maids provided some good fodder for the Soviet security service, especially if they found out that you were experiencing money problems. If you were, it would not be long before someone on the street, at a park or at a gathering of some kind would approach you with the offer of exchanging money at a very favourable rate; say seven or eight roubles for a dollar compared to the official rate of close to one to one. You could buy a lot of extra local items that way, and more than one person fell for it. After several exchanges of money and a few secret photographs of the transactions, the trap was sprung. You then had to weigh the undesirable option of being exposed to your government (leading to withdrawal from the post and likely dismissal at home) or doing some favours for the KGB.

While most embassy personnel were assigned middle-aged maids, UPDK had a different twist for the Australians, who tended to send single men to Moscow, in contrast to the married couples dispatched at the time by Washington, Ottawa and London. Maids assigned to the Australians always seemed to be very young, very attractive, and with the shortest skirts in town. One Australian diplomat told me he had the last laugh as the patented Russian plan to entrap him backfired as he preferred another gender.

Soviet ideologues believed that the West was decadent, and its citizens had inherent carnal weaknesses. The KGB accordingly set up what was called, in the lexicon of espionage and embassy circles, a "swallows' nest" of alluring Russian and Ukrainian women who were willing or compelled to engage in sexual activity. They were deployed regularly in hotel bars frequented by foreign businessmen and other tourists who might be tempted by the prospects of an intimate encounter with a beautiful woman far from home. But inevitably in the Soviet Union it would be followed with you being presented with pictures and audio tapes of your transgressions, with the threat that they could fall into the hands of your family and/or your employer if you did not co-operate. We constantly had to warn fellow Canadians, including hockey personnel, of this danger. More than one distraught Canadian, after being snared, quickly showed up at the embassy to seek help. We had a standard response: No matter how hard it might be to face the music and consequences at home, it was a far easier course of action to follow than to end up dealing with espionage charges. An immediate departure from the USSR was counselled and we provided assistance as required.

Swallows could be deployed anywhere: railway stations and on trains, in stores where Westerners gathered, or often in the lobbies of theatres, the ballet or opera. At these performances there were often beautiful young women in the audience who spoke excellent English and who during intermission in the lobby would strike up a conversation about the quality of the production. They could be genuine enthusiasts of the arts or serious students, but one's antenna was always up, and it was wise to stay clear.

As a Russian speaker from a NATO country, I was on the target list for swallows. One evening at a hotel on the road between Moscow and Leningrad, I had come down from my room to eat in the dining room. It was packed and all the places were taken except for two seats at a four-person booth. I was escorted there, where a couple was already seated on the opposite side. Scant minutes later a stunning woman slipped in beside me on the aisle seat, blocking my exit. The three of them peppered me with questions about who I was, where I was from and what I was doing here; though it was safe to assume they had all the answers before I gave any response.

Russian dining rooms, where they existed, frequently featured live music by small groups playing recognizable tunes, and this was the case here. With the dearth of Russian men following the war, Russian women had taken up the practice of dancing together, and if an unattached man happened to be present, they were not shy about taking the initiative and asking him to dance. Reluctantly and after several protestations, I soon found myself on the dance floor—out of courtesy, I told myself. A couple of fast songs gave way to a slow number, and my attractive table companion pressed her body close to mine and whispered in an alluring Russian accent, "Tell me all about the West." I guffawed and separated myself, saying it was too vast a subject. I motioned to return to the booth, but she pleaded she had to work early in the morning. It was cold and snowy out and there were no taxis, would I please drive her home in the Mustang she knew I had? All my training and instincts told me to say no, but I wanted to confirm my suspicions and so agreed. I was not going to go anywhere near her apartment though, and when we got to the far reaches of her parking lot, I told her this was the end of the line and bid her goodnight. As she got out of the car, I caught a glimpse in the distance of three militiamen peering out the front door of her building. Suspicion confirmed.

In the same lexicon, the KGB also had a smaller "ravens' nest" of young men to be used against gay men and susceptible female spouses of foreigners. Laurielle was an avid and expert tennis player and spent considerable time at the tennis courts at the Lenin sports complex. One evening she told me that quite a handsome young man had shown up unexpectedly at the courts stylishly dressed in whites. He had asked to join in a doubles match and, after being accepted, played very well. Following the game, he offered to buy her coffee and explained he was an army captain from Leningrad who was on leave in Moscow and looking for some exercise. He proceeded to pepper her with questions about her background and what it was I did at the embassy, and then asked if he might buy her lunch. She politely declined and left. After another two failed attempts in following days, he disappeared.

Once in a while there would be a Western male who would scoff at all the goings on and tell us he had thrown the photographs back in the faces of his intended blackmailers because he did not care if the pictures were released. The line of argument often went as follows: "Go ahead and release them. I am divorced/separated, and my mum and granny won't care. Besides I can post the photos up on the clubhouse wall for my golf buddies to admire."

Having a brief sexual encounter with a swallow or raven was one thing, falling in love with a "Romeo agent" was another. They were much more subtle operators and covered their tracks well. There was no rush of emotion leading to a one-night stand, but weeks or months of effort to build trust with their unsuspecting victim. A French ambassador was said to have once fallen under the spell of such an agent. He thought it was his own Gallic charm that had attracted the much younger Russian woman. He suffered the consequences back home. Later, at a Scandinavian embassy, a security guard was said to have become smitten with a local Russian woman. He was sure she genuinely loved him. When a KGB agent informed him she would be executed for her involvement with a member of a foreign mission, he agreed to open the embassy safe in an effort to spare her. He was reported to have been dumbfounded when he found out she had deceived him.

East German intelligence (Stasi) followed the KGB lead and developed Romeo agents of their own. They were particularly successful with lonely West German secretaries at home and abroad, including at NATO headquarters, where I later worked. More than forty women were eventually prosecuted for passing secrets to their lovers, not realizing they were foreign agents. The notorious Stasi chief Marcus Wolf is claimed to have stated that "more secrets would be revealed through love than short sexual relationships."

If money, sex or love did not work, then there was always the ideological approach—trying to convince you why socialism was better than capitalism and why you should come over to the "workers' paradise." One day I received word at the embassy that I was being invited to lunch at the Prague restaurant by someone in the Second European Division of the Soviet Foreign Ministry.[28] It was a strange development, as the foreign ministry rarely issued an individual invitation, particularly to a junior diplomat. Moreover, it was from someone no one in the embassy had ever encountered. Ambassador Ford recommended Ottawa be consulted. Word came back quickly that the invitation was from a suspected KGB intelligence officer, in all likelihood making a recruiting approach toward me. I thought the instruction would be to decline the invitation but instead was told to proceed—to be careful but to size him up, make precise mental notes about what he already knew about me, and to pay attention to his line of argumentation.

The Prague restaurant was among the best on the small list of places to eat in Moscow. My host was awaiting my arrival. He was well-tailored, possibly Saville Row of London, and spoke impeccable English. He knew where I had graduated and my general work history, and as we finished the soup course he went into details about which cars I drove and which position I preferred to play in baseball—all laid out with a convivial smile. He wanted me to know they had built a dossier on me and were adding to it.

The main course was accompanied by attacks on American imperialism. Vietnam was mentioned repeatedly, as was Latin America, the military-industrial complex, the branch plant nature of the Canadian economy, the control of elections by rich elites, and the suppression of minorities and the working class; the latter of which, he said, I should be able to identify with. I counterpunched with the freedom of movement and freedom of expression in the West and our ability to move up the ladder of success despite obstacles; the "gulag" system of political prisoners in Siberia, the Soviet invasion of Czechoslovakia, and the USSR's own upending of governments around the world, as well as Stalin's murder of millions of his own citizens in the so-called interests of the revolution and the state. By dessert, we were at a stalemate and the conversation came to an end. He paid the bill but did not get his money's worth from the luncheon. I never encountered him again.

IT WAS EXTREMELY difficult to meet ordinary Russians, let alone have substantive conversations with them. The vast majority had a deep mistrust, embedded in their bones, of all foreigners after centuries of invasions. This was fuelled first by tsarist and then communist propaganda. All Soviet citizens were instructed to report any contact with foreigners, and particularly with diplomats, to the authorities. Failure to do so could have severe consequences. Each apartment building had a female *dejournaya*, a kind of attendant, on the main floor, part of whose duties was to keep an eye on things and to report any violations by tenants. Shared apartment living also permitted little privacy, so much so that young lovers escaped to parks or bought train tickets, even if they had to share a compartment with strangers. Laurielle and I experienced this one night while travelling on the "Red Arrow," the name of the overnight trains which set off from both Moscow and Leningrad just before midnight. From our lower berths we could hear the personal activities of a couple on one of the berths above us.

People were reticent to speak in public areas, and it was a marvel how, on the morning subway a whole train could unload hundreds of workers onto a city centre platform, where they would walk off in almost total silence. Better not to say anything that could be overheard and misinterpreted. One Sunday afternoon, while out walking the dog past the Chinese embassy and approaching Moscow State University, I encountered three students. Sabu was a conversational icebreaker, and they could tell from my appearance that I was a Westerner. When I mentioned Canada, they became quite animated and wanted to talk about American rock music groups. Did I have any albums? Mention of the band Chicago caused their eyes to flutter. As a good patriot, I put in a plug for Winnipeg's The Guess Who and said I had just been listening to two of my favourites, "No Time" and "American Woman," which I was sure they would enjoy. They were excited and wanted to come to my apartment to listen, but I cautioned they would have to pass the "milibox" and would likely be barred entrance, if not arrested. They countered with the idea that I should come to their rooms at the university, noting that I was young enough to pass as a student and we all could slip by the university guards. I was sorely tempted but could this be another hidden provocation? I also realized that, if they were legitimate and were caught with me inside the university without authorization, their studies would be over or worse. As a compromise solution I left them on the street, walked back to my apartment and returned with the albums, which I gave them as a gift. I never did get the experience of sharing the music together or of hearing their perspective on life.

There were the odd Russian risk-takers, and chance encounters as with the students, but by and large personal contact was with those "authorized to deal with foreigners." However, even among those authorized people there was tremendous caution. Everyone looked to higher-ups to take the lead or to grant permission. When personnel from the foreign ministry and other government departments were invited to the embassy for hospitality purposes, they would arrive together, often surround the buffet table with its imported delicacies, and then depart en masse. One time I was invited to the apartment of an American colleague, for a small luncheon for his fellow co-worker, who was departing at the end of his posting. Also invited were two officials from the foreign ministry with whom the colleague had frequently interacted during his time in Moscow. One showed up on time for drinks and we exchanged banalities. As the clock ticked by and it became clear the second official was going to be a no-show, the first became anxious and said he had to leave. When asked about the lunch, which was about to be served, he proclaimed innocence, saying he had not realized he had been invited for a meal. We were left with two empty chairs, extra food and knowing smiles on our faces: being alone in a foreign apartment was not something a Soviet official wanted to have to explain.

Travelling by car was equally restrictive. You could not drive any farther from the Kremlin than forty kilometres without permission from the foreign ministry, which had to be sought in writing at least forty-eight hours in advance. Often at the very last minute, you would hear that permission was not granted "due to reasons of a temporary nature." It took away any potential for spontaneity except for outings to the so-called "diplomatic beach," which was basically a field next to a tributary of the

Moscow River and only for foreigners. Other parts of the USSR were permanently closed to travel by foreigners; some because of military installations or industrial complexes in the region, but others for no apparent reason. Even when there was no objection to your travel, you were monitored on the roadways by the State Automobile Authorities (GAU) in elevated glass towers on the outskirts of the cities and towns. If you did not pass the checkpoints in a reasonable amount of time, a patrol car would come looking for you. Once, after obtaining travel permission, Laurielle and I stopped alongside the road in an open area for a picnic. A patrol car appeared, and the officials told us to pack up and move on. I showed them my travel authority. That was only to go from A to B, they said, it did not mean we could stop between A and B.

Travel by air inside the USSR also required advance permission. In hotels, the key to your room would be held by a woman monitoring each floor and your movements. Get the key from her upon your arrival and return it to her on your every departure. Cleaning staff would frequent your room more than periodically, and the phone would ring regularly day and night with no one on the other end—just checking to see you were really there. On trips to less frequented cities like Dushanbe, in Tajikistan, for "familiarization purposes," our phone started ringing just as we turned the key in the lock for the first time. A local "cultural aide" would organize your program, stick to you like glue, and paint a rosy picture of local conditions, even if there was nothing rosy to see. If you did venture out on your own during a brief interlude, there would inevitably be someone close behind.

While in the USSR, there was not only the KGB and its various blandishments to deal with, one also had to pay attention to what your fellow colleagues were up to at the embassy. Had any of them been caught in a trap or started to work for the Soviets? Double agents working for the other side were real, such as Kim Philby. Triple agents—wherein you would pretend to work against your own country in order to feed false information to the other side and to find out their operational methods and personnel—were not unheard of. The KGB reputedly thought at first that Philby might be such a triple agent. It was no wonder that in these circumstances you might develop paranoia. Then there was your own back, which you had to watch. The RCMP had its own files on me and my wife, as it did on other embassy members and their spouses. Unusual activity might be noticed, and attention was paid to any suggestion in your reporting that you might have developed "localitis," or "gone native" as the British used to say, by putting Soviet interests before those of Canada. John Watkins, Canadian ambassador to the Soviet Union from 1954 to 1956, died from a heart attack while being questioned by the RCMP (and reputedly the CIA) in a Montreal hotel room in 1964, but was never found to have given in to Soviet blackmail or of having been a traitor.

Recently I was told by a Team Canada hockey player that, during the briefing prior to leaving for Moscow in 1972, the RCMP had mentioned Ambassador Ford was a "communist." Whether this reference was misheard or misunderstood by the player, I saw no evidence of this of any kind at the time or in subsequent years, nor was it ever suggested by any of my closest colleagues. If it was truly said, perhaps the RCMP representative had difficulty distinguishing between *empathy* for the Russians and *sympathy* for them. Admiring world-famous Russian achievements in music, ballet, art, literature and poetry did not mean you were blinded to everything else or that you had become their mouthpiece.

THE EXPERIENCE OF working as a diplomat in the Soviet Union was akin to living in an intense pressure-cooker. Not everybody could handle the stress. Ottawa had determined Moscow was a "hardship posting," which meant that the normal assignment was just twenty-four months (Laurielle's and mine lasted forty months—the Fords were an incredible exception). As a midpoint break, after a year the Canadian government would pay for the equivalent of a return trip to Ottawa for you and your family. Everyone, though, was encouraged on a more frequent basis to "get out" for a few days' break, which normally meant going to Finland for shopping and relaxation. Helsinki at the time was seen as an Eastern city if you arrived from Paris or London, but was most decidedly a Western city if you started out from Moscow, with the Finnish capital's bright lights, colourful advertising, creature comforts and openness.

The roughly fourteen-hour overnight train ride to Helsinki was not overly arduous, with lovely pastoral scenes to be observed once day broke. Just before the border, the train halted and Soviet border guards with German shepherds appeared. Everyone's passports and visas were closely scrutinized, while the undercarriages and roofs of each car were carefully examined. The gate on the border fence then opened and as the train slowly moved forward the guards jumped off. A few minutes later, the train again stopped, this time for smiling Finnish authorities. In the background near the tracks was a smallish building with a bright-red Coca-Cola sign and an ad with the Marlboro Man. The passengers broke into spontaneous applause as the tension evaporated.

CHAPTER SEVEN

TRUDEAU AND KOSYGIN

FATHERS OF THE SUMMIT SERIES

PIERRE ELLIOTT TRUDEAU did not play team sports. He preferred one-on-one or solitary athletic endeavours: judo, swimming, canoeing. These sports had their own individual rewards, and he was never accused of being out of shape or of not being an athlete. He also enjoyed spectator sports and was more than happy to be the centre of attention at large public events, whether it was to drop a puck at centre ice or perform the ceremonial kick-off at a Grey Cup game. Trudeau recognized the power of sport; particularly its political power.

Most Canadians adored sports, particularly winter sports. They were supposed to be our strong suit, reflective of our northern culture. However, Canada's performance at the Winter Olympics had been on a downward trajectory. In 1960, at Squaw Valley in the US, we had won four medals (two gold) and placed seventh overall in the medal standings. At Innsbruck, Austria, in 1964, we had slipped to three medals (one gold) and dropped to tenth overall. At the 1968 Olympics, in Grenoble, France, we still won three medals (one gold) but fell further, to thirteenth overall.

Thirteenth position. At the first Olympics in which we flew the new Maple Leaf flag. Our heads and spirits were low, even though the country rallied around the gold- and silver-medal performances of Nancy Greene in women's alpine skiing.

What really caused national angst was the continuing poor perform-ance in our marquee sport: men's hockey. Our last Olympic hockey gold medal had been in 1952, when the amateur Edmonton Mercurys repre-sented Canada. In 1956 the amateur Kitchener–Waterloo Dutchmen fell to third with a bronze medal, behind the USSR and the USA. In 1960 the Dutchmen again carried the Canadian colours and moved up to a silver, behind the host nation, USA, and ahead of the Soviet Union. The 1964 national team finished fourth, behind the USSR, Sweden and Czechoslovakia. It was the first time Canada had been shut out of a hockey medal. The same format of amateurs and retired professionals in 1968 led to a third-place finish and a bronze-medal performance, once again behind the USSR and Czechoslovakia.

The Department of External Affairs reported that the decline of our hockey capability had serious international consequences, as it had led to a deterioration of Canada's image abroad, especially in Europe. Hockey and Canada's standing in the world were inextricably linked.

The time was ripe for change. When Pierre Trudeau, as the newly chosen Liberal leader, ran for prime minister for the first time in the general election of June 1968, sports became a key policy plank in his platform. He promised to investigate the status of amateur sport in Canada, noting on the campaign trail that "hockey is our national sport and yet in World Championships we have not been able, as amateurs, to perform as well as we can."

With an eye on the voters in British Columbia, he also expressed concern that Canadian cities, including particularly Vancouver, were having difficulty in obtaining NHL franchises. In Trudeau's view, sports were part of culture, and culture was an essential ingredient in national identity and indeed in national unity, which was the major theme of his election campaign. His view proved to be popular.

With Liberal electoral victory and a majority in the House of Commons (the first majority in four elections, going back to 1958), experienced Hamilton East politician John Munro was selected by the prime minister to become the minister of National Health and Welfare as well as minister of Amateur Sport.

In little over a month a four-person task force was set up to study the basic issue of how the federal government could become more involved in sport within Canada. One of its key recommendations was the creation of Hockey Canada, which launched in February 1969, an amazingly fast implementation for government. Hockey Canada's first mandate was to join with the Canadian Amateur Hockey Association (CAHA), which retained jurisdiction over Canada's participation in international hockey, in order to press the International Ice Hockey Federation (IIHF) to agree to "open play," without restriction, so that Canada would no longer have to rely on amateur players.

There was no sense talking about the involvement of professionals, of course, unless they were part of the discussion. Accordingly, a heavy-hitting steering committee was set up comprising all the relevant parties. Chaired by Bill Wirtz, the chairman of the NHL board of governors, it included Charles Hay, the president of Hockey Canada; Joe Kryczka, president of the CAHA; Alan Eagleson, executive director of the National Hockey League Players Association; Doug Fisher, director of Hockey Canada; and Lou Lefaive, the director of Sport Canada, which was part of the Ministry of Amateur Sport.

The pressure campaign began almost immediately, in March 1969 at the IIHF meeting in Stockholm, when the Canadian delegation launched a discussion about the joint participation of both amateur and professional players.

Four months later, in July 1969, at the next IIHF meeting, at Crans-sur-Sierre, Switzerland, Canada arrived with a beefed-up delegation of fifteen people led by the president of the NHL, Clarence Campbell. The delegates were shown a film depicting professional hockey, which ended with an address by Pierre Trudeau proposing that the World Championships be open to all players. The prime minister was still personally engaged on the hockey front.

While the vote went against Canada thirty to twenty, the IIHF congress decided, as an experiment for one year, to allow nine professionals to be included, provided they were from minor pro clubs and not NHL teams. There was the added caveat that those nine players would have to leave their teams six weeks before any tournament in order to regain "amateur status." It was convoluted, rather farcical and represented only the smallest of improvements.

Canada was encouraged to try out the arrangement in December of 1969 at the Izvestia invitational tournament in Moscow, which was now entering its third year as a "winter rehearsal" for the top national teams prior to the World Championships in April. Utilizing five of the nine "pro slots," the Canadian team put up a very credible performance, finishing second and tying the powerful USSR team 2–2.

Even this minimalist formula didn't last for long. When the IIHF met again, in Geneva in January 1970, it reversed the decision, announcing that at the forthcoming World Championships, with games to be split between Montreal and Winnipeg, Canada would not be able to use any professionals of any kind. The IIHF had been heavily influenced by the pronouncement from Avery Brundage, the long-standing American president of the International Olympic Committee (IOC), that mixing amateurs and professionals violated the Olympic code and would jeopardize ice hockey's status as an Olympic sport.

Faced with this intolerable return to square one, Minister Munro was quick to announce that Canada was withdrawing its invitation to host the 1970 Games and would leave international hockey until an open and fair competition was permitted. It was a decision that had widespread support across Canada. Nevertheless, it left the USSR largely unchallenged in continuing its string of Olympic and World Championships. More importantly, it left open the gnawing question of which country was the best hockey nation. The prime minister, though, had more than sports on his mind.

TRUDEAU FIRST CAME to office in 1968, which had been a tumultuous year around the world. Not only had the Soviet Union and its allies invaded Czechoslovakia, but the US was in turmoil. Both Martin Luther King and Bobby Kennedy had been assassinated in the spring, and American cities were on fire as a result of violent civil unrest. Further afield, the US was adding more combat forces to South Vietnam in order to shore up that government and forestall what Washington believed to be a string of potential communist dominoes in Asia and elsewhere. The Middle East had just come through the Six-Day War in 1967, and all the conditions were still there for a further war. General Charles de Gaulle had been forced from office in France by a population fed up with the destructive colonial war in Algeria, while European colonies elsewhere in the world were continuing to struggle with their own newfound freedom. India and Pakistan kept up their efforts to use force against each other as the prime way to deal with unresolved problems on the subcontinent. The two communist giants, China and the USSR, were arguing over ideology and were amassing troops along each side of their extensive border.

There was a lot to be concerned about on the diplomatic and military fronts, let alone matters of trade and commerce and securing international markets for Canadian business. As he did with sport, Trudeau set up a task force. This one was to examine how this rapidly changing and challenging world impacted Canada and to design a foreign policy for Canadians that would protect and advance our national and international interests.

The prime minister was not a fan of conventional wisdom. There was a bit too much of the status quo in the task force report, particularly regarding relations with Europe. Despite strong opposition from External Affairs and National Defence, Trudeau cut Canada's military contribution to NATO in half. He favoured diplomacy over defence, and global engagement over isolationism.

It made no sense to him to ignore the country with the world's largest population, the People's Republic of China, even if it was a communist country crushing its own citizens. Better, in his view, that

China be at the world's tables and subject to dialogue and some form of influence. Early discussions with the Chinese in the neutral location of Sweden led to the establishment of diplomatic relations between Beijing and Ottawa in 1970, and in 1973 Trudeau would become the first Canadian prime minister to visit China.

It was similar with the Soviet Union. Trudeau wanted to move beyond a policy of strict containment and to avoid the practice of "megaphone diplomacy," in which you just shouted at each other and never listened to the other side. In the era of nuclear weapons, miscommunication or miscalculation were too great a risk.

Trudeau achieved another first when he became the first Canadian prime minister to visit the USSR.[29] When the visit was postponed from October of 1970 to May 1971, the purpose remained the same but the circumstances had altered significantly for two main reasons. Firstly, ping-pong diplomacy had broken out between the United States and China. In a strange incident, an American participant at the World Table Tennis Championship in Japan had inadvertently boarded a bus carrying Chinese participants and had been befriended and given a gift by one of the players. News coverage was quickly followed by an invitation from the Chinese government to the American team to visit China, which it did on April 6, 1971. The fact that this had been the first American delegation to visit China in over twenty years was startling news—no place more so than in Moscow, which was still smarting from the bloody battles with Chinese troops on the far eastern border and still traumatized about the prospects of a full-scale war with Beijing.

Whether the Kremlin had any premonition that this ping-pong move would lead to a secret visit by US National Security Advisor Henry Kissinger three months later, to be followed by the surprise visit to China by President Nixon in February 1972, did not matter. Moscow's two principal enemies getting together in any form was bad news for the USSR. In high-stakes poker terms, diplomatic analysts suggested Washington was playing a "China card" against the USSR, while Beijing for its part was playing a "USA card" against Moscow.

Trudeau's impending visit provided the Soviets with the opportunity to play this game, though a "Canada card" was of less strategic significance. Nevertheless, careful note had been taken in Moscow of the prime minister's foreign policy views and his stated desire to obtain more breathing room in Canada's relations with the USA. Canada also had access to North American technologies that the USSR also wished to obtain. For these strategic reasons, the Kremlin pulled out all stops to make sure the Trudeau visit was a success.

The second circumstance that altered the prime minister's earlier postponed visit was not strategic, but personal. Trudeau had married Margaret Sinclair on March 4, 1971, in Vancouver. She was twenty-two years old—twenty-nine years younger than him. Her first official trip abroad as the prime minister's wife would be to the USSR. Not an easy initial destination by any means.

The visit had been expanded to twelve days, starting on May 17, and would cover seven destinations, including springtime Moscow and Kiev; sweltering Tashkent and Samarkand in the Soviet Eurasian subcontinent; and the frigid, normally closed Siberian city of Norilsk. The northern port of Murmansk and former capital, Leningrad (Saint Petersburg), were thrown in for good measure. The unusually large forty-person Canadian press corps, looking mainly for honeymoon photographs and coverage, gave the couple little respite. They were not aware she was fighting off morning sickness at the time; pregnant with their first child, Justin, who would be born on Christmas Day in 1971.[30]

That Trudeau had arrived with his wife had changed the scenario for the Soviets as well. Premier Alexei Kosygin was the approximate counterpart to the prime minister, but his wife had died four years earlier. A female protocol officer might have sufficed to act as the official hostess and to accompany Mrs. Trudeau to various places of interest, but in a personal gesture the normally glum-faced Kosygin asked his married daughter, Ludmilia Gwishiani, to take on the role. It was a deft move. Gwishiani was twenty years older than Margaret Trudeau, but the two women got along well.[31] Personal chemistry is as important in international diplomacy as it is in business or in everyday life.

FOR MY PART, the postponement until May meant I would be on the ground in Moscow and part of the action. The embassy acted as the go-between linking the authorities in Canada (the Prime Minister's Office and External Affairs) and those in the USSR led by the Soviet Foreign Ministry: nitty-gritty diplomatic negotiations about whom the prime minister would be meeting; where exactly and when and for how long; how many officials would be permitted on each side; what agenda items would be discussed and the nature of any agreements each side was seeking to achieve; and then always the question of publicity and access for the media. I was tasked, under the Ambassador's direction, with helping prepare the short, carefully crafted background notes on a range of topics that went into the prime minister's "briefing book," together with suggested "talking points" for meetings and press conferences, as well as proposed texts for speeches and toasts. The prime minister largely knew what he wanted to say in the key meetings in Moscow, but needed context and suggestions as to what to expect from the Soviet side. I worked hard pulling together and writing material for the secondary cities on the trip and on the state of exchanges between the two countries, including the hockey file. Colleagues in Ottawa also had a major input in all the preparations.

The big news item to come out of this particular visit was the signing by the prime minister and Premier Kosygin of the Protocol on Consultations, which provided for regular consultations between Canada and the Soviet Union on a range of international and bilateral issues. It didn't make the countries best buddies, but it was a step in that direction. The world paid attention.

As he had been telegraphing beforehand, the prime minister outlined his thinking at the accompanying press conference. He made it clear at the outset of his comments that Canada is not only a friend of the US but also an ally in NATO with Western European countries and in the North American Air Defence Command (NORAD), which had special responsibility for protecting Canadian and American airspace. But he said, and this was the kicker, "Canada has found it increasingly important to diversify its channels of communications because of the overwhelming presence of the United States. This is reflected in the growing consciousness of Canadians of a danger to our national identity; (from a cultural, economic and perhaps even a military point of view)."[32] He added in a comment ahead of its time, "Canada and the Soviet Union are bound by a community of interests in the development of vast northern territory rich in resources and in which industrial construction is bound to disturb the ecological balance."

Kosygin and other Soviet leaders smiled. Back home in Washington, Richard Nixon did not. Trudeau already was seen as a maverick in Washington, and this would only add significantly to his dossier.

A number of other political and economic issues were discussed in Moscow, including Canada's large commercial sales of wheat—the embassy assiduously followed information about Soviet wheat production in order to help determine what quantities would be demanded so that we could get the best price possible. The subject of hockey and securing Soviet agreement to open international competition was listed as the sixth-most important objective of the visit and was raised informally as a subject of collaboration, with nodding Soviet heads but no commitments of any kind at this point.

It was clear to everyone in Canada that it was the Soviet Union and its allies who were the blocking force behind the IIHF and reinforcements for Avery Brundage's IOC positions denying the playing of Canadian professionals. And why change? The USSR was able to use its "professional amateurs" and to retain the all-important bragging rights of being the perennial world and Olympic champions. So hockey was put into the context of the desire of both governments to improve bilateral relations and the natural affinity both countries had as northern neighbours for winter sports—ice hockey prime among them.

One of the prime minister's senior-most advisors on the trip was Edgar (Ed) Ritchie, a Rhodes scholar, former ambassador to the United States and, at that time, the under secretary of state for External Affairs—the top official in the department. Ritchie, who had exchanged positions with Marcel Cadieux, was not only a brilliant diplomat but also an enthusiastic hockey buff who had played for the Oxford University Blues and who personally would continue to shepherd the hockey file at the highest bureaucratic levels in Ottawa.

My own first brief chat with the prime minister was also about hockey. The ambassador had asked that I greet the PM at the front door of the embassy and escort him and Mrs. Trudeau to the rear garden, where the Fords and other Canadian staff and Canadian residents in Moscow had been gathered. It only took a few minutes to make the passage, but I quickly told him, drawing on an embassy cable from Ottawa, that the Montreal Canadiens had beaten the Chicago Black Hawks 3–2 in game seven of the Stanley Cup final, on a third-period goal by Henri Richard. The PM was attentive and expressed his appreciation for the news. He was aware of the strength of the Soviet hockey system and had asked that the agenda include a visit to a Soviet hockey training facility. Premier Kosygin, who had already had two formal meetings with the prime minister and jointly had attended two reciprocal lunches and a reception with him, organized a small outing to the princely Arkhangelskoye estate outside of the city. It was a major historic tourist attraction—described as the "Moscow Versailles"—but also served as the training base for the Central Army (CSKA) hockey and soccer teams, who resided in two buildings built initially as sanatoriums in 1934 for military personnel. The dry-land facilities were nothing special to observe, but the PM was told it was not the equipment which was important but the training regime, with its emphasis on scientific methods, strength-building and even ballet techniques. Kosygin and his daughter then hosted a private dinner for the Trudeaus, Fords and a few others in a wooden chalet in the nearby woods. On the menu was roast bear. I was obliged to remain outside, contemplating its taste.

THE PRIME MINISTER'S meeting with Communist Party leader Leonid Brezhnev was set for the Kremlin. Attendees would be limited to the PM, Ambassador Ford, Ritchie, and Ivan Head, the prime minister's "special assistant" for international affairs. The ambassador asked that I accompany him, as there was a long hallway to navigate from the elevator and he couldn't rush, whereas the PM preferred the quickness of the stairs. Waiting outside Brezhnev's office door, we were told by a Kremlin official that the general secretary had been advised by his doctor to cut back on his smoking and accordingly had been given a cigarette box installed with a timer that would only open every hour or so. As a result, the official said, Brezhnev had taken to bumming smokes from his guests. If that happened, the prime minister and his party were to refuse the request. The aide was pleased when I informed him none of them smoked. Brezhnev apparently had also been advised by his doctors to cut back on his drinking, but the official said nothing on that front.

With the two-hour meeting over, the PM, Ritchie and Head sprinted down the stairs, while the ambassador and I took the long corridor back to the elevator and down to the waiting cars. When we arrived outside there was no prime minister to be seen. Asked what was happening, a Soviet motorcycle policeman, standing around sheepishly, related that the prime minister had asked to see his bike, climbed on, kicked it into gear, and sped away inside the Kremlin walls. The PM returned before too long an absence with two Soviet protocol officers running on foot in hot pursuit, sweating profusely. The PM gave a thumbs up to the policeman, looked at us with a grin and a shrug of his shoulders, and jumped into the official car. The ambassador had a quizzical look on his face, but there was nothing more for him to do beyond shrugging his own shoulders.

Trudeau seized another opportunity to challenge convention on this trip. The ambassador would tell me afterward that Brezhnev had figured out a way to outfox the timer on his cigarette case and smoked continuously throughout what had been a "good" meeting. The Soviet leader made it clear the USSR wanted to improve relations with Canada, and as part of that discussion, had referred to a marvellous Canadian agricultural seeding machine he had seen that was unlike anything the Soviet Union possessed. He talked for a few moments about his family. Changing gears, he noted that improving the state of the Soviet economy was a key priority of the Communist Party, but it ranked third behind matters of national security and foreign relations. A key discussion point concerned the Soviet's relationship with the US—Brezhnev personally had been involved with five presidents and was frustrated that they all talked about peace but continued to surround the USSR with military bases. He was hopeful some sort of arrangement could be worked out to lower tensions.

The delegation then set off for Kiev, the capital of Ukraine, which is magnificent in the springtime with its streets lined with chestnut trees in full bloom. It was then part of the Soviet Union. Ambassador Ford had asked me to come along for the entire trip to assist him and to provide the large entourage, which included members of parliament, with another Russian-language speaker from the embassy.

The first night of our visit included a casual dinner at a local Ukrainian restaurant. A few large tables were set aside for the prime minister's party, but the Canadian press corps was not invited and had their own festivities. It was a pleasant dinner, with the local patrons looking on with a combination of amusement and pride. Then the music in the restaurant grew louder. It did not take long before a Ukrainian woman from a table nearby was on her feet beckoning the prime minister to join her for a whirl on the small dance floor. With a nod from Margaret, he accepted the invitation and drew loud applause from the entire restaurant clientele and staff for his participation.

The day had been long and tiring. Just after I got into bed past midnight there was a knock on the door of my room at the guest villa. A member of the RCMP from the prime minister's protective service stood in front of me. There had been an incident involving an embassy staffer who had been battling health and stress issues for weeks before the visit and apparently had crossed a diplomatic line that evening. The Soviet authorities did not want to make a public issue of the case due to the prime minister's visit, but they let it be known that the individual had to leave the Soviet Union within forty-eight hours. The ambassador had been informed and agreed that I was to return to Moscow with the staffer and ensure the person's timely departure back to Canada. Two tickets had been secured for the first flight from Kiev to Moscow, leaving in a few hours.

Not a pleasant task. It was tough enough dealing with my distraught fellow employee on the flight, but there also was the requirement to pack up all the staffer's belongings in less than two days and the realization their assignment was suddenly over and that they would have to leave friends and fellow workers behind. The Trudeau visit carried on without me. I returned to the embassy and kept in daily contact with the travelling party as best as possible given the poor Russian telephone and telex systems, reporting back to officials in Ottawa about their progress as well as what was being said about the visit in the Soviet press.

Immediately after returning to Ottawa, the prime minister decided to send a personal message to President Nixon to lay out in his own words the purpose of his visit to the USSR. He knew the president would not be happy but offered no excuses or apology and even indirectly suggested Nixon should follow suit. The confidential telegram of May 28 was sent by Under Secretary Ritchie to Ambassador Cadieux in Washington by "Flash" precedence—meaning it superseded all other diplomatic traffic—with instructions to deliver it to the White House without delay. The essence of the one-and-a half-page message read as follows:

I have just returned from an extremely interesting visit to the USSR. During the past twelve days I have had a good many talks with leaders of the Soviet Union in Moscow and in many other parts of this vast and complex country.

Your country, of course, remains our nearest neighbour and the one with which we have the closest relations. I am sure that both our countries can only gain from more normal relations with that other neighbour to the north. I do not underestimate the difficulties in achieving reasonable relations but I think the effort is essential. I have no doubt that you share this objective.

In general I can say from a Canadian viewpoint the discussions, and the extensive travel in the Soviet Union, were valuable in improving our understanding of each other. More broadly I appreciated the moderate and responsible attitude shown by Mr. Brezhnev, Mr. Kosygin Mr. Podgorny and other Soviet leaders in talking about world problems. While they fully accepted I was from a country which is in NATO and NORAD and which has often disagreed with the Soviet approach or methods, they talked seriously and without polemics.

I believe that a significant advance in developing the bilateral relations between Canada and the Soviet Union may have been made on this trip. While the United States and the Soviet Union are quite capable of talking frankly with each other, I am asking my officials to inform your people fully on any aspect of the visit of interest to you.[33]

Trudeau also offered to compare notes more fully with Nixon during a proposed state visit to Ottawa by the president.

Two weeks later, on June 4, 1971, the ambassador received a letter from Ivan Head, the prime minister's special assistant for foreign affairs. After praising Ford for his deep knowledge, sound advice and strong leadership, he went on to say, "I was most impressed by the professionalism of your officers. I can't recall a prime ministerial visit proceeding in a complete absence of hysteria and panic as did this one. In my assessment there can be no higher praise for competence and confidence." These words prepared the ambassador and the rest of us at the embassy for what was to lie ahead.

Protocol dictated that a state guest would invite his hosts to pay a return visit at some undetermined, mutually agreeable date, so it was that at the conclusion of the Trudeau visit invitations were extended to President Podgorny, Premier Kosygin and Communist Party leader Brezhnev to visit Canada.

The Soviet leaders had a number of pressing domestic and foreign issues on their plates and many invitations as well from other countries, both communist and non-communist. Normally Canada would not have factored into this equation so soon and the return invitations would have gathered dust, but Washington's dalliance with China was picking up steam, and the Trudeau visit had been well received and his remarks about the United States served Soviet political interests.

In surprisingly quick time, word came through that Premier Kosygin—accompanied by his daughter—wished to pay a return visit, which would cover large parts of Canada. The target date was proposed for mid-October 1971—less than five full months after Trudeau had departed the USSR. The embassy and I were back to preparing briefing notes and policy options for the consideration of our colleagues in Ottawa, including counselling against any meeting between Kosygin and the head of the Communist Party of Canada.

While a wide swath of the Canadian population may have supported the prime minister's desire for more breathing room from the tight embrace of the USA—particularly after President Nixon's August 15, 1971, surprise import surcharge of ten per cent[34]—many Canadian individuals and communities had no love, indeed had a real hatred, for the Soviet Union.

The boot of the Red Army, Stalin's bloody ways, and the Soviets' totalitarian practices toward dissent and against human rights were linked to bleak personal memories for a large number of Canadians from the Baltic republics and Ukraine, as well as countries such as Poland, Hungary and Czechoslovakia. In addition, the Canadian Jewish community was up in arms against the perceived mistreatment of Soviet Jews and the refusal of the USSR to permit their emigration to Israel. There also were a plentiful number of Canadians of Eastern European origin clamouring to be reunited with their family members stuck behind the Iron Curtain.

The upshot was that the Soviet leader was walking into a buzzsaw of protest and demonstrations when he arrived in Ottawa on October 17 to begin his eight-day visit. Many thousands of angry people were in the streets of the Canadian capital with placards and bullhorns, spilling onto Parliament Hill, where the Soviet premier had his initial meetings. As Kosygin was exiting the building for a stroll on the lawns with the prime minister, a twenty-seven-year-old man of Hungarian origin[35] burst through the crowd and before he could be restrained jumped on the premier's back, "riding him like a horse,"[36] according to one media account, shouting, "Long live Hungary! Down with the Russians!" before being pulled off. An extreme breakdown of security to be sure. When Kosygin repaired to the Soviet embassy to meet staff, the hostile crowd followed, breaking the glass in numerous windows and doors along the street as they proceeded.

The protests dogged the premier wherever he went; sometimes smaller, sometimes larger. The crowd of demonstrators outside a business event in the Toronto suburb of Don Mills was estimated at thirty-five hundred. Kosygin's stated purpose was to visit large Canadian industrial plants with innovative technology in the pulp and paper, hydroelectric, oil refining and automotive sectors; to meet with various business communities and federal, provincial and local government officials; and to sign a comprehensive Industrial Co-operation Agreement with the prime minister.

Trudeau had resisted the agreement, though, recognizing that such a deal would favour the Soviet side and would further antagonize the US, which was the original source of a considerable amount of that technology. Besides, there already was a more modest economic co-operation arrangement in place. The prime minister opted instead for a "General Exchanges Agreement" dealing with scientists, students and those involved with culture and sports. This umbrella agreement was signed at the end of the Ottawa leg of the visit with details to be negotiated later.

Among the prime minister's briefing papers, there had been a confidential note prepared by External Affairs about Canada–Soviet hockey relations, with five paragraphs of "talking points" to raise with the Soviet premier, either formally or informally. It was similar to what had been prepared for his visit to Moscow. The first sentence stated the obvious: "One of the most important channels of contact between the people of Canada and the Soviet Union has been international hockey competition." The final paragraph referred to the efforts of Hockey Canada and the CAHA, with the Soviet Sports Committee and Ice Hockey Federation, to find a solution to the current impasse. The last sentence of the paragraph stated, "This should be encouraged at the government level by both Canada and the USSR to mutual advantage."[37]

Kosygin was exhausted by the time he completed his business engagements in Vancouver on October 22 and was inclined to skip the NHL game between the hometown Canucks and Montreal Canadiens, which a Canadian official in External Affairs had pencilled into the program. As much as he loved hockey and had played the game himself, Kosygin thought the idea of being subjected to a booing crowd of sixteen thousand hockey fans was one task and one personal indignity too much.

Paul Martin Sr., who had been Canada's previous minister of External Affairs and was now leader of the government in the Senate, had been assigned to accompany Kosygin across Canada. Martin was an astute political observer. In a confidential memo to Ottawa, he reported he had taken the measure of the premier and indicated that Kosygin was not a communist ideologue but someone with whom you could dialogue. In the report, Martin indicated he had found Kosygin lying on his hotel bed the evening of the hockey game in Vancouver not disposed to do anything further, but he and Arthur Laing, the cabinet minister from British Columbia,[38] had been able to convince the premier to attend, saying they were certain the hockey crowd would provide him with a different reception.

Sure enough, when the sixty-seven-year-old premier was escorted to centre ice at the beginning of the game to meet the two team captains—Henri Richard from Montreal and Orland Kurtenbach of Vancouver—he received a large, warm round of applause, a reception

Kosygin himself would describe as "the warmest I have received outside my home country." Kosygin presented the two players with gold tie clips and cufflinks and told them, through an interpreter, that he had a pair of skates at home but was too old to use them now.[39]

For the first time at an NHL game, the Soviet hammer and sickle flew side by side with the Canadian maple leaf.

The premier departed after the Canadiens went ahead 4–0 in an ultimate 6–0 victory, but there had been an instructive exchange with Bud Poile, the general manager of the Canucks. Kosygin reportedly had remarked, "This is a great game, and it should be played internationally between our countries." When asked by Poile if he knew why Canada was no longer playing at the international level, Kosygin said, "No, but I intend to study it."[40]

The *New York Times*, for its part, carried a special news report from correspondent Jay Walz in Vancouver under the headline HOCKEY BREAKS THE ICE AND KOSYGIN SMILES. There was an accompanying photograph of Kosygin standing on the ice with a hockey stick next to Richard.

The light went on for Alexei Kosygin that October night in Vancouver. If the Soviet Union wished to improve its relationship with Canada and enhance co-operation, the way to do it was through hockey.

In early December of 1971, two days of negotiations were held in Ottawa to flesh out the framework of the General Exchanges Agreement. The Department of External Affairs had recalled me from Moscow to participate in the detailed discussions with Soviet representatives, to ensure the projected arrangements would work for visiting Canadians in the USSR. Categories of people covered, numbers, timing, financial and administrative arrangements were all addressed. Importantly for hockey, the "exchange of sportsmen" was included for the first time in a document signed at the highest political levels on both sides.

We all knew that nothing ever happened in the Soviet Union without political approval.

CHAPTER EIGHT

THE SNOWMAN

D IPLOMATIC SUMMITRY WAS working its magic. In the interim there continued to be all sorts of machinations, by various actors at the hockey level, to make something work with the USSR. All to no avail.

Alan Eagleson, who was always thinking and cleverly planning chess moves far ahead of most others, had thought the football (soccer) World Cup model provided the best example to follow, wherein the best players from all nations could participate. Shortly after the creation of Hockey Canada in February 1969 and his participation therein as a senior member, he decided as part of a European holiday one month later, to attend the World Hockey Championships in Stockholm. One of his goals was to seek a meeting with the new general secretary of the Soviet Ice Hockey Federation, Andrei Starovoitov. Despite several promising suggestions that such an encounter was possible, Starovoitov failed to appear. The holiday plans included the USSR in early April, and so Eagleson tried again with the assistance of Ambassador Ford. Eagleson wanted to emphasize that he was not the lawyer for the capitalist owners of the NHL—that was Clarence Campbell—but rather the lawyer for the workers. Ford secured a meeting, but as Aggie Kukulowicz, who assisted Eagleson and acted as interpreter, would later recount,[41] it almost ended in the first thirty seconds when Starovoitov told Eagleson, "You don't represent the CAHA and therefore we have nothing to talk about."[42] Kukulowicz said he found it difficult to find the right words to appropriately interpret Eagleson's angry response.[43] Eagleson left a note typed up by his wife. Starovoitov apparently allowed the contents to wither on the vine.[44] Eight months later Canada withdrew from international play.

In November 1970 Hockey Canada officials sent a message to all competitors in the IIHF championships scheduled for March–April 1971 in Switzerland. The messages carried a challenge to the champion to compete in a tournament in Canada in May 1971 against a team of Canadian choice (i.e., with professional players). This written message was followed up a month later by a visit to Moscow by Charles Hay of Hockey Canada and Gordon Juckes of the CAHA. Both men had thorough meetings with Soviet hockey officials, including Sports Minister Sergei Pavlov, and Juckes came away with three observations: 1) the Soviets would come to play in Canada, but only as the Soviet national team and not as IIFF world champions; 2) the Soviets do not recognize the authority of Hockey Canada and will only deal with the CAHA as the legitimate affiliate of the IIHF; and 3) the Soviets would not compete "for technical reasons" in a May 1971 tournament in Canada but would like a Canadian team to visit the USSR in the fall (that was not acceptable at this point to the Canadian officials).[45]

Bearing in mind the Soviet views, Earl Dawson, the president of the CAHA, proposed to the IIHF that there be two round-robin competitions in Canada in September 1971 involving the USSR, Sweden, Czechoslovakia and Canada. In return, Canada would participate in similar competitions in Europe at a later date. There would be no restrictions on player selection.[46] Straightforward enough, it seemed, but John "Bunny" Ahearne, the obstreperous long-time president of the IIHF made a three-pronged counter-proposal: 1) only the Soviet and Swedish teams would come to Canada; 2) there would be seven exhibition games including professional teams and four games containing only amateurs on the Canadian team; and 3) the Canadian team would undertake three visits to compete with Soviet, Swedish and Czechoslovak teams but not in a single tour.

Ahearne also wanted Canada to return to IIHF tournament play in 1972 by entering a "simon-pure team" of only amateurs in the second-level "B" pool.[47]

It may have seemed strange that a British travel agent occupied such a powerful position in the hockey world, but Ahearne had been secretary of the British Ice Hockey Association dating from 1934 and had been involved in managing the British team to a gold medal at the 1936 Winter Olympics in Garmisch-Partenkirchen, Germany. This unexpected British victory dethroned Canada from the top podium for the first time after four previous Canadian Olympic wins and may have been the start of a long-running animus between Ahearne and Canada. He alternated as IIHF president and vice-president beginning in 1951.

Canadian hockey officials did not accept Ahearne's counter-proposal because of its restrictive nature, and therefore the proposed Canadian tournament was cancelled. Furthermore, it was stated that because none of these three European countries supported Canada with the IIHF, Canada would not send a team to the December 1971 Izvestia Cup in Moscow.

Back to the hockey drawing board.

It continued to be evident that if something were to break this stalemate it would have to come from the Soviet side. The Winter Olympics in Sapporo, Japan, in February 1972 remained their top priority.

Anatoli Tarasov was a giant in Soviet hockey and was often called its "father." After the Second World War, the Soviet Ministry of Sport asked Tarasov to develop an ice hockey program from scratch. No one cast a larger shadow than the long-standing coach of both the victorious and widely celebrated national team and the perennial national champion of the Central Red Army team.[48] He was tough, tenacious and knowledgeable, and his training camps were notorious for their military discipline, intensity and Spartan nature.

And why not have a military-style camp and lodgings when most of the players were part of the military, with military commissions, military salaries and privileges, and military pensions? Being a member of the Central Red Army team meant you were in the Army. Being a member of the Wings of the Soviet team meant you were in the Air Force. The Army and Air Force did not train only seven, eight or nine months of the year like NHL players, but year-round, like the soldiers and airmen they were—not with guns, bayonets and aircraft but with sticks, pucks and skates. The same thing applied to players from Dynamo, who were supported by the police and security forces.

Training techniques were important to Tarasov, and he had met, read and followed Canadian Lloyd Percival's 1951 *The Hockey Handbook*, with its emphasis on hockey fundamentals, diets and year-round conditioning, including dry-land techniques (particularly running). Tarasov's interest in learning from others was so great that he was said to have once attended the training camp of the NFL Minnesota Vikings to see what he could absorb from American football.[49]

Tarasov had no challengers on the ice or behind the bench, and his ego grew with every success over many years. But he may have forgotten at some point that he had a boss. Not a capitalist business owner, like in Canada or the USA, but the State. The Soviet government. The Party bosses.

Tarasov was desperate to prove himself and his teams against the professionals and would often outsource ideas through a variety of parties. In February of 1971, Aggie Kukulowicz informed the embassy that Tarasov had approached him with a request to make a proposal to president David Molson for a series of games between the Montreal Canadiens and Central Red Army, with five games to be held in Canada and five in the USSR. Tarasov said he would leave it up to the Canadiens to decide on a convenient time, but May of 1971 would suit him. Ambassador Ford advised Kukulowicz to caution Tarasov about receiving any positive answer given the conflicting proposals being considered by the CAHA and Hockey Canada.[50]

In early September 1971, Tarasov decided to go public by venting his views in a Russian sports publication. It was dripping with sarcasm and threw down a gauntlet to the NHL and perhaps, as well, to his own authorities. He started by going way back to the mid 1950s, expressing his unhappiness that Canadian hockey authorities had refused to recognize the significance of the USSR's victories at the 1954 World Championships, and the 1956 Olympics. The successes reflected the new school of hockey emerging in Europe, but there had been no invitation to visit Canada until 1957; even then, and afterwards, only weak Canadian teams were pawned off against them. In a magnanimous comment he was willing to forgive Canadians for their lack of respect. Tarasov though wasn't satisfied with beating Canadian amateur teams over and over. His desire, as a coach, to play against professionals should therefore be understood by everyone. The only way the Soviet team could improve was to play against quality opponents. It was his view that the Soviet team was up to the task of challenging the professionals.

There was a long diatribe about various interactions with Canadian hockey officials, including NHL representatives, claiming they all found a variety of excuses about why they couldn't play against the USSR. The real reason was that they were afraid of being defeated and knocked off their self-proclaimed perch. The Stanley Cup, by the way, only involved teams from Canada and the USA. Tarasov went so far as to suggest Canada's withdrawal from international hockey in 1970 was the equivalent of putting up a white flag.

Tarasov carried on and on in a vituperative manner but ended with a bang. Soviet teams were ready to play professional teams either on a club-to-club basis or at a national level provided there were equal conditions, including an equal number of home and away games and neutral referees. If his challenge was accepted, then the ultimate winners of a clash between the two hockey schools would be fans and hockey enthusiasts everywhere.

This was a major statement, no doubt, and the embassy had it translated and sent to External Affairs in Ottawa for onward transmission to the various Canadian hockey officials, including the NHL.[51]

An analysis of the article raised a number of questions. First of all, was he really directing his message to a Canadian audience when he should have known well that Canada wanted to play the USSR with an unrestricted Canadian professional team? Also, did he really believe that the NHL was the reluctant party? Thirdly, was the actual intended recipient of his article the Soviet leadership that had been opposed to encounters with unsanctioned "professionals"? The article was carried in a domestic Russian-language newspaper but not given in its entirety to foreign correspondents or the TASS news agency. And finally, was he speaking on behalf of the Soviet government? The ready, willing and able message on his part, and that of fellow coach Arkadi Chernyshev, was clear enough, but it didn't jibe with everything being said in Moscow at that time.

Pending answers to these questions, it was most instructive to note the conditions which Tarasov had laid out for the proposed matches in terms of equal home and away games, the referees, rules, and national-vs-national or club-vs-club opponents.

Then, startlingly, the Soviet embassy in Ottawa approached the Department of External Affairs on November 18, 1971, with the proposal of a "Championship team" (read Central Red Army) challenging the three Canadian professional hockey teams (Montreal, Toronto and Vancouver) to play on January 9, 12 and 14, 1972. The proposal, apparently, had originated with Tarasov and had some form of official blessing. It was turned down by Canadian hockey officials because of timing, but they suggested that something might be possible in the autumn of 1972.

At the same time, the CAHA was beginning to promote the idea of inviting Soviet "Boys' Teams" to come to Canada to participate in various regional tournaments: the Quebec City Pee Wee tournament in February; the Richmond Hill, Ontario, tournament in March; and an international Bantam tournament in Kamloops, British Columbia. The latter invitation had been directed by the Kamloops organizers to Aggie Kukulowicz at the Air Canada office in Moscow.

There was confusion aplenty. Who was speaking for whom and about what? The Canadian embassy in Moscow decided to seek clarification from the international section of the Soviet Ministry of Physical Culture and Sport, which controlled the Soviet Ice Hockey Federation and, in turn, the Soviet teams and coaches.

I accordingly showed up on December 1 in the office of V.I. Koval, head of the international section. He was not happy. Indeed, he was quite angry, asking me why there should be a response to all the boys' applications when the CAHA was ignoring their requests for Canadian participation in the Izvestia and Sovetsky Sport tournaments. "We want contact at all levels," he snarled, "not only with boys."

I told him he knew the reason why there was no contact at senior levels. He would also recall Canada had been ready to play a series of games with the USSR, but this had been scuttled by the IIHF president, who had received Soviet support. The CAHA therefore had decided to go forward with the junior boys' contests. If the Soviets were prepared to initiate contact at this level, it might generate goodwill and lead to resumed contact at more senior levels.

When asked about the Tarasov article and proposal, Koval said the Soviet coach was "anxious to play against any Canadians." Koval himself, though, was concerned about the consequences for Olympic eligibility for any Soviet players taking part. I pressed him: If that was the case, why then was Tarasov proposing to play games before the Olympics? That set him off again: "It's impossible—these games [as proposed by Tarasov] will never take place."[52]

There was an apparent split in Soviet thinking between the coaches and sports officials about the timing and the nature of any encounter with Canada.

Just over two weeks later the Izvestia invitational tournament got underway in Moscow. Without Canadian or American participation, there were only four teams involved. The USSR, which beat Czechoslovakia and Sweden[53] but lost to the Finns, ended up winning the tournament but only on a highest-total-goals basis. It wasn't an awe-inspiring performance. Tarasov and Chernyshev were behind the bench as usual.[54]

The tournament had been initiated four years earlier to mark the fiftieth anniversary of the October Revolution, when the Bolsheviks had seized state power. Originally called the Moscow International Tournament, by 1969 it had been renamed the Izvestia Tournament, after the official government newspaper that became its sponsor. The main organizer, chief cook and bottle-washer was the paper's principal sportswriter, Boris Fedosov. He was a curly haired, likable individual with a sense of humour and imagination, a rarity in the tense, steely-eyed environment of Moscow officialdom.

Fedosov had helped finalize the official logo of the tournament: a smiling goalie snowman with a large stick in one hand and a catching glove in the other. The chinstrap on his helmet was unfastened in a carefree manner. It created a chuckle when you saw it. The logo was on pennants, pins, posters and other publicity materials, and participants would receive porcelain replicas or wooden dolls in the snowman's image. Fedosov himself used the pseudonym "Snegovik" (The Snowman) when he wrote his regular columns about the tournament and hockey in general. He was estimated to have a readership of about six million sports fans across the USSR.

The day after the Izvestia tournament ended on December 20, 1971, was the eve of the winter solstice, and darkness in Moscow began to fall not long after three p.m. It was snowing outside, and I had put my feet on the desk to begin my obligatory afternoon read of this Russian-language newspaper. It was tough sledding and boring trying to find any real news among the various industrial and agricultural production statistics and stilted accounts of self-selected international and domestic meetings intended to advance Soviet interests. I, therefore, had taken to the habit of reading the paper from back to front, which allowed me to start with the lighter fare of sports. There was Fedosov's column chronicling the wind-up to the tournament, written in his comparatively jaunty style for a Soviet journalist, all of whom had to operate within the limits of official censorship. He described the exploits of various players and their goals but began to reflect on the bigger picture. The tournament lacked the excitement of 1969, when Canada had last appeared and when the tickets had last sold out. Yes, the USSR had won again, as it had over and over again in international play, but the Soviet team needed a new challenge. It was time to play the Canadian professionals, without reservations.

My feet hit the floor and I jumped up. This was not the Soviet coach in a sports journal, but a columnist in the official government newspaper who was also a board member of the Soviet Ice Hockey Federation. The column had to have been cleared by the authorities.

Peter Hancock's office was next to mine. A fellow Russian speaker, keen hockey player and senior to me, with an extensive background in East European affairs, Hancock possessed an exceedingly sharp mind. What did he think? Could be significant, he replied. Why not call up Fedosov and pursue it?

While the Moscow telephone system was bugged and technologically shaky, and numbers were difficult to obtain, I eventually got "The Snowman" on the line. He was pleased and honoured that someone at the Canadian embassy read his columns. Aware of those who might be listening, he suggested it would be better if we met in person to further discuss what he had written. The year-end holidays were upon us, so he suggested a time early in the new year. He would invite some Soviet hockey officials to participate, and we all could have some vodka together. He extended his Christmas greetings. Since the USSR no longer celebrated this religious holiday, I reciprocated by wishing him and his family a Happy New Year, with the hope Grandfather Frost and the Snow Maiden would pay them a visit.[55]

The holidays came and went. The invitation firmed up later in January for an evening encounter at the centrally located Izvestia building.

It wasn't wise to go alone to an event like this, particularly when vodka was likely to flow. Hancock was more than willing to attend with me. We brought a reel-to-reel film, in a heavy metal case, of the 1971 Stanley Cup Final between the Chicago Black Hawks and Montreal Canadiens.[56]

The gathering was held in a standard cavernous Soviet meeting room with a high ceiling and chandeliers, framed pictures of Lenin and Brezhnev looking down from the walls. The lengthy meeting table was resplendent with appetizers of caviar, herring, smoked salmon and black bread, with plentiful bottles of vodka and mineral water. Experienced vodka drinkers knew to eat the fish, its oil coating your throat and stomach linings, before getting into the clear alcohol. Fedosov had invited what he called "interested persons." These turned out to be representatives of the Soviet Ice Hockey Federation and the Figure Skating Association, as well as a sprinkling of Soviet athletic stars, including former national hockey team captain Boris Mayorov, Olympian gold-medallist high-jumper Valeri Brumel, and the current captain of the Soviet football (soccer) team. Anatoli Tarasov was not among the guests.

Excerpts of the Stanley Cup film were shown, which evoked various oohs and ahhs. The head of the Figure Skating Association commented that we must have sped up the film, as she watched Bobby Hull fly down the left wing and let go a cannonading slapshot. The film made a big impression, and they asked to borrow it for a longer period to show their hockey coaches and players, and particularly members of the national team.

With the film at an end and the food largely consumed, but with plentiful vodka still available, Hancock and I were left alone with Fedosov and Andrei Starovoitov, the general secretary of the Soviet Ice Hockey Federation. A former defenceman on the champion Central Army team in the late 1940s, he became a well-respected referee on the international circuit at eight World Championships from 1955 to 1966. He had worked his way up the slippery Soviet hockey ladder through persistence and a knowledge of how to navigate the communist shoals. Now three years into his influential job, he still knew how to measure his words. The impression he conveyed was that of a no-nonsense straight-shooter.

At only five-foot-eight Starovoitov was towered over by his young, ever-present shadow, Viktor Khotochkin, who stood six-feet-four and was well over two hundred pounds. His title was International Secretary of the Federation, and he acted as the official interpreter for Starovoitov when so required. We spoke Russian with them nevertheless. On his own, Khotochkin was discreet and spoke quietly, but you knew he was always listening attentively and watching carefully, as his KGB training had taught him.[57]

We finally arrived at the main topic of conversation for the evening: Was the USSR ready to play a team of Canadian professionals without any conditions? The history of the question was rehearsed by Starovoitov. He wanted to know why Canada had backed out of the series of games that had been agreed upon with the CAHA during the 1971 World Championships in Switzerland. The Soviet team had planned their schedule around this event and had lost quite a large sum of money as a result of Canada cancelling the games.

Drawing on guidance from Ottawa, we explained that the CAHA had every intention of proceeding, but IIHF president Ahearne had intervened with a new set of conditions of his own, which were unacceptable to the CAHA and Hockey Canada. As a result, the games were never held.

Starovoitov replied this was the first time he had ever heard about any Ahearne conditions and then snapped that Ahearne had no authority to interfere in games arranged by two member countries of the federation if the proper rules were followed.

We agreed but said this principle was not always followed and cited the case of the role played by Ahearne in preventing the East Ottawa Voyageurs boys' team from playing games with a team from Finland. When Starovoitov asked how Ahearne had been able to accomplish this, we told him of Ahearne's threat to withdraw the 1974 World Championships from Finland. Starovoitov smirked, saying it appeared Canada was trying to blame Ahearne for all our problems, adding that it seemed a little strange that it was always Canada that was having it out with Ahearne, while other countries in the International Federation got along with him just fine. Canada's differences with Ahearne were well founded, we countered.

On to the subject of professionals. We made the point that there was really no difference between players in Canada that were known as "professionals" and those in the Soviet Union who played for leading teams such as Central Red Army, Wings of the Soviet, Dynamo and Spartak. Each country's players could be considered as professionals, as they received a salary for playing and were occupied most of the year only with hockey. In the case of Central Red Army, it began practising early in July and continued until May, a longer period than the NHL teams.

Starovoitov did not dispute this, but Fedosov interjected to say the difference was that the Soviets did not call their players professionals while the Canadians did, and we were only creating problems for ourselves by using this term. It was an interesting take on the situation, as if everything could be solved simply by having Canadian players call themselves something like "workers" rather than "professionals."

Despite these differences, Starovoitov and Fedosov were unanimous in wanting to re-establish Canadian–Soviet hockey contacts. We said it was our understanding the CAHA was ready to discuss this and urged him to contact the Canadian delegation at the Winter Olympics and speak to the CAHA representative, who we expected to be present even though we had withdrawn our hockey team (the first time Canada had not been represented since ice hockey was made an Olympic sport in 1920).

Starovoitov undertook to do so. Fedosov, for his part, urged Canada to return to the Izvestia games with any sort of team it wanted.

When we returned to the embassy the next day, taking a little time to pull our thoughts together after the previous night's festivities, Hancock and I prepared an account of what Starovoitov had to say and met with Ambassador Ford to discuss the ramifications. Ford had never played hockey himself due to his polio, but he was a keen fan and was astutely aware of the political importance of the game to Canada's relations with the USSR. He also was no stranger to the downside of hockey exchanges, having had to speak sharply to the Allan Cup-winning Sherbrooke Beavers in January 1966, during their visit to the USSR, when they initiated a bench-clearing brawl after being badly outscored by the Soviet national team. Ford also had threatened to take action to cancel the Beavers' remaining two games unless their deportment improved. Tarasov would say later this was the only time he willingly encouraged his players, including his goalie, to take the gloves off with Canadians.

Our message to Ottawa, which Ford wanted to sign to give it added weight, made two key points. Firstly, Soviet sports representatives were enthusiastic to resume hockey contacts with Canada in a context that would set aside the contentious issue of IIHF and Olympic eligibility.

The term "exhibition series" was mentioned. The format could either be national team vs national team or club vs club after the coming Sapporo Olympics. Secondly, such games would have a major impact on the Soviet public, which was well informed about Canadian hockey and would line up by the thousands to obtain tickets for a Canada–Soviet match. The Sovetsky Sports Club tournament in September '72 and the Izvestia national team tournament in December '72 offered ready-made vehicles in the USSR.

The ambassador added that it was important to move beyond the realm of good intentions. The next step had to be for the Canadian side to make a firm set of proposals, including dates, for the Soviet side to consider. Ford also emphasized that the embassy had developed a good relationship with Starovoitov and the Soviet Sports Ministry and, if it was agreed upon by Canadian hockey authorities, the embassy could begin more detailed discussions in Moscow with the hope that a signed agreement could be reached by the time of the IIHF Congress and World Championships in Prague in April.[58]

The ice hockey matches at the Winter Olympics in Sapporo, Japan, February 3–13, came and went.

A starburst went off shortly thereafter, but not about the medals or the negotiations with Canada. The Soviets had won their fourth consecutive gold medal in the six-team "A" bracket competition, with the USA claiming the silver and Czechoslovakia the bronze. The USSR record was four wins with a tie against Sweden, but the Soviets didn't dominate as they had in the past, even though Valeri Kharlamov had won the scoring title by a wide margin. It was noted that the Soviet Union had the oldest team, with an average player age of twenty-six years and four months.

It was this announcement, on February 24, 1972, which shook the Soviet hockey world to its core: Tarasov and Chernyshev were out.

TASS carried the news in three terse paragraphs. The Presidium (the standing executive committee) of the USSR Hockey Federation had appointed Vsevolod Bobrov as senior coach and Nikolai Puchkov as coach of the USSR national team. They would be in charge of preparing for the World and European championships in Prague. Tarasov and Chernyshev, who were members of the chief council of coaches, would remain as coaches of Central Red Army and Dynamo respectively and would compete for the national championship.

Bobrov's achievements were touted. He had been a member of the 1954 and 1956 World and Olympic championship teams and named best forward in 1954. He had gone on to coach Spartak, which won the national title in 1967 under his leadership. He was reported as being forty-nine years old.

Puchkov also had played on the 1954 and 56 teams and been named best goalie in the 1959 World Championships. At forty-one years old, he was the current coach of the Army team in Leningrad.

No explanation was given by the Presidium for the decision. No explanations were ever given when announcing personnel changes in the USSR.

Chernyshev himself was trotted out in an attempt to smooth the waters with the Soviet public the next day, February 25, in an interview with TASS. He and Tarasov had resigned their positions, he said. They had led the national team for many years already, witnessed the emergence of many star players and had won multiple World Championships, and Olympic medals. The tournaments had involved "great physical and nervous strain." The two of them, Chernyshev said, had a combined age of one hundred and ten (Tarasov was fifty-three and he was fifty-seven). The strain had increased with each passing year, particularly as they also had to deal with their own individual clubs. This was the first time wherein the Olympics and World Championships were stand-alone competitions, so it made for a good moment to make the move to younger coaches. Chernyshev then lauded the experience and skills of Bobrov and Puchkov, saying they had participated in and observed many international matches and together had coached the second national team. He was "sure the Federation was correct, when on our recommendation, it has been gradually training them to take on this new responsibility." Just to reassure the Soviet hockey audience, Chernyshev added, he and Tarasov would continue to make a contribution to the national team by training their respective club players.[59]

There was no interview with Tarasov. He would see the sudden evaporation of his long-time dream of coaching the Soviet national team against a united squad of Canadian professionals or even being behind the bench for a Central Army game against an NHL team.

What actually happened? This wasn't a resignation but a firing.

The age story did not hold up. Bobrov was only a few years younger than Tarasov, and mid-fifties was not old by any standard—particularly not compared to the advanced age of the Soviet leadership. And the national team Tarasov had coached, with Chernyshev as the senior coach dating back to 1948, was still winning even if it had slipped a bit.

There had been rumours in Moscow that the two of them had angered senior officials by demanding higher financial compensation for their players and that they had allowed their players to be paid by Japanese business for two exhibition games prior to the Olympics.

Tarasov had publicly run afoul of senior Soviet political authorities before. In 1969, in the presence of Party leader Brezhnev, he had pulled his Central Army team off the ice for forty minutes in an important match against Spartak to protest the referees' decision about a non-goal. He wouldn't listen to an order to immediately resume play and was stripped of his "Merited Coach" title by the Hockey Federation Presidium on orders from above.

One thing surely would not have been appreciated by those at the very top, and that was Tarasov's multiple solo efforts to orchestrate games against Canada in a way that could have jeopardized the Olympic status of Soviet players. In the end his individualism and egotism lost out to the collective interests and will of the Soviet state.

Bobrov, though, wasn't helped by the sudden departure of Tarasov. There was little time to prepare for the World Championships, and the majority of his players were from Tarasov's Central Army team, while Bobrov was a Spartak man.

One of the top scorers on the national team and three-time league MVP, Anatoli Firsov had been a staunch personal supporter of Tarasov and his methods and did not get along with the new coach. Firsov would not accompany the team to Prague just over a month later, when the USSR would lose its World Championships title after nine consecutive victories. Host Czechoslovakia won the tournament, playing on national emotion, by beating the USSR squad 3–2 after an earlier 3–3 tie game. Firsov's presence might have made the difference.

The embassy continued to wait for follow-up instructions to Ambassador Ford's February message about the Soviet willingness to play a Canadian team of professionals. Finally, on March 23, a message was dispatched from Ottawa with instructions to propose a "double round-robin tournament of twelve games in Canada in September 1972, involving unrestricted teams from Canada, the USSR, Sweden and Czechoslovakia." The instructions contained a fallback position of bilateral games should the tournament proposal not work, but we were told not to deploy that option yet.

Starovoitov was away in Switzerland until April 3, but in order to get the proposal on the Soviet table as soon as possible I secured an appointment on March 28 with D.I. Prokhorov, deputy chief of the international department of the Ministry of Physical Culture and Sport, who was accompanied by a junior official from the hockey department.

Prokhorov was noncommittal, saying a response would have to await a meeting between the Sports Committee and the Ice Hockey Federation scheduled for April 4 as a prelude to the IIHF championships in Prague. Nevertheless, he warmly welcomed the prospect of resuming Canadian–Soviet competition, as Canada had been missed in international play. It was necessary to emphasize to him that Canada's proposal had nothing to do with the IIHF nor with Bunny Ahearne. We were not proposing a "World Championship" but a competition among the best hockey teams the four countries could assemble. The USSR was sensitive about putting its World Championship on the line.

Then a bit of diplomatic stickhandling was required, as Prokhorov wanted to know whether the Canadian proposal was being put forward to the Swedes and Czechoslovaks at the same time or if the USSR was being consulted first. Simultaneously, was my response, but I added that Canada–Soviet hockey contacts naturally had a "special place in Canada's view." Prokhorov then wanted to know whether Canadian–Soviet contacts would depend on the acceptance by all parties of the round-robin proposal. I said there was no reason why progress on a bilateral basis should depend on the responses of third countries. The fallback position, as instructed, was not mentioned.

Prokhorov then asked if Canada would attend the Sovetsky Sport tournament in September as well as the Izvestia tournament in December. I noted the first was for clubs, not national teams, and anyway it would conflict with our proposal for September. He asked about the makeup of the Canadian team. (Best available, was my reply.) Who would coach it? (I had no information.) Would there be one or two Canadian teams in the tournament? (Likely one.) Prokhorov agreed such technical details as the location(s) in Canada and financial arrangements of the round robin "would not be material to the Soviet decision." It was noted that Hay, Kryczka and Lefaive would be in Prague ready to discuss the round-robin proposal further, but it would help facilitate matters greatly if we could have a Soviet response before that date.

The final sentence of my classified return message to Ottawa, based on this discussion and other encounters with Soviet hockey authorities, was "we see every predisposition to seek play with Canada's best, if not in the tournament format, then on a bilateral basis."[60]

Following up with the State Committee, the embassy was able to inform External Affairs on April 7 that "Soviet authorities agree in principle to resumption of hockey contacts ... subject to some technical questions to be discussed in Prague."

We had another discussion with the Sports Committee on April 17 to urge a Soviet decision. There was some confusion among their officials about exactly what was happening in Prague, but we drew the conclusion that Starovoitov appeared to be empowered to reach a deal. Regardless, the embassy counselled that any agreement be in writing.[61]

Then, on April 18, 1972, in Prague, a page-and-a-half "Letter of Agreement" finally was signed by Joe Kryczka, the president of the CAHA, and Andrei Starovoitov, general secretary of the USSR Ice Hockey Federation. Kryczka had played hockey at the University of Alberta with the Golden Bears, graduated as a lawyer and gone on to become a widely respected judge, where he was commonly known as "Justice Joe." With a reputation as a skilled hockey negotiator, he soon found himself moving up the administrative ranks. There were only two other names on the Prague Agreement: most importantly Fred Page, the IIHF vice-president responsible for North America and former CAHA president, and Bunny Ahearne, who wrote in large script at the bottom "Approved."

The agreement listed the terms and conditions governing "an exchange of visits between a selected unrestricted Canadian hockey team assembled on behalf of the CAHA and the Soviet National Hockey team named by the Soviet Ice Hockey Federation for the purpose of playing a series of exhibition matches in Canada and in the USSR."

The agreement was pretty straightforward and closely approximated what Tarasov had sketched out back in September in his *Sovetsky Sport* article, except for some detailed financial arrangements, which Starovoitov obviously had put in, wanting foreign currency and fearing the CAHA might have another reason to back out of the deal. Along these lines, the CAHA's Gordon Juckes would later tell External Affairs officials that the financial issue was the only real stumbling block in the negotiations. Previous international arrangements had called for a fee of two hundred and fifty dollars per game, and he had advised Hay and Kryczka that in this case a doubling to five hundred dollars per game might be in order. Juckes strenuously objected however when Starovoitov demanded ten times that amount, five thousand dollars per game, but he was overruled, as neither Hay nor Kryczka wanted the series to founder over a matter of money.

Alan Eagleson had not been present at the negotiations in Prague but was due to arrive in the city shortly. He had been a significant part of the

Hockey Canada endeavours back home and had agreed to support the series, but it wasn't overly long before he began to pick away at what had been signed by others. Before returning home, Eagleson had been among a variety of Canadian hockey officials to witness the USSR–Czechoslovak and Finland–Sweden final matches to size up the forthcoming international opposition. Swedish coach and former Toronto Maple Leaf Billy Harris was quoted by TASS, from Prague, as saying, "The Soviet National team is ready to hold its own against the Canadian professionals."[62]

The Canadian embassy in Prague had alerted External Affairs in Ottawa in advance of the public release of the agreement, and the department in turn advised the office of NHL president Clarence Campbell, as well as Sam Pollock, general manager of the Montreal Canadiens, and Harold Ballard, owner of the Toronto Maple Leafs.[63]

The accompanying press conference in Prague attracted quite the international crowd. One report said there were more than four hundred journalists present. Kryczka and Page were the only Canadians on the stage, with Kryczka taking the lead in speaking for Canada. He reviewed the terms of the agreement and informed the assembled throng that the Canadian team would stop off in Sweden before the games in Moscow for a four-day training session and two exhibition matches, part of the fiftieth anniversary of hockey in Sweden. He also mentioned the strong possibility of one or two exhibition matches in Czechoslovakia. Timing for these had not been firmed up, but Kryczka acknowledged Czechoslovakia had played seven games in Canada over time and there was "a Canadian debt to be repaid."[64]

Ahearne, who had for so long disparaged Canada and Canadians and been a major roadblock to Canada returning to world play with a professional team, was now as cuddly as a plush bear. All of a sudden he was revealing that it had been his long-time dream to see Canada and the USSR play without restrictions and it had only taken him "three seconds" to sign the agreement.

Starovoitov must have gotten to Ahearne about not trying to block a bilateral exhibition series, because Ahearne was still singing his old negative tune in a separate interview with a local Czech journalist, as reported by our embassy in Prague. In that account, Ahearne stated that as long as he was in office, he would vote against any attempt to have an "open tournament" with professionals, as it would unbalance the federation in favour of Canada and the USA. That stated position must have included the CAHA proposal, which was still under discussion in March, for a "double round-robin tournament" in Canada, in September 1972, of twelve games involving the USSR, Sweden and Czechoslovakia. Ahearne referred to Kryczka as "a young, respectable man" who might change his mind about pushing to involve professionals in IIHF matches and might revert to amateurism, but then noted the CAHA president likely would be gone in a year, adding he had dealt with twenty such Canadian representatives during his tenure as IIHF president.[65]

The Soviet print media, radio and television stations, buzzing with excitement, carried the story the same day, focusing on the eight-games series. TASS, in its English-language service, mentioned the twenty-thousand-dollar performance bond each team would post, of which five thousand dollars would be paid out to the visiting team for each game it showed up for and completed. The Russian-language papers gave this aspect a pass. Money was a capitalist matter even if Starovoitov considered that matter to be of particular importance.[66]

The embassy telephones began to ring that night with multiple enquires from the foreign expatriate community about the availability of tickets.

The following day TASS reported the announcement "had stirred up literally the whole of Canada" and that one Canadian journalist had contacted Soviet coach Puchkov seeking a reaction. His response: "There will be competition but whatever the results, it will be ice hockey that will benefit."[67]

TASS also carried a statement from Clarence Campbell that the NHL fully supported the CAHA and Hockey Canada in this series of matches and that the three Canadian clubs (Montreal, Toronto and Vancouver) would make players available for the Canadian team, and Canadian players of us-based clubs would be included if they wished to meet the Russians.[68]

Boris "The Snowman" Fedosov was hot and cold with the news. Happy that the Canadian professionals would be playing the USSR, but disappointed it would not involve his Izvestia tournament. A few days earlier he had written a scalding column, following his visit to Canada, about the Americanization of the NHL. Fedosov wrote that the NHL had expanded from six teams to twelve and now fourteen, but there were only three Canadian cities among them, even if the vast majority of players on each of the fourteen teams were Canadians. He also suggested that the purity of the game was being compromised in Canada in the name of spectacle and ticket sales. Marvelling at all the music played throughout NHL games—as opposed to the largely unaccompanied matches in the USSR—he commented that its main purpose was to keep the spectators entertained. He also observed that a fight would be staged by lower-grade players if a game wasn't interesting. NHL owners were characterized as croupiers in casinos in Monte Carlo or Las Vegas, and they, not the fans or players, took all the winnings.

Professional hockey was moving away from sport and had turned itself into a gigantic profit-making enterprise, Fedosov said. He had met with Jack McLeod, the former coach of the Canadian national team, and asked him where hockey was headed in Canada. McLeod's only comment, apparently, was to hold up a copy of *Macleans* magazine that had a cartoon of Clarence Campbell holding a dollar sign instead of a puck. Hockey and its president were portrayed as marionettes in the hands of big business.[69]

This was a hard-line, anti-capitalist Soviet view expressed by Fedosov, but its sentiments and even several of its choice words would be used by Canadian fans themselves three months later, when it became known some star Canadian players, like Bobby Hull, would be excluded from the Canadian team. American financial dominance of the NHL would become the target of Canadian ire.

THE PRAGUE AGREEMENT specifically called for the Canadian embassy in Moscow to be involved in two aspects: the selection of hotels and the financial performance bond. (As the embassy representative, I was designated to hold their money in roubles, and the embassy would pay Team Canada the dollar equivalent of five thousand dollars for every game played in Moscow.) It was evident from the start, however, that this would just be the beginning and there would be a massive administrative burden ahead for the embassy as the agreement was fleshed out in greater detail and actually implemented.

In order to avoid confusion and logistical snafus, the embassy proposed that all messages and instructions coming from Canada (including from the CAHA, Hockey Canada, the NHL and NHLPA) be co-ordinated with and sent via External Affairs' telegraphic means and in confidential code as required. The embassy would then deal directly with Starovoitov, officials at the Sports and Foreign Ministries, and any other Soviet bodies as required.

This was a brand-new arrangement with an extremely high profile on both sides. It would not just be a standard hockey-organization-to-hockey-organization matter but would involve a government-to-government overlay. Embassy personnel cancelled all holidays and brought in the reinforcements.

As jarring as it might have been, hockey was put on the embassy back burner in the second half of May. President Richard Nixon was coming to town with a massive entourage for six days of crucial meetings with the Soviet political leadership. Nixon had been to China in February and had used that diplomatic breakthrough for leverage purposes in dealing with the Kremlin. It was the first ever visit by a sitting US president to Moscow and was exactly a year from the time when Prime Minister Trudeau had blazed the same trail. Although a fractious pair, Trudeau and Nixon had the opportunity to exchange their own views beforehand during the president's state visit to Canada in mid-April.

The Canadian embassy in Washington and our political and military delegations to NATO headquarters in Brussels had been keeping our embassy abreast of the general state of the pre-negotiatons between the Americans and Soviets. It was a very big deal and major step forward in the détente process when the president and General Secretary Brezhnev signed two landmark nuclear arms control agreements: SALT I freezing the number of strategic ballistic launchers at existing levels, and an ABM treaty restricting both sides to only two sites for anti-ballistic missiles. Canada possessed no such weapons itself, but their flight paths were over Canadian territory and we were a potential target.

There were also other agreements of importance to Canada, including: incidents at sea, environmental protection, future space co-operation between the Apollo and Soyuz programs, and a joint declaration of plans to avoid a military confrontation.

I participated in the embassy's analysis and reporting of the visit, which had global implications. It emphasized the scale at which the Americans operated and their pre-eminent importance to the leadership in the USSR. Then it was back to hockey. In Canada there were a massive number of administrative issues to address, none more important than the selection of coaches and the construction of a team. The USSR, having its coaches and core players already in place from the existing national team, was way ahead in this important area.

Alan Eagleson and Harry Sinden had their first telephone conversation in early June about the coach's position. Sinden was invited to meet in Montreal with the nine-person steering committee of Hockey Canada. The job was his, and he quickly moved to bring John Ferguson on board as assistant coach and to have a team of thirty-five players. Sinden's rationale for the surprising large number was that he needed enough players to compete against each other, as two squads, as there were no other NHL teams available as competition in August.

Soon signs began to emerge that not everyone on the Canadian side was on the same page. The embassy received a confidential telegram from External Affairs in Ottawa indicating that the Canadian players (read Alan Eagleson and the NHLPA) were not happy with the September dates and wanted the embassy to inquire about postponing the series until November, when it was argued everyone would be in better shape and game ready after the summer layoff. At the same time the embassy was aware Hockey Canada and the CAHA stood by the dates of the April agreement. September also had been the date that Canada had put into play earlier for the proposed round-robin tournament.

The embassy was put in the awkward position of being an intermediary on a matter that should have been resolved in Canada and was evidence of a looming power struggle back home. We took our instructions to mean we were to suggest a postponement—not to demand one.

Two separate meetings were arranged with Starovoitov and Romesky on June 15, involving Hancock and me, and again on June 22, when I participated on my own. When I advocated on both occasions that the USSR might find it more convenient to postpone the games to avoid the conflict with the Munich Olympics in early September, Starovoitov wasted no time in stating unequivocally that the September dates had been agreed in Prague and Soviet planning was going ahead on that basis. Moreover, the Soviet team already had other engagements scheduled for November. The only problem he had with the September dates was the Vancouver game, due to air connection issues returning to Moscow, and a couple of times he suggested reversing the order of the games in Canada, to start in Vancouver and end in Montreal. Starovoitov was interested in Canada's idea of a rest day in Banff, Alberta, and moving the Vancouver game to September 9, but again said it all hinged on being able to fly back to Moscow on a regularly scheduled Aeroflot flight.

In our return confidential message to Ottawa, we stated the embassy believed it had "completely met" the wishes of Eagleson and the Players' Association to ask for the games to be moved to November and that it would be "extremely unwise" to keep pressing the matter if the agreement and the series were to remain intact.

We also reported we had told Starovoitov that reversing the schedule in Canada to start in Vancouver would cause us difficulties and another solution would have to be found to his flight problem—perhaps by using Air Canada, which had a joint pooling arrangement with Aeroflot.

Player limits were also discussed. We told Starovoitov that Canada's interpretation of the Prague Agreement, with its ceiling of thirty on the number of players and officials, meant that the number should not be exceeded at any one time and that we were considering some players on the team in Canada might be replaced by others in Moscow. Starovoitov confirmed that was his understanding as well and said the USSR would likely want to make three or four changes between the games in Canada and those in the USSR. His concern was to avoid a situation where Canada would bring in additional players at home, beyond the limit of thirty, giving it an unfair advantage. The Soviet team would already have to cope with the transatlantic flight and time change, and he was of the opinion both teams should be governed by the same conditions in Canada.

Our return message to Ottawa said this particular point "seems reasonable." As a possible option, we raised the possibility of increasing the ceiling, on a reciprocal basis, and that Starovoitov appeared agreeable to such a proposal.

Uniform colours had been an issue as well, with the Soviets shifting back and forth on whether they would wear red or white sweaters in Canada. In the end, it was finally agreed that the home team in each case would wear red and the visitors white. Starovoitov gave us examples of both of their uniforms used in international play, which were sent by diplomatic bag to Ottawa. We would provide examples of the Canadian sweaters when they were ready. It would be a new design.

Starovoitov was also keen on exchanging coaches to witness each other's training camps and proposed that two Canadians arrive in the USSR on August 15 to witness the finals of the Sovetsky Sport Tournament (involving club teams) and attend one full week of training camp for their national team. It was agreed to discuss this further.

An exchange of hockey films was also agreed upon. The Soviets would provide Canada with 35 mm copies of films showing major Soviet teams in action as well as their national team in international competition. In exchange, Starovoitov requested we provide 35 mm copies of NHL games (his preference was for the New York Rangers, Boston Bruins and

Montreal Canadiens, whom he thought were the strongest teams—he left out the Black Hawks for no apparent reason) and TV videotapes of regular league games that could be shown on Soviet television to acquaint the Soviet audience with professional hockey.

The Canadian Commissioner of the National Film Board (NFB), Sidney Newman, had recently been in Moscow and had proposed the co-production of a film with the Soviet State Committee on Broadcasting that would show all aspects of the series, beginning with the players assembling at training camps and ending with the games in Moscow. While Starovoitov and Romesky showed interest in this idea, they in effect quashed the collaborative element by suggesting the Canadian crew should film in Canada and a Soviet crew would do likewise in the USSR, and then the film could be "blended." The idea never went any further. Blending wasn't attractive to Western directors, while the Soviet Union did not want Western film crews operating in the USSR unless under strict supervision with the content reviewed.

Broadcasting the games on television was another agenda issue to which the Soviets had not paid much attention. Starovoitov's view was that each country would be responsible for the transmission at home, which they would share freely with the other side. Each host would be responsible for delivery to third parties in the US, parts of Europe, and other locations where there might be interest in the series. He also reminded us that five per cent of the Canadian TV revenue would have to be shared equally with the IIHF and North American Federation, while the USSR would provide all five per cent of its revenues to the IIHF. What he hadn't thought about was where TV announcers would be situated (would play-by-play man Foster Hewitt be sitting in Canada dealing with a feed from Moscow for instance?) and how this idea meshed with ongoing CBC/CTV contractual obligations. This was a matter for a lot more discussion, and it was decided to let the broadcasting experts on both sides tackle it.

The issue of the press, in general, continued to be a major hair-puller. Starovoitov reiterated that only three Soviet journalists would go to Canada to cover the games there. He nevertheless accepted our point that the demand from the Canadian media would be far, far greater: as many as one hundred representatives would need to be there. Starovoitov indicated he was hesitating not because the USSR didn't want Canadian media but the press box and related facilities at the Sports Palace were being repaired for the 1973 World Championships and they simply couldn't handle such large numbers. He wanted the Canadian authorities to decide what would be the "necessary number to ensure adequate coverage" and those persons would be given "special seats and proper direct communications with Canada." Any additional members of the Canadian press corps would not be given official accreditation and would have to use Intourist services for obtaining phone lines to Canada and seats in the arena. In any event, all Canadian media would have to avail themselves of the Air Canada/Aeroflot/Intourist package plan. Alexander Sedov, the deputy head of propaganda (information) for the Physical Culture and Sports Committee, also laid down a marker that they would require a full list of journalists planning to attend and all their requirements at least one month prior to the first game in Moscow.

The issue was kicked back to Canada. I did not want to be in the shoes of whomever was going to have to decide which members of the Canadian media were "necessary to ensure adequate coverage" and which weren't.

The embassy suggested to Ottawa that we might want to see if we could arrange an alternative press centre in the Intourist hotel where all the journalists could be lodged, collective communications made available, and where we could keep the costs in check. Our experience was that Soviet hotels on their own would charge exorbitant rates unless there was some sort of government agreement in place.

Then there was the big question of how to manage the logistics of spectators and ticketing. With Montreal-based Morley Ryder and Kukulowicz of Air Canada (Aggie was now a "special advisor" for the company) we were able to secure a guarantee from Intourist for two thousand tickets per game in Moscow. Three hundred and fifty were to be set aside for Hockey Canada's purposes and two hundred and fifty for the embassy (for the Canadian community in Moscow and important political, commercial and cultural contacts of Ambassador Ford). That left fourteen hundred to be marketed to Canadian fans through Air Canada's partner wholesalers: package deals, costing only between six and seven hundred dollars Canadian, included airfare, ten days' accommodation, all meals, and tickets to all four games, as well as tickets to the circus, ballet and other attractions. They were gobbled up in Canada as soon as they went on sale. Demand greatly outweighed supply.

Although there appeared to be agreement in Canada to funnel all communications concerning the September series via External Affairs and then to the embassy, it didn't appear to be the case with proposals for other hockey matches. Starovoitov surprised us with news that Gordon Juckes of the CAHA had sent him directly invitations for a team of "Moscow Selects" to participate in a tournament in Quebec City in mid-December 1972, and for Dynamo to be part of another tournament, a couple of weeks later, involving club teams from the USA, Czechoslovakia and Sweden, as well as Canada and the USSR. We had no comment to make. Starovoitov did not pursue the matter, but interestingly, in reiterating their previous intention for a Canadian team to participate in the December Izvestia tournament, now said Canadian professionals would no longer be able to take part. (This was a significant backtrack from the position Fedosov and Starovoitov had stated earlier and may have been part of a deal with Ahearne of the IIHF that, in exchange for his agreeing to bilateral exhibition matches with professionals, there would be no professional participation in international tournaments.)

The negotiating table was jammed with a multitude of thorny items—all becoming increasingly urgent to resolve, with little more than two months before the anticipated start of the series.

Our reporting telegram, sent on June 22, 1972, to External Affairs, lamented Eagleson's scheduling difficulties with Hockey Canada and concluded it was the embassy's opinion that "the Soviets are intent on holding these games and that major obstacles to completion of the series will not be created by them."[70]

CHAPTER NINE

THE EAGLE LANDS IN MOSCOW

CANADIAN HOCKEY UNITY continued to fray. What appeared to have been common cause between the CAHA, the NHL and NHLPA when Hockey Canada was first formed in 1969, no longer seemed to be the case. In addition to negotiating with the Soviets, the embassy continued to monitor the unfolding drama in Canada with the assistance of newspaper accounts and detailed reports from our colleagues in External Affairs.

Canada had been arguing for so long to ice a national team of professionals, you would have thought it would be an easy matter to do so once an international agreement had been reached with the USSR and with the blessing of the IIHF. This was not the case. Issues emerged with respect to insurance, injury and finances. This particularly troubled the American NHL owners who were being asked to lend their Canadian-born players to a Canadian national team while all the publicity and revenues would accrue to the owners and others in Canada. On the other hand, having the NHL involved in an international series against the Soviets would give the league an advantage over the newly created North American professional league, the World Hockey Association (WHA), which was threatening to expand its operation into Europe, as its name implied. The WHA was already a nemesis of the NHL with its bigger salaries attracting NHL players in increasing numbers.

Alan Eagleson skilfully stickhandled his way through this thicket. The owners would receive some form of profit-sharing from anticipated lucrative TV commercial sales, which were controlled by Ballard–Orr

Enterprises, a company Eagleson had helped set up. Its principals were Toronto Maple Leafs owner Harold Ballard and Eagleson's hockey client Bobby Orr. The company had secured the broadcast rights to the games from Hockey Canada. NHL players would get a concomitant significant boost to their pension fund from the owners. Insurance of the players would be guaranteed if everyone had a signed contract with an NHL club.

Exact details of this arrangement were not clear but were not of direct consequence to my job in Moscow. What was of importance was that there was agreement to ice a team of Canadian professionals.

At an exceptionally well-attended press conference in Toronto on July 12, 1972, Douglas Fisher of Hockey Canada was given the unenviable task of announcing the bad news that those players who had signed with the WHA would not be permitted to play for Canada. As justification he pointed to a pre-existing agreement with the NHL requiring players to have signed NHL contracts before they could attend training camp. Stellar players like Bobby Hull, Gerry Cheevers, Derek Sanderson and J.C. Tremblay, who had been on Sinden's initial notional list, were out.

Harry Sinden followed Fisher to the podium with the good news: the eagerly awaited announcement of the thirty-five outstanding players who had been invited to join Team Canada starting on August 13 at Maple Leaf Gardens. All of them were professionals. Some names rang louder than others, but it was a star-studded line-up including Ken Dryden and Tony Esposito in goal; Bobby Orr, Brad Park and Serge Savard on defence; and Phil Esposito, Yvon Cournoyer and Frank Mahovlich among the sharp-shooting forwards.

This bad and good news was blasted and ricocheted around every corner of Canada. This was news of the highest order and commanded Canadians' attention. The media was quick to focus on the pointed exclusion of the WHA players, which removed some of Canada's hockey legends from the team. A public outcry ensued, particularly about Hull's exclusion, and the prime minister urged reconsideration of the decision—but to no avail. Phil Esposito, in an off-the-cuff moment, would later refer to the new squad as "Team NHL"; as did Bobby Hull.

A restricted report of the press conference, prepared by an officer in External Affairs, noted that both Sinden and Eagleson on several occasions had referred to the "autonomous identity of Team Canada." It was also noted that the staff of this newly minted and newly named organization was composed of the same people who ran the NHLPA, and that a subsidiary called Team Canada Productions had been set up by Eagleson to handle the public relations, financial arrangements, the sale of rights to photographs, uniform costs, advertising costs and other operational expenses associated with the team.[71] The report added the observation that Eagleson "appeared to have an unhidden disdain for the role and operational methods of the organization (Hockey Canada) of which he was one of the Directors."[72]

Separately, in the media and elsewhere, there was speculation about how many of the thirty-five players selected had Eagleson as their agent, with numbers ranging from seven upwards.[73] Three additional clients, who had been drafted in June of 1972 (John Van Boxmeer and Michel "Bunny" Larocque by the Montreal Canadiens, and Billy Harris by the New York Islanders), were invited to the training camp. This brought the roster number to thirty-eight, so there would be two squads of nineteen each for practice purposes.

Hockey Canada was hobbled at this time by the illness of its president, Charles Hay. Eagleson, holding the trump card of player availability, had quickly established himself as the dominant hockey power on the Canadian side, with a leading hand in virtually every decision.

THE DAY AFTER the Toronto press conference, a meeting was held in Ottawa in the office of Under Secretary of State for External Affairs Ed Ritchie. Eagleson was there with Sinden and Ferguson, along with administrator Bob Haggert and Eagleson's executive assistant, Mike Cannon. Doug Fisher and Chris Lang were among those representing Hockey Canada, and there were a few officials from External Affairs, including a new actor in the form of Patrick Reid.

Reid was a big man with an ever-ready smile and quick glad hand. He had done a first-rate job in Japan as the commissioner general of Canada's pavilion at EXPO 70. Reid was without a specific job after Expo and knew nothing about hockey, but he was an expert at projecting Canada's image abroad and was selected to lead Ritchie's and the Trudeau government's new policy of public diplomacy.

Ritchie called the meeting to ensure that everyone had a clear and explicit understanding of the interest of the Department of External Affairs (and that of the Prime Minister's Office) in the political dimensions of the series and in any further negotiations with the USSR, Sweden and Czechoslovakia. This message was directed primarily at Eagleson and company, who had decided with little notice to come to Moscow to meet with Starovoitov to review the state of negotiations and to press for an increase in the ceiling on players.

Reid's recollection of that meeting, which he later recorded in an autobiography,[74] was that Eagleson was happy to receive all the diplomatic assistance he could. Reid's initial impression of Sinden was less positive, which was reciprocated following Reid's admission about his lack of hockey knowledge. As Reid put it, "Sinden appeared to have little comprehension that life had dimensions beyond the rectangle of a rink and the round of a puck."

It was a snide comment. Who could blame Sinden for focusing completely on the rink, the puck, the players and the games? Someone had to and it was essential that he, as coach, did. That was his job.

Unbeknownst to the embassy and to Eagleson and Sinden, the head of Sport Canada and Hockey Canada director, Lou Lefaive, it seems, had persuaded CAHA president Joe Kryczka to send an independent message to Starovoitov. It stated that the CAHA had decided Team Canada would play a game in Prague on September 20, after the stopover in Sweden and before the team's arrival in Moscow. The timing of the Prague game had been temporarily suspended previously, and there had been agreement in Canada to discuss the subject in Moscow during Eagleson's visit. Kryczka and Lefaive were firing a pre-emptive shot across Eagleson's bow, attempting to re-establish control of international decision-making and to guard the integrity of the April Prague Agreement that Kryczka had signed.

On July 17, the night of the delegation's departure for Moscow, Eagleson held another press conference in Toronto. Members of the now self-named "Team Five"[75] were on the podium, resplendent in matching crested blue blazers, grey-chequered slacks, white shirts and stylish paisley ties. The five were Eagleson, Sinden, Ferguson, Haggert and Cannon, who formed a tight-knit group. An Air Canada representative also was at the table, along with a vice-president of CTV, which had agreed to televise the series at a cost to Ballard–Orr Enterprises of $1 million. Absent from the podium and standing at the back of the room was Lou Lefaive of Hockey Canada. A written External Affairs report the embassy received later indicated that on the flight to Moscow there were unpleasantries exchanged between Eagleson and Lefaive and that Eagleson had been "childish" and "extremely rude" toward a senior Soviet Trade delegation returning to Moscow from Canada.[76]

Eagleson and delegation landed in Moscow the following day. Although tired, the "five" did look sharp in their new outfits. Included in the group were Johnny Esaw and Oliver Babirad of CTV, who were going to deal with the issue of television broadcasting, and Tony Chernushenko from the information division of External Affairs, who worked for Patrick Reid.

Ambassador Ford and I were at the airport to greet them, but the ambassador only had fifteen or so minutes, as he himself was departing for long-planned consultations in Ottawa and vacation leave, which he could not change. Ford's message to the group was threefold: to reiterate the diplomatic importance of the series; to state that the embassy had an excellent working relationship with the Soviet hockey authorities; and to outline the possible negative consequences of a pre-Moscow game in Prague.

Eagleson and I had never met before, but I had studied his hockey background as well as his active involvement in politics: his unsuccessful federal run for the Progressive Conservatives (PC) in April 1963 against popular Liberal incumbent Leonard "Red" Kelly, the star centre-ice man for the Toronto Maple Leafs; election later that same year to the Ontario Legislative Assembly in the new Toronto riding of Lakeshore and defeat four years later in the same riding by the NDP candidate; his major role in fundraising for the PC's and his ongoing presidency of the PC party of Ontario as of 1968.

We rode into the city centre together in a chauffeur-driven embassy sedan, and I had the opportunity to bring him up to speed on what was happening in Moscow. I reported that everything had been going well until Kryczka's telegram had landed on Starovoitov's desk, and Gresko, from the Sports Committee, in turn had called me at the embassy to express his displeasure at this last-minute development. Gresko wanted this matter to be the first item on the agenda the next day. Eagleson's initial reaction was to cancel the Prague game but then agreed with me to keep our powder dry until we saw how the negotiations would unfold the next day and attempt to push it to the end of the agenda. The issue might provide us with some trade-off leverage.

THE DIPLOMATIC FUNCTION of "innkeeping," as defined by Ambassador Allan Gotlieb, paid dividends that evening when, at our apartment, Laurielle prepared a tasty buffet dinner and I supplied generous portions of imported beer. Normally the Russians would shy away from accepting hospitality in a diplomat's private quarters, but not on this occasion. Gresko, Starovoitov, Sedov and Khotochkin all came along from the State Committee and Hockey Federation, as well as Soviet head Coach Bobrov. The full Canadian delegation was in attendance. The dinner turned into an excellent ice-breaker between the two sides, with much merriment all around and keen enjoyment of the diplomatic food and drink. Eagleson had gifts of Team Canada ties, tie clips and cuff-links to present, which were received with wide smiles and generous words of appreciation. We were off to a good start.

The Russians left first. And before the Canadians departed, I gave them some friendly advice that the Intourist Hotel, where they were staying, was a notorious "Viper's Nest" of black marketers and sex workers, both of whom were controlled by the KGB. The "Night Bar" at the hotel had a particularly well-earned reputation for trouble.

Negotiations began the next morning in good spirits, with a smirking Starovoitov saying he and his communist colleagues found it amusing that a capitalist country would permit Eagleson, the head of a "union," to lead its delegation on a matter of such importance. Starovoitov had remembered Eagleson making much of his union role to him at their previous awkward meeting in 1969. This time everyone on both sides just laughed.

The long face-to-face negotiating table, with the Canadian and Soviet flags at one end, was loaded with mineral water, ice buckets, porcelain coffee cups and bowls of oranges.

Boris Fedosov from *Izvestia* had joined the Soviet side of Gresko, Starovoitov, Khotochkin, Sedov and Bobrov. Aggie Kukulowicz from Air Canada joined our side, composed of Eagleson, Lefaive, Sinden, Ferguson, Cannon, Haggert and me. While Gresko was senior to Starovoitov in the Soviet hierarchy, he let the latter lead the discussions, as Eagleson did for Canada. Khotochkin did the bulk of the interpreting, with Gresko, Kukulowicz and me chipping in. The initial agenda items went fairly smoothly and largely in accordance with what had been settled earlier in June. There was no trouble increasing the number of players and officials. Canada could have up to thirty-five players at home with a Soviet official party of thirty-five, of whom thirty could be players. In return, for the four games in the USSR, the Soviets would be permitted thirty-five players while Canada could have thirty players and an official delegation of thirty-five. If Bobby Orr was fit enough to play in Moscow, then the Canadian player number would be increased to thirty-one. This was a nice gesture by the Soviets, who recognized Orr's superlative skills and stature in the hockey world, though they were fully aware that his knee surgery in June was so recent it would be difficult for him to resume play in time for the series. A final list of players was due by September 1, and it was agreed that for each game nineteen players would dress, of which two would be goalies.

The issue of wives accompanying players was a one-way street. No Soviet spouses would go to Canada, but Eagleson and Sinden had promised the Canadian players their wives could come to Moscow as part of the "holiday inducement" to sign on with the team. The Soviets agreed the spouses would be located in the same hotel as the players and would be invited to one or two official receptions, with their husbands.

In terms of uniform colours, red for home games remained, but Starovoitov objected to "Hockey Canada" being on the back of the Canadian jerseys. He requested only "Canada" appear, again reflecting his concern that his federation's official relationship was with the CAHA and not Hockey Canada. He did not wish to create an unneeded issue with the IIHF. It was agreed Team Canada and Hockey Canada would work this out (in the end only "Canada" appeared).

Regarding rules, there was agreement, as per the Prague Agreement, on IIHF standards, with a two-referee system instead of the North American variant of one referee and two linesmen. Icing would be called as soon as the puck crossed the goal line (something the NHL would adopt much later), but a team could ice the puck if it was playing short-handed (this was a deviation from then IIHF rules).

In a further sign they were being obliging, the Soviet side agreed to provide full accreditation for up to fifty Canadian journalists, which would include telex and telephone lines and free tickets. Additional press would have to use Intourist facilities. Canadian members of the press arriving from the Olympics in Munich, which were due to end on September 11, or those based in other European cities, would need to make their arrangements through Intourist but would not have to purchase the package tour. We were told over a hundred additional requests from European journalists had already been made to the Sports Committee. The media numbers were going through the roof, and this didn't even begin to count requests from Soviet journalists, which were said to number two hundred or more.

The exchange of coaches was an agenda item. The Soviets advised they had selected former national coach Arkadi Chernyshev and current national assistant coach Boris Kulagin to go to Canada, as of August 13, to watch the Canadian training camp in Toronto. Eagleson said no decision had yet been reached on the Canadian side but mentioned the names of Gordie Howe and Jean Beliveau as contenders.

We finally got to the contentious issue of the Prague game. Before the negotiations with the Soviets started that day, Eagleson, Sinden, Lefaive and I agreed there were several reasons not to raise the matter ourselves: First, the Soviets were annoyed at this development and we needed their full and positive co-operation with all the logistics surrounding the Canadian fans and media and on other agenda items; secondly, the tightness of the travel schedule in Europe and trying to move the mighty hockey armada in such a short period of time between Stockholm, Prague and Moscow; and finally Sinden's belief that the players were keen for games with the Russians but not very interested in matches elsewhere. This wasn't a big issue with what Sinden described as the "relatively weak" Swedish team, but he was concerned Team Canada could lose to a keyed-up Czechoslovak squad, thereby making the games in Moscow more difficult and an anti-climax.[77]

Starovoitov took the initiative and asked Eagleson if Canada intended to play in Prague and, if so, whether the USSR would have to rearrange the schedule of games in Moscow. It was a slick, loaded question with the hint that everything that had been agreed with the Soviets would have to begin all over again. Starting a diplomatic dance, we asked what the Soviets thought of the idea, knowing they didn't want their fellow Warsaw Pact members to learn that they had scuttled plans for a game in Prague. Starovoitov didn't want to fall into that trap and retorted that this was a matter for Canada itself to decide, but the USSR wanted a decision before this meeting ended.

Lefaive picked up the cudgel, saying the CAHA had a commitment to the Czechoslovak Hockey Federation, but Starovoitov replied he was puzzled as to why a high-powered, all-star, professional team had any commitment to the Czechoslovaks in the context of this series. It was a rhetorical question on his part but drew no response from our side, not even from Lefaive. The matter was left aside as Starovoitov suggested we adjourn and walk down the street to the famous Metropole Hotel for lunch. Caviar and blini and numerous vodka toasts awaited us.

THAT AFTERNOON, AFTER lunch, one of our secretaries informed me there was a telephone call from Under Secretary Ritchie in Ottawa. Surely, I protested, it must be for a senior officer like the chargé d'affaires[78] but was told no, Ritchie had wanted to speak directly with me. It was akin to the CEO of the Royal Bank in Toronto personally asking to speak directly to a junior employee in a far distant branch and bypassing the manager.

I picked up the phone and he came on the line after a slight delay. The under secretary had been concerned about the growing tension between Hockey Canada/the CAHA and Eagleson and wasted no time in asking the question: "What the hell is going on over there?" It was a nerve-wracking enough experience having to deal with Canada's senior-most diplomat, let alone dealing with his direct question, and so I immediately apologized for not having had the time yet to file a written report to Ottawa on the day's proceedings.

The under secretary was pleased to learn the negotiations had gone remarkably well—that we had avoided any blow-up with the Soviets over Prague, and that there had been no fisticuffs among members of the Canadian delegation. I told him about the press conference scheduled for the next day and speculated that some of our problems might disappear if the proposed match in Prague was held after, rather than before, the games in Moscow. He quickly signed off, expressing his thanks and reminding me my principal job was "to keep the series on the rails."[79]

That evening Gresko, Khotochkin, Sedov and Fedosov invited everyone to Lenin Stadium (capacity 100,000) to watch the Olympic elimination trials in the men's high jump and women's 3,000-metre events, and a soccer game between Moscow Torpedo and Dynamo Kiev. Lefaive, Esaw, Babirad, Cannon and Chernushenko attended, while the rest of us stayed back to review what had been agreed and what still needed tweaking. During the course of the game, Khotochkin took Esaw and Babirad to inspect the cameras, control van and quality of the colour transmission of Soviet television. They were impressed with all three.

There was finally time to get off a reporting message to Ottawa on the day's proceedings, including comments about the contentious game in Prague. A return telegram came back signed personally by Under Secretary Ritchie: "Thank you for your useful message and helpful work you have done on this delicate question."[80]

The following morning, we met again briefly for a review of everything and then went to the Hall of Journalists for a press conference. Gresko read out a prepared statement of what had been decided (including the ongoing discussions with the State Committee for Radio and Television) for the benefit of the approximately thirty Soviet journalists who were permitted to attend. Milt Dunnell of the Toronto *Daily Star* had come from Canada to cover events and was there along with David Levy, a freelance journalist based in Moscow who followed the USSR for a number of Canadian newspapers, particularly the *Montreal Star*. Eagleson, at the microphone for Canada as the head of the delegation, firstly thanked the Soviets for their hospitality. He then stated his conviction that, in spite of "certain scepticism in Canada,"[81] the negotiations led by Team Canada were successful—a reference was added to my "able assistance." Major objectives had been achieved to raise the number of players and make provision for Bobby Orr "in view of the interest in his presence in the Soviet Union."

What particularly caught my attention, though, was Eagleson's remark that the agreement in April, signed between the CAHA and the Soviet Ice Hockey Federation, could be considered the first step leading to true international hockey competition, while this agreement between "Team Canada" and the Soviet State Committee for Sport could be considered the second step. This provoked Gresko to intervene, saying

it should be made clear to the press that the agreement on a Canada–
Soviet series was a bilateral agreement only, and that any discussion of
international competitions involving several countries would have to be
taken up with the IIHF.

There was no mention of the Prague game by either side, and the
Soviet press made no reference to any such discussions having occurred.
There were inquiries about the absence of Bobby Hull from the Canadian
line-up, to which Eagleson responded with the explanation used in
Toronto with the Canadian press. Sinden mentioned that the five administrative members of Team Canada would be proceeding to Sweden the
next day (without Lefaive) for discussions with Swedish ice hockey officials about arrangements for pre-Moscow workouts and game(s) there.

Esaw and Babirad of CTV and Chernushenko, for their part, were
running into difficulties with their separate discussions with the State
Committee for Radio and Television. The Soviets initially refused to
meet with the group, arguing their exchange agreement with Canada
had been signed with the CBC and not with CTV. It was another case
of the rigid nature of Soviet bureaucracy. After a considerable delay, a
telegram from Spencer Moore of the CBC was secured and the doors
then opened.

That morning, while we reviewed the hockey details, Esaw was able
to secure agreement on a number of technical matters: including colour transmission; use of an additional, fifth, camera for presentation
of strictly Canadian programming during intermissions; availability of
slow-motion, stop-action machines, and a video recorder for replays, as
well as clear line arrangements for the transmission of the picture either
via the Moscow–Kiev–Berlin (Reisting) route, or the Moscow–Tallinn–
Helsinki (Eurovision) route.

At midday it was agreed to put these elements into a Russian and
English text and then to discuss the always contentious issues of costs
and revenues.

After the joint press conference, Esaw asked if I could come along
to assist at his meeting and to bring an embassy translator who could

verify the language in the texts prepared by the State Committee. Lefaive agreed to participate as well.

Surprise, surprise, the Soviet side said it could not provide us with the promised cost estimate for the requested extra equipment as, following discussions with more senior officials, it had been decided that the questions would have to be "studied more closely."

Then there was a disagreement on the issue of rights to the broadcasts. The original Soviet suggestion had been for each country to maintain the rights for the broadcasts emanating from their own country. Esaw instead suggested CTV was familiar with the North American market, and it could subcontract the Soviet broadcast in the USA while the Soviets could do the same in Europe for the Canadian broadcasts. As this was being discussed, Lefaive offered up a simpler solution: draw a line down through the Atlantic Ocean with Canada having all North American rights and the USSR all rights in Europe. The Soviets, of course, knew the biggest money lay in the North American market so countered that they could agree to the Atlantic demarcation but only if all revenues would be pooled and shared equally by both sides. That left Lefaive saying he couldn't make the decision himself and it would have to be discussed further in Canada. The Soviets had their own counter, stating this all was now a matter of policy and would have to be taken up with the Sports Committee.[82]

The discussions became messy, and it was finally decided to kick this question down the road once again for further consideration. Firm cost estimates for the extra equipment and staff, requested by Esaw, were promised though, to be put into a letter within a week and delivered to me at the embassy for onward transmission to CTV by diplomatic bag.

In assessing the overall outcome of the visit, it was my opinion that it did not change the fundamental structural bedrock of what had been agreed to in April in Prague in terms of who was playing, the number of games, their location, the timing, the financing, the rules and the refereeing system. Granted there were some alterations achieved in terms of numbers and a variety of items were nailed down, but these had all been discussed in June by the embassy with Starovoitov and Gresko and could have been accomplished in the regular course of business. The sole exception was the broadcasting agreement which needed the help of specialists.

DURING THIS VISIT, Eagleson was highly personable and professional—someone who took advice (at least in the Moscow context) and played his cards well with the Soviets. There were no verbal outbursts. Whether it was his initial objective or not, by the time the meetings were over, it was obvious to the Soviet side that he and Team Canada were now, de facto, their principal hockey counterpart for the series and no longer Hockey Canada nor the CAHA.

Lefaive was pleasant enough, but pensive, and seemingly overwhelmed by Eagleson. It was as if Eagleson was a speeding train that Lefaive could not stop, let alone slow down. Sinden had yet to become a team's general manager, with the larger administrative portfolio which went with that job, and so was happy enough focusing on players and on-ice matters and enjoying discussions, through an interpreter, with Coach Bobrov. Sinden would say the visit had been a "good dry run" enabling him to meet his opposite number, other sports officials and to see the arena, as well as Moscow. Ferguson was generally in the background, interacting with Sinden as required.

Haggert was cheery and content to be an onlooker, while Cannon, as Eagleson's executive assistant, always appeared eager to overachieve the wishes and thoughts of his boss. Kukulowicz, as always, got on well with everybody and was both helpful and productive. Esaw and, to a lesser extent, Babirad were of good humour at all times, despite the challenges and difficulties they faced, and were greatly excited with the prospects of being responsible for broadcasting what they knew would be a monumental series.

Throughout the negotiations I kept an eye on the Soviet side to watch the dynamic between the stalwart and competent Starovoitov and the slicker secret-police personage of Gresko. Nothing really discernible yet as to who was really calling the Soviet shots, but some tension between them seemed to be in the air. Nothing yet manifested, that is, as with the distrust I could see between Eagleson and Lefaive, as well as Kryczka.

Before their departure for Sweden, Eagleson, Sinden and I had one last chat about what would be required for the well-being of the players in Moscow beyond decent accommodation and good care of all their spouses. The embassy could bring in fresh milk from Finland, and we had adequate supplies of imported beer and soft drinks. We just needed to know quantities, which Sinden agreed to provide. Sinden had not been impressed with the quality of the beef steaks served up at the Intourist hotel. Steaks were an important part of the players' diet and so he planned to bring meat from Canada, though this would raise storage issues and would necessitate dealing with various Soviet import restrictions. Both of them also mentioned the possibility of bringing along a chef from Canada to cook the team's food.

THE DELEGATION SPLIT up and departed on its separate ways. It looked like there might be a bit of a breather to get some other work done at my desk, but the embassy telephone operator rang me to say there was a very unhappy Canadian hockey journalist on the line asking to speak with the person responsible for hockey at the embassy.

Renowned *Montreal Star* sportswriter Red Fisher was sitting alone and frustrated in his Moscow hotel room. Fisher told me he had made arrangements with the Soviet consulate in Montreal to come to the USSR to interview the Soviet coaches and players and witness them training. His editors at the *Star* wanted to get a jump on the other Canadian newspapers. The air ticket had been organized with Aeroflot on the Montreal–Paris–Moscow flight, and he had been told Soviets sports officials would meet him at the airport upon arrival and look after his every need. He related that his flight inexplicably had been diverted to

Kiev, and when he showed up in Moscow at ten-thirty p.m., six and a half hours late, there was no one to greet him. He had been given no phone numbers nor contact names and was at a loss as to what to do. Could the embassy help?

It was a Friday, and I contacted the Sports Committee and asked Gresko to be in touch with Fisher. A meeting was set up for the Monday. In the interim Gresko told Fisher he could enjoy the tourist sights of Moscow over the weekend. When the meeting finally occurred, Fisher related that he had encountered a room full of officials but no coaches or players. Where were they, he asked. Why was he not met at the airport? If you pushed Gresko, he would shove back. He said it was Fisher's own fault for arriving a day late. Back and forth they went, repeating the same questions and comments. Fisher was on unfamiliar ground, and Gresko took great relish in countering Fisher's perceived impertinence by saying he knew where all the players and coaches were: Valeri Kharlamov was in East Germany, Alexander Yakushev was enjoying the Black Sea, Coach Vsevolod Bobrov was at the Caspian Sea, and Boris Mikhailov and Alexander Maltsev were training outside Moscow. The only one in Moscow, Gresko smiled, was Fisher himself. In the end, with a little more embassy persuasion, Bobrov and a few players were produced later in the week, and Fisher got to meet Starovoitov. These two would come together again in Montreal after Fisher wrote that the Soviets didn't have a chance in the series.

Gresko's attitude and gamesmanship would reappear more than once.

Many years later, in the late 1980s, when the Soviet Union was becoming more transparent, Fisher recounted this episode in a newspaper column he wrote, adding he had now been told by a Soviet source that Gresko was "a full Colonel in the KGB."

CHAPTER TEN

TRYING TO STITCH IT ALL TOGETHER

Tᴵᴹᴱ ᴡᴬˢ ʀᵁᴺᴺᴵᴺᴳ out. Just over a month now before the first puck was to be dropped in Montreal.

The foreign ministries in both Ottawa and Moscow were swinging into high gear. Not because of what was to happen on the ice—but off it, in Canada and in the USSR respectively.

The burgeoning number of Canadian fans planning to go to Moscow for ten days was now a matter of considerable concern to the Department of External Affairs. The Soviet Foreign Ministry, meanwhile, was worried about anti-Soviet political events in Canada. Both ministries had worked hard to improve relations between the two countries, in keeping with the directives received from Prime Minister Trudeau and Soviet Premier Kosygin—but what about "wild cards"?

As the number of Canadian fans heading overseas rose above two thousand, the Canadian media was full of stories anticipating a raucous delegation arriving in Moscow that would partake in heavy drinking, hi-jinks and hoopla—something akin to the festivities surrounding Canadian football's Grey Cup. But riding a horse into the lobby of a hotel, as a Calgary Stampeders fan did in Toronto in 1948, would not be laughed off in Moscow, as it had been in Canada. Both the rider and the horse would be hauled off to jail—or much worse.

On July 27 in Ottawa, External Affairs Under Secretary Ed Ritchie convened a large meeting of his officials to address political, security, consular and public affairs matters. The main agenda item was the fans:

how to make them aware of potential problems they would expect to encounter "within a society whose organization and practices were frequently a source of bewilderment and frustration, even to seasoned travellers."[83] External Affairs decided to work with Air Canada to create a brochure entitled "Dos and Don'ts in the USSR." Additional personnel were also assigned to Moscow to set up information desks in the lobbies of each hotel, with at least one Russian speaker per desk, to act as points of contact and steam-release valves. Each desk would also be supplied with bags of maple leaf pins to be given to the fans to wear and for trading purposes. It wasn't just Canadian officials who were concerned about sending a mass of Canadian sports fans to Moscow; so were politicians in Ottawa.

When Senator and Minister of Veteran Affairs Arthur Laing was assigned to replace John Munro as the Government of Canada's senior representative to the games in Moscow, he wrote a "Private and Confidential" letter to External Affairs Minister Mitchell Sharp. In it, Laing exclaimed the job "could be a whopper of a task." He described his worry:

> There are going to be 3,000 Canadians in Moscow, all at once. Very few Canadians really know the Soviets, or vice versa. Our press, and the Hockey Canada organization, has built this into a great PR show with 'Canada's prestige at stake'. Nonsense of course. Because Soviet cities are drab and dull; because few of those 3,000 Canadians will secure accommodation or service that satisfies them, and, above all, because vodka can be bought for 90 cents a bottle, hard currency; our attempt at 'friendship' could suffer a serious setback instead.[84]

Laing called for an all-out effort to inform the Canadian fans what they would be facing in the USSR.

Forwarding Laing's letter to Ed Ritchie, Sharp added his own cover note: "I agree with Mr. Laing that a serious problem probably exists.

Charles Hay of Hockey Canada made the same points with me in Toronto yesterday."[85] Ritchie was ahead of both ministers.

In Moscow on July 28, Soviet officials in the Foreign Ministry's Second European Division, of which Canada was then a part, invited several of my more senior embassy colleagues and me for a "friendly luncheon." They didn't normally do this, and less so with Canada, concentrating instead on the Soviet Union's relations with the UK, France and West Germany.[86]

Most of the conversation was about the impending series. Our senior host indicated they had heard from their embassy in Ottawa that the prime minister planned to be involved in the opening ceremonies. There was a "good chance" Secretary General Brezhnev would play some role in the Moscow opener. Some other senior leaders who were "old friends of Canada" might also participate, as would Premier Kosygin.

This was all fine and good, but the Soviet officials were concerned that an "unfortunate event" might occur during the games that could "offset" current positive developments. We thought they were referring to the Canadian fans coming to Moscow, but they indicated they would have "sufficient militia/police forces available to deal with any trouble in the USSR." No, their concern was about the situation in Canada where they were aware that "great emotion was being generated by the games, with a strong nationalistic aspect to it, and that certain ethnic groups might attempt to direct this emotion against the Soviet Union." A concern obviously precipitated by the vast number of demonstrators Premier Kosygin had faced during his visit to Canada the previous year involving Canadians with origins in Ukraine, the Baltic States, Poland, Hungary, Czechoslovakia and other countries, as well as members of the Canadian Jewish community.

Our reply was there would have to be further discussions with the Soviet Foreign Ministry about how to "minimize potential trouble" between the militia and the Canadian fans. There would need to be a focus on both parties. In terms of the situation in Canada, there was indeed large interest in the games, and Canadians were strong backers of their team and hoped it would win, but it was "unlikely" this enthusiasm would go beyond this point. This was particularly the case, we said, since a majority of Canadians appeared to support an improvement in bilateral Canadian–Soviet relations.[87]

While hockey was dominating everything else on my agenda, it wasn't the only thing.

The Canadian Eskimo Art Council had organized a major world tour entitled "Sculpture/Inuit: Masterworks of the Canadian Arctic." It had started out in Vancouver in November 1971 and made its way to Paris and Copenhagen and then on to the world-famous Hermitage Museum in Leningrad from June 19–July 27. I had been involved in the arrangements there, but the next stop was to be in Moscow, at the Pushkin Fine Arts Museum, and there was much work associated with the exhibition's opening on August 10 and its scheduled month-long stay.

Aside from the sculpture, two of the artists had been sent from Canada to be present during the opening week. They were expecting considerably warmer weather than in the Canadian Arctic but were surprised to be greeted with the hottest Moscow summer in thirty years, with the temperature reaching thirty degrees Celsius almost every day. It was so hot that Russian schools had delayed their opening until October 1, and in early August smoke was enveloping the capital from out-of-control peat-bog fires.

The artists didn't let the weather bother them. One had a way with words and imagery as well as sculpting. When asked how his flight had been, he described it as "dancing with the sun," which went up and down and moved from side to side as he looked out of the aircraft window.

The exhibit drew large, admiring Russian crowds, reinforcing the view that the Arctic and hockey are the two most common factors between Canada and Russia.

Hockey didn't disappear from my radar for long.

BY AUGUST 16, I was having another face-to-face meeting at the Sports Committee with Gresko and Sedov. The three of us were all wearing short-sleeve shirts to offset the unusually oppressive summer heat. This time I was informed the Soviet head of delegation to Canada would be Deputy Chairman Georgi Rogulsky. He was pleasant, had a sports background, wasn't overly senior, and was less likely to draw the ire in Canada than a more political Soviet figure. Sports Committee Chairman Sergei Pavlov, his immediate boss, would instead lead the Soviet delegation to the Munich Olympics.[88] There was the hint of a suggestion the Soviets preferred keeping the hockey series in the shadow of the Olympics, just in case the outcome might be negative.

Gresko noted there would now be nine officials and twenty-seven players going to Canada; an increase of one from the number agreed upon during the Eagleson visit. The USSR, in turn, would raise the Canadian number to thirty-six, for which they would cover the costs in Moscow.

The question of who was coming from Canada and when was becoming increasingly complex and confusing. We now had an official delegation, led by Minister Laing and Under Secretary Ritchie; a Team Canada delegation of players and coaches, plus Eagleson and associates; a sizable Hockey Canada delegation led by its president, Charles Hay, which would include CAHA president Kryczka; the players' wives; thirty news reporters and twenty-five CTV personnel accompanying the team from Sweden, and another twenty-five journalists arriving direct from Canada.

Gresko indicated he had already reserved a hundred rooms plus lounges and special eating areas for the Canadian delegation at the Intourist hotel and was now ready to increase that number to a hundred and seventy to ensure all of the above were included.

He and Sedov pushed for "complete data" on the Canadian media, including names, newspapers and, more importantly at this stage, what facilities each would require. They noted that, in addition to Canadian and Soviet journalists, the international press corps based in Moscow wanted accreditation, including the *New York Times* and *Washington Post*.

They also had received requests from seventy European journalists, and seventeen European countries had requested television coverage of the games in Moscow via Eurovision. Happily, Hockey Canada was sending two gentlemen from Canada within the week to help sort out the press situation: Len Knott and John Alexander, two seasoned executives from the advertising firm Vickers and Benson, would focus on the delicate question of establishing who, from the ever-expanding Hockey Canada group, should be accorded priority treatment for hotels and tickets.

I also returned to the question of a Canadian crew coming to the USSR to make a film on all the off-ice activity, including training camps. As with the previous suggestion from the National Film Board, this again ran into opposition. Sedov dismissed it, saying simply, "This would be difficult for the USSR." Once more the counter-suggestion was made that each side do their own film in their respective countries and the two parts be melded together for a final product. I explained, for the second time, that the end result of such a plan would be two different films rather than one consistent and better quality production. Sedov retorted that the matter should be taken up in Canada with the Soviet embassy and the Novosti news representative there. This was a backhanded way of saying our proposal was dead in the water.

Gresko then raised the matter of tickets for the Soviet ambassador and embassy staff in Ottawa for the games in Canada. The Sports Committee had provided twelve free tickets for each game in Moscow to Ambassador Ford, and on the basis of reciprocity, he wanted to confirm that Ambassador Boris Miroshnichenko would receive forty-eight complimentary tickets as well. His request was they be front-end loaded, as Montreal was the closest destination from Ottawa and they knew Prime Minister Trudeau would be attending Game One at the Montreal Forum. Gresko also requested additional tickets be available to the Soviet embassy for purchase, as had been the case for the Canadian embassy, and at an equivalent price. He had thought they were fifty dollars a pair in Canada and was surprised to learn a pair only cost fifteen dollars. This was almost the same as the six roubles a ticket being charged in Moscow (seven dollars and twenty cents a ticket or fourteen dollars and forty cents a pair at the official exchange rate).

I said I would pass both ticket requests to External Affairs and Hockey Canada and said it shouldn't be a problem. Gresko, after all, was attempting to do his best to overcome our difficulties; at least on administrative matters.[89]

THE NEXT DAY, Ottawa sent a telegram with a message from Mike Cannon of Team Canada about the food and drink. The embassy was asked to acquire two hundred and fifty quarts of milk and thirty-two cases of Coca-Cola—a total of seven hundred and sixty-eight bottles. There was an additional line that there "may also be a storage requirement for imported beer," but no reference to the embassy's supplies. A third paragraph stated, "Please arrange for the storage for three hundred pounds of meat to arrive in Moscow September 20 under arrangements being concluded between Team Canada and Canada Packers." There was no mention of a chef.[90]

Another meeting with Gresko was required on August 18 after the Air Canada station manager, Rudy Hucl, called the embassy to say he was having trouble matching numbers with Intourist. Air Canada by this point had sold 2,435 complete packages, but Intourist had only confirmed 2,355. This meant there were eighty Canadian fans who had paid but were without either accommodation in Moscow or hockey tickets.[91]

Whether this was a case of Air Canada overselling or Intourist underdelivering, Hucl was hoping the embassy could assist in resolving the matter. Intourist wasn't being helpful.

Gresko called in the deputy head of Intourist's North American department and, including Hucl and me, the four of us went over all the numbers again for the tourist packages and all the other Canadian groups, counting off hotel rooms and tickets as well as noting who would be guests of the USSR and who would be paying direct to Intourist. In the end, we appeared to have it straightened out with the Intourist manager, who was doing his best to find eighty additional packages. His concern was that the Soviet leadership had called a meeting of the Central Committee of the Communist Party for September 19–22 inclusive. Hundreds of delegates would be coming from across the USSR, requiring hotel space, and he presumed they would generate their own heavy demand for hockey tickets.

THAT EVENING, FRIDAY, August 18, at eight-thirty p.m., after a four-hour delay in Kiev (shades of Red Fisher), the two Canadian "coaches" arrived via Aeroflot for a visit to watch/study the Soviet team. They weren't Gordie Howe and Jean Beliveau, as hinted at by Eagleson and Sinden a month earlier, but representatives of the Toronto Maple Leafs: coach Johnny McLellan and chief scout Bob Davidson.

Both men had a quick late dinner with Kiril Romesky of the Sports Committee and left at midnight on the Red Arrow for Leningrad, where Soviet Coach Bobrov was attending the Sovetsky Sport Tournament of club teams. They returned to Moscow that Monday morning, and McLellan called the embassy to report that all had gone well in Leningrad. There was, though, a major glitch in their departure plans. Unbeknownst to the embassy, Juckes, from the CAHA, had apparently sent a telegram to the Sports Committee saying that the two Canadians would be departing on Wednesday, August 23. The Sports Committee, accordingly, had made arrangements for the pair of them to watch a blended intra-squad match of the national and Central Army teams on August 22—the only occasion on which they would see all the players of the national team in action. Problem was, their tickets called for them to depart on the 22nd, and both McLellan and Davidson had prior engagements in Canada on the 23rd.[92] Neither was pleased about the foul-up, but they agreed to stay over the extra day. They asked the embassy to inform their spouses and the people at Maple Leaf Gardens (Harold Ballard, their boss, and Team Canada, which was training there).

The three of us, along with Alexander and Knott, who had just arrived, then went to watch the Soviet national team in an intra-squad game at a smallish practice facility. There was a lot of fast skating, passing, stickhandling, turn backs and regrouping, but little in the way of serious body-checking. I was no expert, and certainly not in a position to even carry the water for McLellan and Davidson as a hockey analyst, yet I told them it didn't seem like the Soviet players were going full tilt, based on what I had previously witnessed of them in game conditions. Lanky Vladislav Tretiak from the Central Army squad was in one net and was the presumptive goalie for the national team. Only twenty years old, he had already won two World Championships and an Olympic gold medal and had accumulated fame across the USSR, being featured on the cover of several sports magazines and the recipient of dozens of admiring letters from fans. But on this night, he seemed like a sieve, letting in eight goals. Sure, we were told he was getting married the next day and wasn't fully concentrating on the game for obvious reasons, and that there had been a loud party the night before hosted by his teammates, but Tretiak was being beaten high and low, on both glove and stick sides.

McLellan and Davidson chose to rely on their own eyes—not on past international achievements by a non-NHL player. Both men were subsequently criticized by Team Canada coaches, players and the Canadian media for their scouting report, which was said to have significantly underestimated the Soviets' abilities and particularly those of Tretiak. Still, the Soviets themselves believed goaltending was a comparative weakness for them versus Team Canada, and according to a major Soviet sports journalist,[93] Bobrov was so uncertain about Tretiak that he had two additional goalies on his roster of twenty-seven players in Canada and added one more netminder for the games in Moscow, to bring the total to four. Bobrov was a Spartak man, and his only previous experience coaching Tretiak internationally was at the World Championships in Prague that April, when the USSR saw its string of nine consecutive championship victories come to an end.

If there was a fault in McLellan and Davidson's observations, it might have been due to their limited exposure to the Soviets and the European game. Certainly, their time in the USSR was astonishingly short and punctuated by a difficult travel schedule.[94] By contrast, their Soviet counterparts, coaches Chernyshev and Kulagin, only had to visit one location, Maple Leaf Gardens, where they watched one Team Canada practice after another for the full two weeks.

As McLellan and Davidson departed Moscow, Knott and Alexander swung into action. Alexander had arrived in my office with one of those ear-to-ear smiles that light up a room. He sat down and without saying a word plunked an airport souvenir on my desk of two gnomes, under which the words "Together, we can do anything" appeared.

He, the equally impressive Knott, and I then had two critical meetings with the Sports Committee on August 23 and with the people at Intourist on August 24, to get down to business. Alexander wrote up a detailed seventeen-page report of the proceedings for Hockey Canada, which included a multitude of suggestions and guidance for those coming to Moscow.[95] The report—perhaps not surprisingly since he was working for Hockey Canada—was focused on Hockey Canada's "constituents." This included four hundred and thirty people: the Team Canada entourage, their wives, all the media, various Hockey Canada officials and contacts, the NHL president and club owners and associates, as well as clients and associates of Vickers and Benson and Alan Eagleson. The four hundred and thirty would all be lodged at the Intourist hotel, which despite its "Vipers' Nest" reputation was only two years old and even had air conditioning.[96] Everyone in this select group would be seated together at the arena near centre ice in section nine of the Palace of Sports. Intourist was anxious to know whom among these four hundred and thirty guests were the hundred and fifty "Super VIPs," so they could be assigned the very best rooms and guides that the hotel had to offer. Higher costs would be involved. In this sense, there was no difference between communism and capitalism.

The remaining independent Canadian fans—just over two thousand—would have to be accommodated elsewhere, including at the National and Metropole hotels, which though once elegant had their best days behind them, and the less-than-stellar Hotels Ukraine, Bucharest and Berlin. Some would have to be lodged three or four to a room rather than the standard two to a room. The only other good hotel, the Rossiya, had been booked completely for the Soviet Central Committee gathering. The seats for these Canadian fans, who were being shepherded only by Air Canada, would be scattered around the arena as best as possible.[97]

The Intourist hotel would become the centre of the action, and the major information booth in the lobby would have three representatives: one from Hockey Canada for its party; one from Air Canada to handle ticket and flight information and liaison with Intourist; and an embassy representative to deal with matters related to passports, entry-exit visas, foreign currency declarations, health, commercial inquiries and any encounters with the Soviet security forces.

Transporting everyone around Moscow and not losing anyone was going to be a challenge unto itself. We expected that more than eighty buses would be required. In discussing how to identify individual buses, other than by forgettable numbers, I recalled from my Expo 67 days that the Montreal authorities, who had received over fifty million visitors, had come up with the idea of using animal symbols in the parking lots. It was a big success, being far easier to remember that your car was in the Bear lot rather than lot 481.

Intourist and Air Canada adopted the idea, and so the Canadian fans would become Bears, Beavers, Otters and Moose, etc., and their bus and luggage tagged accordingly.

Alexander's report mentioned the two likely main sources of confrontation with the Soviet law enforcement: excessive drinking by the fans, and "women of adventure," who could potentially lead Canadians astray outside of the hotels (bearing in mind no one had a single room). As a result, Alexander was "quite convinced thirty-five Canadians will end up in jail" but expressed "the hope none of them will be our 430."

Alexander added it was his "strong recommendation" that each individual or couple bring along "a roll of toilet paper, a couple of bars of soap, deodorants, toothpaste, cookies and more especially Rise N Shine or Tang crystals (as an orange juice substitute) as none of these articles are in abundant supply." A subsequent Hockey Canada letter to the spouses of the players added personal hygienic items and a can of bug spray, "not for listening devices but to combat the notorious Moscow cockroaches."

He concluded his report with this observation: "I think if we try and communicate to at least our constituents that the service is not too good and meals are not too bad, or not that good, and try and take it easy, that it will be a very pleasant stay, although I guarantee you that after ten days, pretty near everybody will be glad to get out of the place."

It was a jam-packed week.

Following his return to Canada, Alexander wrote a gracious letter to me on August 28, copied to officials in Hockey Canada, External Affairs and to Ambassador Ford, thanking me for the effective manner in which his and Len Knott's visit had been organized. He commented favourably on my ability to operate within the Soviet Union, adding generously, "I believe your input into this series' operations will wind up being a major pillar in the success of the entire series."

EARLIER IN JUNE, hockey equipment maker Cooper Canada Inc. had contacted the embassy with an offer to provide the Soviet team with thirty complete sets of protective equipment, four goalie sets and several dozen Hespeler sticks, all with the compliments of the company. The Soviet Ice Hockey Federation accepted the offer, with thanks, and asked if delivery could be made before the team departed for Canada. The shipment arrived via air-freight on August 22, together with the additional sticks we had offered to purchase for the Moscow Maple Leafs. The embassy truck delivered the gear to the Soviet practice facility.

John H. Cooper, the company's vice-president for sporting goods, had asked for a few pictures of the players wearing the equipment, and when I showed up at the arena for the official handover there were two Soviet photographers standing around. Out skated three of the Soviets' best players—Tretiak, left winger Valeri Kharlamov and defenceman Alexander Ragulin—all in their Cooper finery of pads, gloves, helmets and sticks.

John Cooper would have been pleased, but before the photos could be sent to him by diplomatic bag, I received a call from the Sports Committee saying that while the USSR was grateful for the equipment, it did not wish the photos to be used for "commercial advertising." Being seen in the equipment during a game was one thing, but having Soviet players "pose in the products of a commercial firm" was another and "could lead to those players being barred from Olympic competition."

Another diplomatic dilemma. Here I had a powerful photograph on my desk that, if published, could possibly knock three of the top Soviet players out of the Olympics and World Championships. At the same time, such action would anger the Soviet government and likely lead to the end of my posting in Moscow. Another consideration was the requirement of a Canadian diplomat to pursue the interests of a well-known Canadian company, whose sole simple request was for a picture of its complimentary equipment being worn. In the end, my return letter to the vice-president explained the situation and added, "I am sure you understand their position and would not wish to affect the state of good will that now exists toward your firm as a result of the gift."[98]

Not the best reply perhaps, but it was evident the company would receive much favourable publicity when the Soviet players hit the ice in Canada wearing Cooper products. Still, Cooper offered to have a representative present in Canada to check the equipment and "to present additional items if required." The company also extended an invitation to have Soviet officials and players visit Cooper's new manufacturing plant while they were in Canada to see how sporting goods are produced. The Soviet delegation declined due to time constraints.

THE LAST FEW days of August saw the embassy trying to cope on two fronts: with the Soviet team in the last stage of departure plans for Canada, and with the ever-increasing demands related to the pending Canadian invasion of Moscow.

The Sports Committee called on August 29 to confirm that its head of delegation, vice-chairman Rogulsky, wished to visit all the facilities and see any associated plans related to the 1976 Montreal Olympics. (The USSR was contemplating bidding again for the 1980 Olympics, after it failed to beat out Montreal in 1976.) We were also told Rogulsky was an avid and good-quality tennis player and had expressed the specific wish to play tennis every morning while in Canada. He would be bringing his own equipment, and it was stated his opponents could be drawn from Canadian hockey officials or players from local tennis clubs.[99]

The issue of the performance bond was raised again by Starovoitov, who reiterated he wanted to receive the five thousand dollars immediately after each game or the full twenty thousand dollars while in Toronto after Game Two. It was necessary to remind him that the Soviet embassy in Ottawa had the line of credit and could do what was required. Since this matter remained an important but seemingly confusing issue for Starovoitov, we asked if Hockey Canada or External Affairs officials could help him with the formalities at the bank.[100]

Logistical issues continued to pile up. On the Moscow front, the CTV crew announced it would have seven spouses as part of its party. Intourist was already struggling with the wives of Team Canada, requesting that they be clearly identified and arrive together as a group rather than individually to avoid them being assigned to the wrong hotel.

The Intourist hotel also had a limited number of "deluxe duplex" rooms (suites), which Alexander had requested for Eagleson, Sinden, Hay, Kryczka, Lefaive and Clarence Campbell, as well as leading members of Hockey Canada. Air Canada was requesting the same rooms for its top clients, and the embassy was asked again to decide upon whom should receive priority. We undertook to sort it out once again with the two Canadian entities.

The commercial section of the embassy was already dealing with a large-scale agricultural equipment exhibition and ongoing contract negotiations but began to field an increasing number of requests from Canadian fans with a business background who wished to establish contacts with Soviet ministries. Ambassador Ford also reminded External Affairs that in September there were planned visits by the president of the National Research Council of Canada, a seven-person academic delegation, another visit by a five-person education delegation, which included a provincial minister of education, as well as a delegation from Atomic Energy of Canada for discussions about nuclear reactors. Throw in the arrival of the first exchange students and professors under the terms of the new General Exchanges Agreement, and it became more than a handful of obligations.[101]

THROUGHOUT THAT LONG, hot summer of 1972, when outdoor mushroom vendors along the streets wore three-pointed hats made of newspapers, the attention of Soviet sports fans was not on Canada and hockey but on the Icelandic capital of Reykjavik and the national obsession of chess—a game of the mind, without physicality, but one that requires as much mental toughness and stamina as hockey. It was a sport which the USSR had dominated for decades. The reigning world champion, thirty-five-year-old Boris Spassky, was being challenged by an erratic, petulant American whiz kid by the name of Bobby Fischer, and the Soviet public had been mesmerized since the first of twenty-four scheduled matches had begun on July 11. Large billboards had sprouted up in public areas in many Moscow neighbourhoods. Replica chess pieces were moved by hand on them to depict the proceedings. People came and went, milled around, or sat gossiping or doing their knitting as they watched each move gradually displayed in front of them. Russian newspapers and television were consumed by the proceedings.

The drama and the excitement, fuelled by Fischer's unorthodox behaviour, generated a worldwide audience, and the championship became dubbed "The Match of the Century." Three games were planned per week, but with various adjournments they often found themselves facing off at the table on additional days. On they went, until August 31, when Spassky adjourned the game and did not return the next day, September 1. Fischer was declared the new (and first American-born) champion with a 12½ to 8½ victory.

Spassky's defeat, particularly by an American, had been excruciatingly hard to take for the local population. But as we moved into September, here was another chance for a Soviet world champion to show its international mettle—this time as a team on the ice against a second North American foe: the professionals of Canada.

CHAPTER ELEVEN

TO CANADA WITH THE SOVIETS

AEROFLOT FLIGHT SU-301, an Ilyushin-62 jetliner, took off from Moscow's Sheremetyevo Airport in the afternoon of Wednesday, August 30, bound for Montreal and the long-awaited first game of the Summit Series.

The passenger list was limited. The twenty-seven players of Team USSR; senior coach Vsevolod Bobrov; team doctor Samuil Belakovsky; Georgi Rogulsky, the deputy chair of the Sports Committee and titular head of delegation; Kiril Romesky, listed as chief, Division of Sports Committee and deputy head of the delegation; Andrei Starovoitov and official translator Viktor Khotochkin; as well as Georgi Avseenko, a "masseur," and a second assistant Nikolai Smirnov, listed as "technical guide and director."

Assistant coach Boris Kulagin, who had been observing Team Canada during its training period, had remained in Canada and would join the Soviet team in Montreal. His addition would bring the Soviet side to the new agreed number of thirty-six persons.

Rogulsky's appointment as "head of delegation" was a last-minute decision as a fill-in for Sports Minister Pavlov, who had been invited by the Canadian government. Pavlov told us he was needed at the Munich Olympics, which was of "higher priority to the USSR," given the Olympic medals that needed to be won. Alexander Gresko also occupied himself with the Olympics, obviously knowing he was not going to receive a Canadian visa due to his previous expulsion from Britain for his KGB recruitment activities.

There was, though, a thirty-sixth passenger onboard.

A Canadian.

Me.

Alan Eagleson had suggested that I be named as the Canadian government's official escort and liaison officer to the Soviet team, apparently due to my Russian-language ability, intimate knowledge of the negotiated agreements and, in particular, the excellent working relationship I had developed with Starovoitov. Eagleson also thought that knowing what was to happen in Canada would be invaluable to assisting him and Team Canada when it came time for the return matches in Moscow. Normally, a seasoned protocol officer in Ottawa would have been tasked with the job, but Under Secretary Ritchie at External Affairs readily agreed to Eagleson's proposal, as did Ambassador Ford, who was my immediate boss.

While I was well known to Starovoitov and Khotochkin, and less so to Coach Bobrov and Romesky, I was not a complete stranger to the Soviet players. They had seen me when they were introduced to Canadian scouts McLellan and Davidson during their intra-squad game and again when I had come to present them with the Cooper hockey equipment and to take pictures.

The day before departure, Bobrov had given a press conference to announce who had been selected to go to Canada from the list of thirty-four candidates. He was careful to say the decision had not been made by him alone, but by the "Main Coaches' Council." It had been based on past performance and recent games against the number-two national team as well as against Central Red Army, Dynamo and Spartak. (These pre-series competitive matches were an advantage Bobrov had that Sinden didn't.)

There would be three goalkeepers among the twenty-seven players selected: Vladislav Tretiak, Viktor Zinger and Alexander Sidelnikov.

Four groups of five (demonstrating the USSR preference for units of five rather than separate forward lines of three plus an assortment of two defencemen, as in the NHL): Gennadi Tsygankov/ Alexander Ragulin, Vladimir Vikulov/ Alexander Maltsev/ Valeri Kharlamov; Viktor Kuskin/ Alexander Gusev/ Boris Mikhailov/ Vladimir Petrov/ Yuri Blinov; Evgeni Paladiev/ Yuri Lyapkin/ Evgeni Zimin/ Vladimir Shadrin/ Alexander Yakushev; Vladimir Lutchenko/ Valeri Vasiliyev/ Yuri Lebedev/Vyacheslav Anisin/ Alexander Bodunov.

As a reserve defenceman, Coach Bobrov selected Yuri Shatalov, and for extra forwards the young Vyacheslav Soloduhkin and two experienced players, Vyacheslav Starshinov and Evgeni Mishakov, who would deal with short-handed situations and "tense moments during the game."

"We are sure they wouldn't let us down," Bobrov added.

Bobrov also addressed the sensitive issue of why left winger Anatoli Firsov (and defenceman Vitali Davydov) had not been included on the team. The Coaches' Council had wanted both because of their "rich experience," he explained, but they were injured. It was true Firsov had practised with the national team, but he had injured his knee beforehand, and it wasn't sufficiently healed to engage in hard competition. It was his and the Coaches' Council's hope Firsov would recover enough to be ready to play when the series returned to Moscow. Team Canada had the same hope for Bobby Orr, but Harry Sinden meant what he said. Bobrov's carefully crafted comment was intended to mask Firsov's personal dispute with him—in essence Bobrov was saying he wanted to include Firsov, but he couldn't.

While this was billed as the USSR team, representing all fifteen republics, in fact there was only one player who was not born in Russia: Evgeni Paladiev from the Republic of Kazakhstan.

The issue of whether the Soviet players were amateurs or really professionals in all but name was a longstanding bone of contention for Canada, so it was interesting to read the official visa applications that were submitted by the Soviet foreign ministry to the Canadian embassy. Occupations of some of the players were listed as follows:

Tsygankov — Metal Craftsman

Kharlamov — Student, Institute of Physical Culture

Yakushev — Student, Moscow Pedagogical Institute

Shadrin — Student, Oil Institute

Maltsev — Student of Moscow Electro Technical College

Bodunov — Student of Machine Building Technical School

Tretiak — Student, Institute of Physical Culture

Basically, just a bunch of students with no reference to their connections to the army, air force, police or anybody else who might be paying them a salary and expenses; except perhaps for the metal craftsman. This argument carried on for years in relation to the Olympics and World Championships, but it no longer really mattered in determining which country was the hockey power with the best team. That question was going to be answered in the coming days and weeks.

It was no surprise the Aeroflot flight was not full. There were no wives, girlfriends, parents, other family members, friends, fans or reporters aboard. The Soviets followed a policy of "no distractions." The vast majority of them in any event could not have afforded the costs involved—particularly in Canadian dollars ("hard currency" which they did not possess). But the real reason was that they could not obtain exit visas from the Soviet authorities.

None of the Soviet sports personnel, ballet or opera stars, musicians or writers who were permitted to travel abroad to showcase Soviet culture or sports excellence were allowed to bring loved ones with them. They might decide the bright lights and affluence of Paris, London, Broadway, or even King Street in Toronto, were so alluring that they would consider defecting to the West and to capitalism. Everyone knew what unpleasantness would befall their families in the USSR if they jumped ship, so it was a solemn, persuasive reminder for them to stay on the straight and narrow.

The flight lifted off in silence. No loud bantering or fooling around, as might be expected from a plane-load of young athletes who know each other well. Everyone was prim and proper. Soviet officials up front and the players arranged behind them. All were clean-cut and wearing double-breasted navy-blue blazers, white shirts and specially designed reddish-coloured ties, like their fellow countrymen attending the Munich Olympics.

I had a row to myself at the back of the players. My hair was long by comparison, in keeping with early seventies style, and my blazer was also blue but with large red checks. Some might have considered it to be "loud."

The only one not in a blazer was Kiril Romesky, who wore a sharp grey suit that complemented his salt-and-pepper hair. I had picked him out as one of the KGB "minders," not just because of his sartorial elegance but based on his self-confidence, swagger, and the ever-changing job titles with which he was identified. He would keep an overall eye on everyone, including Georgi Ragulsky, the titular head of the delegation, with whom he was always in close contact, and because the KGB trusted no one at home and particularly on trips abroad. His fellow KGB associate, Viktor Khotochkin, the official translator, likewise was always with Starovoitov. The "technical guide and director" and the "masseur" could likely be added to the minder list but would be focused on the players.

The general silence continued as the flight progressed, with only low-volume exchanges between seatmates. An unremarkable meal was served, with mineral water and fruit juices being the drinks of choice. None of the players, without permission, was going to initiate a conversation with me, the foreign diplomat, even if I was of their own age group. I decided to break the ice by standing up in the aisle and asking in Russian whether any of them had any questions about Canada, the Canadian players or arrangements in Montreal.

Finally, from across the aisle, Evgeni Zimin, the young right winger from Spartak, perked up and asked, "Why is Bobby Hull not playing for Canada?" The other players turned their attention toward me. It was a tough question. It was a question millions of Canadians had asked. It was a question the prime minister had asked.

A complicated situation, I replied. Hockey Canada had made an arrangement with the NHL to permit their professional players to participate in this exhibition series. Bobby Hull was no longer with the NHL and therefore was not invited to be on Team Canada.

Zimin reflected on this for a moment before continuing, "But if we are playing against Canada's national team, and Hull is a Canadian and the best player, he should be on Team Canada, shouldn't he?"

Zimin then asked whether this had anything to do with the NHL being made up mainly of US-based teams, perhaps reflecting an observation made previously by Soviet sports journalists, including Boris Fedosov.

No, I replied. The vast majority of players on all NHL teams were Canadian. This was primarily an issue between the NHL and the World Hockey Association, its new competitor.

Zimin still had a difficult time understanding the situation, noting that in the USSR, if government officials and coaches said you were to be on the national team, then you were on the national team.

And what about Gordie Howe? Zimin continued. He was a Canadian and a world-famous hockey player? Why wasn't he on the Canadian team?

That was a different story. For sure one of the greatest Canadian hockey players of all time, but, I replied, you wouldn't get to play against him either, as he retired after the 1970–71 season.[102]

I asked him how much he knew about the Canadian players. They had no real firsthand knowledge, he replied, beyond their scouting reports. Bobby Hull was known because of his 1967 book *Hockey Is My Game*, which had been translated into Russian with a written introduction from none other than coach Vsevolod Bobrov himself. All the players had read it. They had also seen the 1971 Stanley Cup film that Peter Hancock and I had provided the Soviet hockey authorities at the beginning of the year, featuring Hull's Chicago Black Hawks against the Montreal Canadiens. They knew from the advance line-ups they had been provided with that both the Black Hawks and Canadiens would be strongly represented on Team Canada. It was Hull, however, who had captured their attention with his "skating ability, strength and incredible shot."

Zimin said it was his dream to play against Hull. It was "disappointing" this was not possible.

Other members of the Soviet team were now more engaged in the conversation. In response to my query about which other Canadian professional hockey players they had heard about, a couple of them also mentioned Gordie Howe, which set several heads nodding.

This precipitated their naming of Phil Esposito, Bobby Orr, Frank Mahovlich, and Brad Park. Stan Mikita's name was also mentioned as "the Czechoslovak-Canadian." This was said more as an observation, without spoken malice or reference to their heated on-ice battles with the Czechoslovakian team. And, of course, none of the Soviet players would make any public comment to me about the invasion of 1968. Then more questions came.

Why had Canada dropped out of the World Championships and Olympics?

Because we couldn't use our best players, like other countries could, including the Soviet Union. I gestured to the players around me saying, "Like you."

How much interest was there in Canada in the series? Enormous. Press interest? Enormous. Television? Enormous. More interest than the Olympics? By a long shot. This was a massive event that had captured the imagination of the whole country, I emphasized, which they would see for themselves upon arrival.

A beaming face appeared over the seats from the row in front of me. It was Evgeni Mishakov, introduced by the players as "our jokester." He had one of those warm, open smiles that instantaneously endeared him to others. Mishakov struck me as the Soviet equivalent to Peter Mahovlich, a player always willing to bring good humour and cheer to his teammates. His questions were about opportunities off-the-ice for shopping, particularly for music.

Not everyone was as jovial as Mishakov or as inquiring as Zimin. Valeri Kharlamov appeared moody, not displaying any of the zest of his Spanish-born mother. Alexander Maltsev had his scowl and Vladmir Petrov remained glacial, reflecting his position as the leading Communist Party member on the team and responsible for political and ideological discipline. Tretiak was an exemplary member of the Komsomol (Young Communist League) and conducted himself accordingly. Boris Mikhailov was reputed to have an acerbic, humorous wit—he was known to be a leading voice on the team—but it wasn't on display this day. Most stayed to themselves, perhaps recalling this was not a holiday flight but serious business with their country's reputation on the line, and they were part of an official Soviet delegation. There was also the old dictum, communist or otherwise, that it was always safer to say nothing.

I wasn't aware at the time, and there was no mention of it by the players, of a reputed analysis prepared by the Soviets a few years previous in which Soviet hockey strengths had been compared to those of Canadian professionals. Boris Mikhailov was said to have been involved with the five-point grid system. All the details weren't clear, and Mikhailov had never actually played against professionals, but the Soviets apparently had the following advantages: (a) physical preparation: 5-4; (b) team spirit: 5-4; (c) passing: 5-3; and (d) power play: 4-3. Team Canada was seen as stronger in (a) shooting: 4-3; (b) force/aggressiveness: 5-4; (c) goalkeeping: 5-3; and (d) defence: 4-3. Equal grades were given to skating: 4-4; individual puck control: 4-4; shorthanded performance: 4-4; and game character: 5-5. Mikhailov's numbers were said to work out to a Soviet advantage of 53.5 to 51.[103]

The figures showed the Soviets only real advantage was in passing, while their largest deficit was analysed to be in goaltending.

Apparently, this was an attempt by a widely respected player to make the case to Soviet authorities that the USSR would not be outmatched by Canadian professionals. It was hard not to see Anatoli Tarasov's hand in the background.

There was no mention in the analytics report of having to fight against the Canadians or of Tarasov's prior training in skirmishing—the so-called "cockfighting five minutes."[104] I had heard from Ambassador Ford about Tarasov and the bench-clearing battle in 1966 against the Sherbrooke Beavers in Kalinin. There were no references to that here either.

About an hour before we arrived at Dorval airport in Montreal, I chatted again with Ragulsky and the other Soviet officials to review what was expected to happen upon arrival. Whether they took my comments on board or not, as soon as the aircraft pulled up to the gate and the officials and players looked out the aircraft windows, they were greatly surprised by the flashing lights of police motorcycles and cruisers. Equally noteworthy for them were the Canadian and Soviet flags flying from an ultra-modern bus. Then the aircraft door opened and an immigration official came on board to collect the passports. Cameras went off and the whole area was lit by television crews. A welcoming party that included Alan Eagleson and Aggie Kukulowicz was sandwiched into the arrival corridor, and handshakes were immediately extended.

There was no need to line up to clear customs or collect personal baggage as the Soviet team had to in other countries. That would all be looked after. Passengers simply had to walk outside and board the waiting luxury bus. It was a speedy trip to the prestigious Queen Elizabeth Hotel. The players were impressed. Alexander Yakushev would say they had never had such a warm and expeditious welcome before—not even for the Olympics. Others made mention of a perceived prestigious Hollywood- or NHL-like reception, with great fanfare. Another would say quietly that we may lose this series but we are sure going to be treated well. It was just a portent of things to come.

Everyone was tired after the close-to-ten-hour flight, and it was now three-thirty a.m. Moscow time, a seven-hour time change. The Queen Elizabeth staff was highly efficient, though there were numerous onlookers in the lobby. One of the players remarked that all the gawking made him feel as if he was from outer space. Finally upstairs, the players were assigned two to a room. The Soviet officials had privacy.

Before going to bed myself, I put in a transatlantic call to Laurielle to let her know I had arrived safely, without incident. I needed as well to attend a meeting with the protocol people from the Department of External Affairs about events planned for the next day. I was told later by other departmental colleagues that an unexpected legal crisis was threatening to derail the series before it had even started.

A Canadian citizen had filed a legal claim in Quebec stating that his rental car had been demolished by a Soviet tank while he was in Prague in 1968. The local rental agency had demanded fifteen hundred dollars from him to cover the approximate value of the vehicle. His efforts in the intervening years to seek restitution from either the Soviet or Czechoslovak governments led nowhere. With news of the impending arrival of the Soviet hockey team in Montreal, he saw his chance to take action—legally impound the Soviet hockey equipment to force payment. A Quebec lower court judge had allowed the claim to proceed, and the Soviet ambassador in Ottawa was furious, demanding the Canadian government deal with the case immediately and threatening to send the team back to Moscow. The claim though became public and naturally was given widespread coverage in the Canadian press. The prime minister became involved, as did Alan Eagleson and Hockey Canada. External's lawyers made it clear that existing international law prohibited civil lawsuits against a sovereign country like the USSR, and Minister Mitchell Sharp would issue a formal "Certificate of Immunity" to this effect to the Quebec courts. In the interim, any direct payment to the claimant, though possibly seen as expeditious, would undermine this position. Instead, Hockey Canada filed a refundable bond with the court blocking the equipment seizure. As part of this arrangement External Affairs lawyers, in private, agreed with the claimant and would assist him in pursuing his claim in Prague and Moscow.[105]

Case dismissed. We could get on with hockey.

THERE IS NOT much sleep to be had on an adventure like this, so after only a few hours of rest I was back at it. First up was a swim in the hotel pool. The players were surprised to see me jump in with them and join in the light chatter. They were in excellent shape.

This was followed by a luxurious buffet breakfast. When the players entered the breakfast room you could see the delight in their eyes. They feasted in particular on the fresh juice and copious supplies of tropical fruit. The latter was very hard to find in Moscow and became a magnet for them throughout the Canadian trip. Somehow the USSR could put a man into space and develop all kinds of weapons systems but couldn't put fresh fruit on the tables of their citizens.

The Soviet players then went off to practise in nearby St. Laurent. A Canadian assistant had been asked to help with logistics and was taken aback to learn the Soviet players were accustomed to carrying their own bags and sharpening their own skates. Not much time passed before reports started to make their way into the press—comments from Canadian players who had a firsthand look at their opponents. It wasn't their passing or skating that caught most attention, but the state of the Soviets' equipment. Outdated skates and gear, everyone wearing funny beanie-like helmets, Tretiak's bird-cage mask. All fed into the growing overconfidence that the series would be a cakewalk for Team Canada.

No one thought that the equipment manager might have cleverly dressed the players in the old gear to create a false impression for the Canadians or just in case equipment of some kind had to be turned over in the court case.

Jacques Plante, the legendary Montreal Canadiens goalkeeper and first NHL player to wear a mask, unexpectedly appeared after the practice with an interpreter wanting to speak with the "tall boy" who would be in the Soviet net. Apparently, he felt sorry for Tretiak or had a simple affinity for a fellow netminder but, using a chalkboard, he passed along some suggestions about how to face some of the key Canadian shooters. Plante took some flack in the Canadian press for supposed disloyalty, but it was seen by the Soviets as "a remarkable gesture of true sportsmanship."[106]

Meanwhile, the Soviet officials and I were obtaining our credentials in the form of plasticized bilingual photo ID cards issued by Hockey Canada. In one corner was my photo, next to the information: "Canada-USSR Series/Series Canada-URSS," "Training Camp-All Canada Games-Moscow." In French and in English. Diagonally across it, in red bold caps, "U.S.S.R. HOCKEY TEAM—ÉQUIPE DE HOCKEY U.R.S.S."

What a juxtaposition. A Canadian working for the Canadian embassy but officially listed as part of the Soviet team for "financial and administrative purposes."[107] Turns out it was the best of both worlds, as it provided unhindered access to both teams and to all events in Canada and in Moscow. The pass also meant there was no need to enter any of the arenas via the normal entrance procedures but rather through the players' and officials' gates with or without the players. As a result, my seat tickets for all eight games remained intact and unmarked.

To meet the extreme public demand for tickets, Hockey Canada instituted a national lottery system wherein Canadians could fill out a form and mail it in expressing which game they wished to attend. Thirty thousand tickets were made available: two-thirds capacity for each rink in Montreal, Toronto, Winnipeg and Vancouver. Season-ticket holders and Hockey Canada personnel had access to the rest. Those lucky enough to have their names drawn from the lottery then had the opportunity, via a coupon system, to purchase two tickets at fifteen dollars for the pair.[108] The tickets did not come with any transportation or hotel benefits. You were on your own to get to the rink and back home, wherever in Canada that might be, but that requirement didn't appear to bother anybody.

H.A. Watts Ltd, the company organizing the draw, reported in a media event at the end of July 1972 that they had received roughly 285,000 submissions and were in the process of opening another 65,000 or so envelopes that had just arrived before the deadline. The approximate breakdown of requests was interesting: Toronto (about

91,000), Winnipeg (about 83,000), Vancouver (about 73,000) and Montreal (about 38,000). The Watts people were all surprised by the low level of interest shown in Quebec.[109] That was strange, given the long love affair Quebeckers had with hockey and the rabid Canadiens fan base. After all, Team Canada had six players who played for Montreal, plus the assistant coach, John Ferguson.

Nick Auf der Maur, a Quebec journalist, would explain in a CBC radio interview that English speakers in the province were upset that Foster Hewitt had been brought out of retirement and chosen to announce the games on television across Canada. Their local broadcasting favourite, Danny Gallivan, had been shunted aside. Even the radio broadcasts would be the sole responsibility of Foster's son Bill. Auf der Maur would add that Ballard-Orr Enterprises, who made the decisions, had inadvertently done a great service for French-English relations in the province, as English speakers would now watch the French-language coverage of the series with renowned francophone broadcaster Rene Lecavalier.[110] Such action would cut across the two solitudes in the province.

Quebeckers were also smarting from the NHL/Hockey Canada decision to exclude local francophone fan-favourite J.C. Tremblay from the team and the NHL's refusal to grant a franchise to Quebec City. Tremblay had jumped ship from the NHL to play for the city's WHA franchise, the Nordiques.

PROTOCOL OFFICIALS FROM External Affairs were super busy organizing a major lunch for up to five hundred persons in each of the four-game cities. They were rather extravagant affairs, costing up to twenty dollars a plate, with top-notch food, wine and champagne toasts. The departments of External Affairs and National Health and Welfare shared the total bill. Guests were stipulated to be "as many players, hockey officials and sports personalities as possible with appropriate representation from provincial and municipal governments." To show its political importance, all guest lists were to be approved by the prime minister's executive assistant, Tim

Porteous. Prime Minister Trudeau would host the luncheon in Montreal, while local members of the federal cabinet would perform this function in Toronto, Winnipeg and Vancouver. Invitation cards stated, "In Honour of the Visit to Canada of the National Team of the Union of Soviet Socialist Republics."

Run-of-the-mill government-sponsored lunches were often a hit-and-miss affair in terms of attendance, but in these cases, with hockey mania spread across the country, there were very few, if any, who declined an invitation. Some guests were disappointed to find out that star players and coaches would not be in attendance, but each luncheon was scheduled for a game day, and it had been agreed beforehand they could excuse themselves, given their pregame routines and preparations. Those players not scheduled to be in the line-up did participate in the luncheons, and I sat with the Soviet players to help with interpretation. The attendees paid them scant attention in Montreal and Toronto, focusing instead on Team Canada, as one might expect, but interest in the Soviets picked up as the series progressed. The large attendance and manner of proceedings did not allow me to have much interaction with the Canadian players at these occasions. They were good natured enough, but it appeared awkward for those who were not playing to have to repeatedly explain the intricacies of what had happened on the ice during the games.

Ragulsky and Romesky would be seated at the head table at each event, and Ragulsky would be called upon for remarks, which Viktor Khotochkin would interpret. This routinely included expressions of appreciation for the hospitality, a reference to the excitement of the games, and the wish that the series would lead to better understanding, co-operation and friendship between both countries and their peoples. The federal cabinet ministers spoke along the same lines. I heard the word "friendship" over and over. The night before each game, the provincial governments of Quebec, Ontario, Manitoba and British Columbia also got in on the act, each hosting a dinner of their own. The culinary tour kicked off in Montreal at the Beaver Club, located in the Queen Elizabeth Hotel, with Prime Minister and Mrs. Trudeau in attendance, along with the Soviet ambassador and his wife. Ragulsky, Romesky and Starovoitov all received the distinct honour of being inducted as honourary members of the fabled club. The Soviet players looked on. I was at one of their tables. Several expressed disappointment there were no gestures of friendly acknowledgement by the Canadian players—only constant glowering. As one put it, they looked like bulls and we looked like sheep.

There was a further manifestation of the great marriage between hockey, politics and diplomacy. Hockey Canada officials at the dinner had handed out copies of their attractive two-dollar official program. Prominently displayed was a full-page photograph of Prime Minister Trudeau across from a signed message from him bearing the Canadian coat of arms. It read, in part, that he was very pleased to offer his greetings and best wishes to all those participating in this "historic hockey series." Millions of people in both Canada and the Soviet Union and throughout the world, he continued, would share "his deep enthusiasm for this international event that is bringing together in exciting matches across Canada and the Soviet Union some of the finest hockey players of our time." He looked forward to "exciting and challenging matches."

SUDDENLY, AFTER A chaotic few weeks of intense preparations and months of planning, it was Saturday, September 2. Labour Day weekend. Game One finally had arrived.

The temperature in Montreal that day hit eighty degrees Fahrenheit. Not really hockey weather, but hockey was very much in the air. Nobody could talk about anything else. Scalpers flogged tickets on the streets at an aggressive markup—a fifteen-dollar pair of seats surged to two hundred dollars or more. One journalist reported of a rabid American fan who had come north for the game shelling out two hundred dollars for a single ticket.

The Soviet players had spent the late afternoon in their rooms resting and watching the Olympic coverage from Munich or cartoons, as they were inclined to do, with no French or English language capability required. Having colour TVs was a bonus for them. By the time their Canadian assistant had shown up to collect them, the players had all moved to the hotel dining room for their pregame meal of sandwiches, pastries, black coffee and bottles of Coca-Cola. The assistant was nervous about getting to the Forum on time. They were nervous about what faced them and quiet as they assembled in the lobby. No rah-rah bravado. All serious now. They knew they were the underdogs—playing against the storied professionals for the first time, on smaller ice, on a strange rink in a foreign country, with North American referees and still jet-lagged to boot. The big defenceman Vladimir Lutchenko admitted to having trembling knees. He and his roommate, Vlacheslav Anisin, had talked all night and had not had a wink of sleep.

It was a large, unknown stage. Who wouldn't be nervous? On the other hand, they were a team. They knew each other. They were in shape and well conditioned. They had trained and played together, with a few exceptions, for years. They had won countless international titles—together.

When we got to the Montreal Forum the coaches and players headed to the dressing room to suit up while Ragulsky, Romesky, Starovoitov, Khotochkin and I were taken to a reception area under the stands to meet with various political dignitaries and hockey officials. It wasn't long before the prime minister appeared, looking tanned and relaxed in a beige sports jacket, striped open-necked shirt with ascot, and brown slacks. A rose in his lapel, as usual. Margaret Trudeau looked elegant in her summer attire. Most members of the electrified crowd, at least in the lower seats, were wearing suits or blazers, women in their finest attire. This was no regular hockey game.

We took our seats. Khotochkin and I were right behind the Soviet bench, adjacent to the hallway to the Soviet dressing room. In the next block of seats, over on the other side of the hallway, sat Prime Minister and Mrs. Trudeau in the front row, with the Soviet ambassador and his wife next to them, followed by Rogulsky. Hockey Canada president

Charles Hay and his wife were on the other side of the prime minister. Former prime minister Lester B. Pearson, Romesky and Starovoitov were in the row behind. Further along, in another section, Alan Eagleson could be seen seated between Progressive Conservative leader Robert Stanfield and David Molson, the owner of the Montreal Canadiens. The prime minister had dropped the writ for the federal election the day before, on September 1, with the election called for October 30, and therefore it was political game on. Each leader wanted to be seen by the crowd and vast television audience as supporting Team Canada.

Then came a surge of energy that galvanized the Forum. Out onto the ice came the Soviet players, dressed in red pants and visitors' white sweaters with cccp in red lettering across their chests. They weren't the ragamuffin outfits and equipment of practice, but crisp new uniforms with new skates, a gift of Canadian skate manufacturer Bauer. In their hands were new sticks with top brand names—Victoriaville, Hespeler, Koho. Most of the Canadians carried Sherwood. Zimin, Tsykankov and Petrov could be seen wearing the square-designed Cooper helmet instead of the round one favoured by the majority of their teammates. Tretiak was sporting a Cooper blocker and catching glove, as well as the goalie pads that Cooper had sent to Moscow as gifts. Front and centre on Tretiak's bird-cage helmet was the word "Montreal."

Other equipment was on offer by additional Canadian companies who had seen a good publicity opportunity when they first heard about the possible legal confiscation of the Soviets' kit.

Team Canada wore home red sweaters with a large white stylized maple leaf in the centre, like a sunburst, designed by the advertising firm Vickers and Benson. Even though Canada's national colours were the same as the USSR's, the pre-tournament agreement negotiated in Moscow called for Team Canada to wear black pants to avoid confusing the players when they had their heads down and only had glimpses of who else was on the ice.

Both teams lined up on opposite blue lines, eyeing each other with a combination of suspicion and nerves. One by one they were introduced, starting with the virtually unknown visitors. Applause for them was more than polite—it could even be described as warm—but the reception paled in comparison to the raucous welcome accorded Team Canada. The Forum cheers were greater for assistant coach Ferguson than for head coach Sinden, in recognition of Fergie's successful tenure with the Montreal Canadiens, with whom he won five Stanley Cups. Sinden looked the most nervous of the four coaches during the introductions. He had stepped on the ice before his visiting counterparts, thereby breaking protocol. Sinden obviously had a lot on his mind. Hometown heroes Yvon Cournoyer, Frank Mahovlich and Ken Dryden received an ever-increasing round of cascading cheers, significantly surpassing those for fellow Habs Guy Lapointe and Peter Mahovlich. Phil Esposito, as a member of the rival Boston Bruins, certainly wasn't a local favourite during the regular season by any means, but he garnered the loudest applause of the non-Montreal players, in excited recognition that his many talents would now be brought to bear in the common cause of Team Canada.

During the long introduction of the Canadians, defenceman Alexander Gusev, who was closest to the boards, edged over to the Soviet bench for a word with Valeri Vasiliev, who wasn't playing that night. Gusev, after having looked at the size of the Canadians and their "mugs," expressed the hope "the Canadians will not kill us all." Vasiliev was said to have retorted, "Don't worry, they wouldn't kill you dead" and then wished Gusev good luck with a laugh.[111]

The red carpet had been arranged on the ice in the standard T shape, and then out stepped the prime minister. He gestured for Rogulsky to walk beside him, but both Rogulsky and Hockey Canada president Charles Hay gave pride of place to the PM and fell in behind him, followed by the four coaches. Three players from each team greeted them at centre ice: alternative captains Phil Esposito, Frank Mahovlich and Jean Ratelle for Team Canada, and Victor Kuzkin, Alexander Ragulin and Vladimir Vikulov for the Soviet team. Pennants were exchanged. Esposito and Vikulov took the ceremonial faceoff; but instead of just gently touching the puck, as was tradition, Esposito fired it down the ice and was obliged to go retrieve it before presenting the souvenir to the prime minister. Esposito was as jacked up as everybody else—if not more so. Game on.

THE PREVIOUS DAY I had been over to the Chateau Champlain, where Hockey Canada reps and Team Canada were lodged. An elevator door had opened, with Don Awrey inside carrying a case of twenty-four beers. The amber brew was a staple for most of the Canadian players, but I wondered how that would work out now that he was one of only five defencemen for Team Canada. Sinden had decided to load up on offense with four complete forward lines and to pare back on the defence. He was expecting a turkey shoot and wanted as many players to participate in the attack as possible.

Bobrov took a different, more cautious approach, dressing only ten forwards while utilizing seven defencemen. It was a significant difference in coaching.

Sinden wasn't wrong, at least to start with. Esposito opened the scoring in Game One with only thirty seconds gone after the opening faceoff. Just over five minutes later, Paul Henderson made it two to nothing. The expected blowout was on, or so it seemed. The Forum organist played the funeral march. For some unexplained reason, I felt a touch of sorrow for the Soviet players. The match was going to be a humiliation for them.

Bobrov called his players over to the bench. They were shell-shocked by all the pomp and circumstance of the lengthy opening ceremonies. No Soviet leader had ever dropped a puck at centre ice. I could hear Bobrov, supported by Mikhailov, tell the players to settle down, to skate, to play their own game. Yakushev would later say that the long, tumultuous introductions, raucous crowd and presence of the prime minister had left them temporarily dazed and overwhelmed. It was hot in the packed Forum. The omnipresent lights required for enhanced television coverage seemed to raise the temperature even further. The ice was on the soft side and mist started to rise. Conditioning was going to play a big role in the outcome.

Then, at 11:40 of the first period, Evgeni Zimin, the Soviet player who so admired Bobby Hull, put the puck into the net to cut the lead in half. He became an instant hero in Moscow as the first Soviet player to score against the Canadian professionals. Petrov followed suit with a short-handed goal at 17:28, and all of a sudden, the game was tied. At first intermission the crowd was buzzing with wonderment. *How could this be? Who were these guys with CCCP on their jerseys?*

By the end of the second period, the Soviets had scored two more unanswered goals, both by the sudden sensation Valeri Kharlamov—assisted each time by another speedster and slick stick-handler, Alexander Maltsev. The USSR was now up 4–2. Ken Dryden, in net for Canada, was used to moving out of the crease to cut off the angle of shooters in NHL games, but the Soviet forwards weren't shooting into his pads but holding onto the puck and then passing to line-mates who had an open net. The fans' wonderment turned into disbelief, then deep concern.

At second intermission, I encountered Eagleson behind the boards near one of the nets and asked him, "What the hell is happening, Al?" He was frantic. I obviously touched a raw nerve. Everyone was asking him the same question. We had been working well together for the many weeks leading up to this moment, but now he exploded and accused me of being "a fucking commie just like they are."[112] He hurried on. So be it, I thought. He knew better, but handling insults was all part of the life of a being a diplomat.

The third period went from bad to worse for Team Canada. The players began to wilt. The five defencemen could not slow down the Soviet forwards, who went around and through them. Awrey and Rod Seiling had a particularly tough time. Boos began to emerge from the upper reaches of the Forum. Bobby Clarke cut the deficit to 4–3 at 8:32 and gave a brief moment of hope, but three quick Soviet goals by Mikhailov, Zimin (his second) and Yakushev brought the curtain down on the drama, ending it in a 7–3 Soviet rout. Gloom, despair and utter shock settled over the fans.

The belief in professional invincibility had been shattered in the very first encounter.

Team Canada headed for the dressing room in quick order, as was NHL practice after a defeat, except for Red Berenson, Ken Dryden and Peter Mahovlich. The Soviets ,waited on the ice for the traditional hand-shake after every international match. A breakdown in communications. Sinden claimed not to have known but must have forgotten the agree-ment in the heat of the moment that the game was being played under IIHF rules.

The Soviets' officials decided to go into the team dressing room immediately after the game, with me in tow. The players were stretched out along the benches, mineral water at hand, looking exhausted but with big grins on their faces. There was no shouting, just an atmosphere of great satisfaction. Clasping hands all around. This outcome was unexpected. Rogulsky summed it up best when he called what had just happened a *"ckazcka"*—a fairy tale. There was no evidence at that point of the traditional victory vodka toast.

During the post-game media interviews with the coaches, Starovoitov sought out Red Fisher of the *Montreal Star*, who had come on his own to Moscow in July. When Starovoitov tracked him down, he made the sarcastic comment that Red might indeed be right: there could be an eight-game sweep, but not for the team Fisher had predicted.

Not wanting to give further incentives to Team Canada to redeem itself, Coach Bobrov did not beat any drums. Sinden took it on the chin, acknowledging Team Canada had been outplayed in every respect. But he vowed the next game in Toronto would be different. As head coach, though, defeat and humiliation fell primarily upon his shoulders, as it did on Eagleson. Both were subjected to a massive amount of public criticism for having misled the country and letting it down.

A story later emerged from the Team Canada dressing room that Dryden was missing one of his goalie skates. It had been wedged into the door frame to stop the door from closing and to allow in some air. This had drawn a retort from a player that the door was the only thing Dryden had stopped all night.[113] A cutting remark alright, but the sort of locker-room banter needed to generate a laugh, clear the air and help the team move on to the next game.

Eagleson's stinging comment to me was eased when it became known that assistant coach Ferguson had approached the insightful Canadian television colour commentator Brian Conacher in the hall and called him a "commie lover" over his praise for the Soviets' techniques and comments that Team Canada had yet to jell and pull together.[114] I was in good company. It was odd that one's fellow Canadians were under verbal attack for being communist sympathizers of various stripes when the real followers of Karl Marx and Vladimir Lenin had so far been spared this invective in any face-to-face dealings with them.

Soviet television hockey commentator Nikolai Ozerov, who was as legendary in the USSR as Foster Hewitt was in Canada, ended his broadcast that night from Montreal with the following remarks (from the Russian): "This is a great achievement for our hockey. A brilliant victory. I can hear the stupefied Canadian announcer trying to analyse it. What is it? Magic or luck? This is neither, my friends. It is incredible will and flawless training."

The Soviet media in Moscow, meanwhile, was overcome with the ecstasy of winning the first encounter.[115] There were only three Soviet journalists in Canada to cover the games in person, one of them being Ozerov; all the others relied, for detailed coverage, on what they saw on television and in the wire services.

Many, like M. Blatin of *Komsomolskaya Pravda* (a paper intended for younger Communist Party members), which carried the headline "Maple Leaf Under a Hurricane," repeated Sinden's words: "The Russians outplayed us in all respects—they had a better goalkeeper, defencemen and forwards; they were better in skating, more precise in shooting, were better in body-checking—in other words they played better hockey."[116]

Blatin went on to use the now familiar Soviet line that the NHL and its players, "in a high and mighty way," had cut themselves off from the rest of the hockey world and had not noticed its rapid development in Europe. They were now paying the price for this.

Pravda, the main Communist Party paper, in an unsigned article, strung together the headlines from several Canadian newspapers to tell the story to its readers: "Canada is in Mourning, the Hockey Myth Gone" (*The Globe and Mail*); "Russians Have Ruined the Myth About the Superiority of Canadian Hockey" (*Montreal Matin*); "Soviet Hockey Players Completely Outplayed the Best Canadian Professionals in the First Personal Fight" (*Sunday Express* in Montreal).

Many Russian readers didn't believe what *Pravda* had to say on its own but did pay attention if foreign newspapers from the West were quoted, so for good measure *Pravda* added the headline from *Helsingen Sanomat*, a Finnish newspaper: "Another Myth Has Been Dethroned."

TASS hockey correspondent Vsevolod Kukushkin wrote from his perch in Moscow that the best moment for him was "watching the Soviet team standing triumphantly at centre ice after the game and seeing the Canadians fleeing in defeat, ignoring the sportsmanlike tradition of congratulating the winner."

At the concurrent Olympic games, Soviet sports officials had wondered, after the score was 2–0 for Canada, whether they should turn in their valued Communist Party cards right there and then in Munich rather than face an ignominious return to Moscow. By game's end, a Russian-language news report of the surprise victory had been posted in the Soviet athletes' common room. Suddenly, hockey had come out of the shadows and was the subject of excited talk among all those who specialized in summer sports.

From a diplomatic perspective, the embassy also noted another story in *Pravda*. This one detailed the scoring and intricacies of the game but finished with two significant paragraphs about honour and respect. The first stated that the Canadian public had given a warm welcome to the Soviet players and that Prime Minister Trudeau had been present and dropped the puck at the first game. The second was a simple statement: "The Canadian Government gave a reception in honour of the Soviet united team."

Both paragraphs would have caught the attention of Brezhnev, Kosygin and other Soviet leaders for the high level of Canadian respect that was being shown to their team.

Lost in the sheer drama and raw emotion of the day was the selection of the respective outstanding stars of the match: Valeri Kharlamov of the USSR and Bobby Clarke of Canada.

SUNDAY, SEPTEMBER 3, IN Toronto was a new day. The city was alive with excitement, even more so than in Montreal. Every cabbie, bus driver, restaurant employee and person on the street had nothing else on their lips, and there was no other subject in the newspapers and on TV and the radio than the forthcoming game the next day—Labour Day, Game Two.

The Soviet team was now feeling confident. The players had passed the all-important first test. It was no longer just a case of "playing for dignity." Nevertheless, they knew the element of surprise, the element of the unknown, had passed. Team Canada would regroup and be waiting for them with fresh determination and more grit.

The External Affairs protocol people had inserted a courtesy visit into the program wherein the Soviet officials and players met Mayor William Dennison and viewed the new clamshell-designed Toronto City Hall. Then a stop on the steps of nearby Old City Hall to meet Dick Beddoes, *The Globe and Mail* sports reporter who had boldly proclaimed he would eat his words if Team Canada lost a single game. Now the man who made his living by words stood by his word and ate his words. A true display of integrity. The column was crumpled, given a little extra shredding by Valeri Vasiliev, and mixed in a bowl of borscht while amused Soviet players and a Soviet journalist looked on.

There was time to visit a record store on Yonge Street. Each Soviet player had been given two hundred dollars of hard currency to purchase personal items to bring back home to the USSR. Those who were married or with girlfriends tended to look for blue jeans, high boots or fancy clothing. The single players preferred music, and a photographer from the *Toronto Star* captured them looking through racks of LP records. In this sense they were like young people around the world—interested in the latest rock-and-roll band or pop star.

The federal government luncheon the next day, game day, was held at the Royal York Hotel. Mitchell Sharp, the Secretary of State for External Affairs and Liberal MP from a Toronto riding, hosted the event. Health Minister John Munro of Hamilton, whose portfolio included sports, was also in attendance. It was good politics to be seen in this hockey milieu, and politics of one kind or another was never far from the scene, particularly now the federal election campaign was underway. Alan Eagleson, a well-known member of the Ontario Progressive Conservative Party himself,[117] had wanted to have the luncheon held at the Sutton Place Hotel, which he favoured and where Team Canada was lodged, but he could not convince federal officials.

THE SCENE IN Toronto for Game Two was very different than that for Game One in Montreal. The carefree circus atmosphere of the fans on opening night in La Belle Province was now replaced with nervousness, concern and even fear. Could Team Canada, which was no longer the absolute favourite if it was still the favourite at all, reverse course and give the Soviets their comeuppance?

Sinden and Ferguson knew the battle was now beginning. Time to tighten up with players whose trademarks were checking and tough corner work, like Wayne Cashman, Bill Goldsworthy and Jean-Paul Parisé, with the experienced Stan Mikita added in for good measure. The lunch bucket brigade.

Gone was the NHL's top offensive line from the New York Rangers—Vic Hadfield, Jean Ratelle and Rod Gilbert—nicknamed the GAG line for scoring a goal a game during the preceding season. In

Montreal they had come up empty, without a point. They were supposed to be quick, but the Soviets had outdone them. Red Berenson and Mickey Redmond also sat out. The defensive corps was expanded to six players. The rock-solid duo of Bill White and Pat Stapleton, from the Black Hawks, replaced Awrey and Seiling, while the master of the spinarama, Serge Savard, put in his first appearance and was paired with his Canadiens defensive teammate Guy Lapointe. The hope was to slow the Soviets down in Canada's end and avoid being deked out by the slick Soviet wingers.

Soviet coaches Bobrov and Kulagin made only minor changes to their line-up (the veteran Starshinov instead of Vikulov, and Anisin in for Blinov). They stuck with their winning formula of ten forwards and seven defencemen. And why not?

The temperature inside the arena was hot again. This time not because of the weather outside but because the owner of Maple Leaf Gardens, Harold Ballard, as part of his efforts to cut operating costs, was said by the press to have eliminated the air-conditioning system inside the building. The fans were heated as well. There had not been a game of this magnitude at the Gardens since the Maple Leafs' Stanley Cup run five years previously, in 1967.

Prime Minister and Mrs. Trudeau were again in attendance, seated with the Soviet ambassador, Opposition leader Robert Stanfield, though not known for his athletic prowess, was not going to let the prime minister steal a political march on him and was again front and centre in the audience.

My assigned seats[118] were not directly behind the Soviet bench for this game, but not too far away. I stood beside the boards as the introductions were being made. The announcer inexplicably failed to call out the name of the second Soviet player standing along the blue line, Vladimir Lutchenko, and I could see his head sink as he was passed over. It wasn't a big deal, but protocol called for all the players to be named, so I hustled around the end boards, spotted Eagleson on the other side and told him about it. He immediately spoke with the nearby announcer, who corrected the situation after he had reached the end of the Soviet and Canadian list of players. Small crisis averted.

Eagleson was like that—one minute full of emotion and name-calling, loaded with expletives, and the next gracious, even-keeled and obliging, even on minor matters.

He had a lot to be pleased about that night. Eagleson had not been on the ice in Montreal nor had he been introduced to the crowd at the Forum. Toronto was his hometown, however, and here he stood at centre ice with former Prime Minister Lester B. Pearson, an enthusiastic sports fan, to award the newly launched NHLPA Pearson trophy for the "most outstanding player in the NHL, as voted by fellow members of the Players' Association." Jean Ratelle, in blazer and tie because he wasn't playing that night, stood alongside them as the first annual recipient.

Not only did Eagleson personally garner the attention of the sixteen thousand or so fans in the audience, and that of the vast television audience across Canada and abroad, he also craftily generated untold publicity for the Players' Association, which he headed.

Sinden, continuously nervous, would remain in the dressing room area throughout the pre-game ceremonies, pacing back and forth.

The Soviet team had been given a warm reception; Team Canada, a standing ovation. This was a different hockey game from the get-go, with Team Canada sticking close to the Soviet players, bumping, grinding and forechecking at every opportunity. The aggressive tactic threw the Soviets off their game, even as Mikhailov and Mishakov tried to match the Canadian hitting. By the end of the first period, it was scoreless. Team Canada had outshot their opponents ten to seven, despite having drawn the only two penalties in the opening stanza.

At the first intermission, the tension was palpable. Nobody in Toronto—or in Canada, for that matter—wanted to go down by two games. The Soviets had withstood the expected opening barrage by Team Canada but now what?

The USSR took two penalties back-to-back in the early minutes of the second period, and then Phil Esposito opened the scoring, for the second game in a row, with a tally at 7:14. Back and forth they went with Team Canada peppering Tretiak from all angles and out-shooting the Soviets by a wide margin of sixteen to five.

Phil's brother Tony Esposito, who caught with his right hand, as opposed to Dryden, who used his left, which was more traditional, was playing well in the Canadian net and had made some outstanding saves. Still, it was only one to nothing when the second period ended, and the nervousness continued. The USSR had scored seven goals in Montreal but were shut out so far in this game. Could their high-flying wingers be held off the score sheet for the rest of the game? The good news for Canadian fans on that front was that Gennadiy Tsygankov had taken a slashing penalty at 19:54 and, in an ensuing scrum, Kharlamov had bumped a referee, said something to him, and was given a ten-minute misconduct.

The Soviet coaches and officials, who had been so calm and collected until this point, erupted when their best player was sent off for almost the entire first half of the pivotal third period with the score so tight. Starovoitov was incensed, yelling out to the referees in protest. Displaying his soccer skills, he kicked a metal container beside the bench. In his view, the referees were doing what Team Canada couldn't do and that was to neutralize Kharlamov.

It didn't take long for winger Yvan Cournoyer to score a power-play goal at 1:19 of the third period. Then Bobby Clarke was called for slashing at 5:13, and Yakushev scored for the USSR forty seconds later on a pass from Zimin and Liapkin. The game tightened with the Soviets down again by only one goal. Stapleton was then sent off twenty-one seconds later for hooking. Was this to be the moment when the flood gates opened?

Not this time. In one of the most terrific plays of the entire series and indeed in hockey history, Peter Mahovlich took a pass from Phil Esposito and faked a slapshot as he crossed the Soviet blue line. The Soviet defenceman, Yevgeni Paladiev, moved his feet together to block the impending shot and in an instant Mahovlich flew by, leaving him flailing with his stick. Tretiak had played brilliantly up to this point, but Mahovlich deked left and then right, leaving the Soviet goalie down and out as he slipped the puck into the net, running over Tretiak in the process.

The crowd erupted. There was the absolute beauty of the goal—the artistry of Mahovlich's moves, all achieved while short-handed in pressure-packed circumstances—but there was also the joyous realization that Canada was back on top by two goals. The roof of Maple Leaf Gardens seemed in danger of being blown off in that moment.

I had been focusing on Peter's older brother, Frank, during the game. He had been a marvel to watch, with his long strides, end-to-end rushes and goal-scoring prowess, which he had demonstrated many nights here in the Gardens as a Toronto Maple Leaf, and in Montreal at the Forum after having been traded to the Habs following a stint with the Red Wings in Detroit. That was in the past. Every time he skated by the USSR bench this evening his attention wasn't on the ice but on the Soviet players sitting there, and he would shout out to them angrily.

Both Mahovlich brothers had grown up in the Timmins area of Northern Ontario, in a family of Croatian descent. Croatians had been badly treated by the USSR after the Second World War because they had sided with Germany, and there was a resultant strong streak of anti-communism in them. Peter didn't seem to manifest it, but Frank, who was eight and a half years older, did. It was on display during this game.

Stan Mikita had similar anti-communist views and had talked about getting back at the bastards who had invaded his country of birth. His uncle in St. Catharines, Ontario, had adopted him in 1948 at age eight as part of a family decision to give him a fresh start in Canada. He had left behind his birth name of Stanley Guoth and his hometown of Sokolce, in the Slovakian part of Czechoslovakia.

Just as I was beginning to wonder how these attitudes might affect the game and Sinden's thought process about them, Frank put paid to the issue by scoring Team Canada's fourth goal at 8:59 on an assist from Mikita and Cournoyer. Neither Mikita nor Frank Mahovlich would take a penalty during the match. The three-goal margin would remain until the game's end as Team Canada outshot the USSR 10–9 in the closing frame. Tretiak was selected the top Soviet player in the game, while the Esposito brothers shared the honour for Team Canada, despite Peter Mahovlich's thrilling goal.

Both teams shook hands before departing for their dressing rooms. IIHF protocol was honoured this time.

Everyone went home happy that night. Team Canada had staged the comeback Canadians wanted so badly, and the series was now tied at one. It also had been a great game of hockey, and fans of the sport far and wide had now developed an avid taste for international hockey at the highest level.

Everyone was happy; that is, except for the Soviet coaches, who complained long and loud at the post-game press conference about what they believed to be the biased nature of the North American referees. It was not just the "unjustified call" that removed Kharlamov from the game for ten whole minutes, but also all the rough stuff by the Canadians that *didn't* get called. This wouldn't be the last time referees would become a major bone of contention for one team or the other.

THE TORONTO AND Montreal games started at three a.m. Moscow time, and so by the time they ended, many Soviet papers had missed their publication deadlines for that day and the stories had to be carried over to the next edition. Geivandov's article in *Pravda* therefore appeared on September 6 under the heading "Canadians Have Taken Their Revenge."

There were no pleasantries this time.

From the moment the Canadian professional stars stepped out onto the ice, he wrote, they were out for vengeance. He noted that nine new Canadian players had been added, mainly those who were known for their "tough" playing. The Canadians played as they had in the last period of Game One, "trying to knock the Soviet goalkeeper off his feet or hitting a rival with a stick after the referee's whistle."

Geivandov summarized his observations by quoting a Canadian journalist: "The professionals demonstrated in this game something akin to what the *Toronto Daily Star* wrote in its editorial yesterday, 'Team Canada added disgrace to its humiliation on Saturday when its players started bullying the Soviet players, who showed splendid self-control.'"

Geivandov concluded by noting that Tretiak had been named the best Soviet player of the match (no reference to the Esposito brothers for Team Canada), and despite the defeat the Soviet team had demonstrated "a high class of playing again."

GAME THREE AT the old 9,600-seat Winnipeg Arena was a blur. The Soviet team was lodged at the Fort Garry Hotel and Team Canada at the North Star Inn. It became the least remembered game of the series, perhaps because it was played in the smallest city or maybe because it produced the only tie game.

Winnipeg had been chosen mostly for its position in the middle of the country, to help compensate the city for its loss of revenue from the cancellation of the 1970 IIHF World Championships, and to recognize its location as the newly created national office of the Canadian Amateur Hockey Association.[119] Some in the Soviet delegation thought the real attraction was what was said to be the world's largest portrait of Queen Elizabeth II, which was hanging on an arena wall.

Coach Bobrov knew Team Canada would continue to fight back hard, as it had done in Toronto. There would certainly be more aggressive forechecking, body-checking and rough-housing. He knew his team was not built for dust-ups in the corners—or anywhere else on the ice, for that matter. It was a team built for speed, for open ice. So, his solution to the Canadian aggressiveness was to generate more speed. To assist in this process, he added a forward to his roster alignment, increasing the number to eleven, and dropped back to six on defence—the same number combination employed by Sinden.

(Top) Regulations: Author's USSR driver's licence and coupon required to purchase gasoline.

(Above left) Crossover: Author's Hockey Canada identity card, issued in Montreal, August 31, 1972, registering the Canadian diplomat as a member of the USSR hockey team.

(Above right) A Bargain: Tickets to Game Two at Maple Leaf Gardens. Price $7 per ticket. Toronto, September 4, 1972.

Diplomatic Hospitality: Author and wife, Laurielle Chabeaux, learn the trade in Moscow, hosting a Christmas dinner for Canadian embassy personnel, December 1971. *Jan Drent*

Sweet Ride: Author on the road to Leningrad in April 1971, after picking up a new Mustang in Helsinki, Finland. *Laurielle Chabeaux*

(Top left) Seeking Common Ground: Pierre Elliott and Margaret Trudeau are greeted by the author and his wife as they arrive at Vnukovo airport in Moscow, May 18, 1971, to begin the first visit to the USSR by a Canadian prime minister. *Canadian Embassy Moscow*

(Top right) Hockey Diplomacy: Soviet Premier Alexei Kosygin (with hockey stick) talks through an interpreter with Montreal Canadiens captain Henri Richard prior to a game against the Vancouver Canucks in Vancouver, October 22, 1971. It was the first time the Soviet flag was flown in an NHL arena. *Associated Press*

(Above) Excitement: Author with Prime Minister Pierre Elliott Trudeau at the Canadian embassy in Moscow, May 1971. *Ronald Cooke*

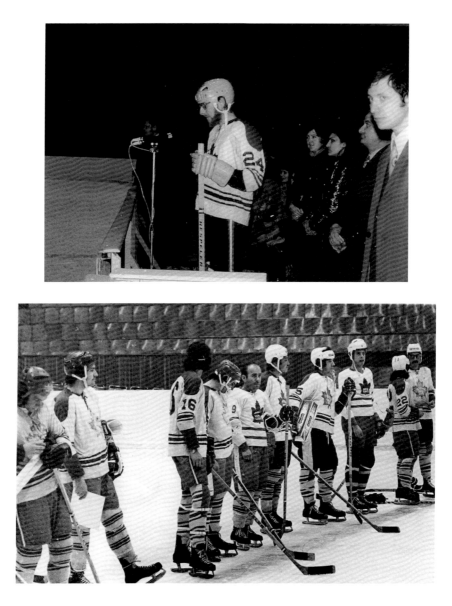

More Hockey Diplomacy: Canadian embassy First Secretary, Peter "goal a game" Hancock, addresses the audience in Russian/English/French at the Sports Palace following a hockey game between the Moscow Maple Leafs and the USSR press agency (TASS). Moscow, March 1972. *Laurielle Chabeaux*

Beer League: The Moscow Maple Leafs embassy hockey team. Author is fourth from right with a case of beer under his arm. Moscow, December 1973. *Les Cundell*

Nailing Down Details: Negotiators for both sides line up after the conclusion of discussions to finalize arrangements for the series. General Secretary of the Soviet Ice Hockey Federation Andrei Starovoitov (*centre*) is flanked by Alan Eagleson (*left*) and Hockey Canada's Lou Lefaive (*right*). Alexander Gresko, Deputy Chief of the International Department of the Soviet Physical Culture and Sport Committee is to the right of Lefaive. Interpreter Victor Khotochkin is back right. Author is in light suit, fifth from left. Moscow, July 1972. *Victor Akhlomov, Izvestia*

Soviet Kingpin: General Secretary of the Soviet Ice Hockey Federation Andrei Starovoitov (*centre*) is flanked by Air Canada's Adolph (Aggie) Kukulowicz on the left and the author (*right*) following the negotiations in Moscow, July 1972. Alan Eagleson and John Ferguson are visible in the background. *Victor Akhlomov, Izvestia*

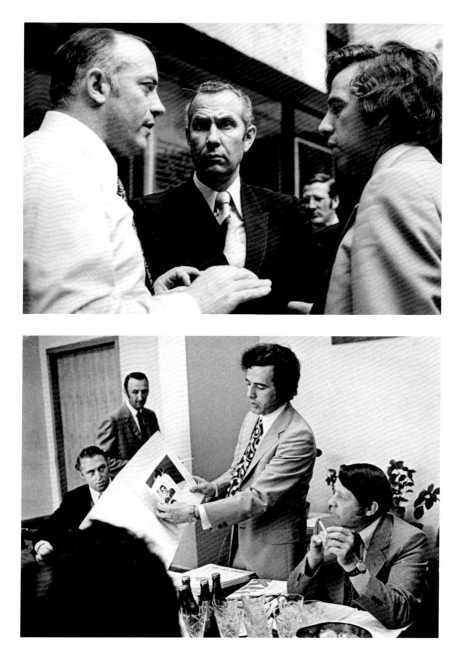

The "Snowman": *Izvestia* hockey columnist Boris Fedosov (the "Snowman"), *centre*, listens intently as Soviet Sports and Physical Culture deputy chief of propaganda, Alexander Sedov, *left*, makes a point to the author during Moscow negotiations, July 19, 1972. Alan Eagleson is in the background. *V. Cherbakov, Izvestia*

Taking the Floor: Author, during the negotiations, presents examples of publicity photo requirements for the series. Moscow, July 1972. *Victor Akhlomov, Izvestia*

(Top left) Innkeeping: Welcoming dinner hosted by the author and his wife for both negotiating sides to break the ice. Soviet national coach Vsevolod Bobrov, (*second from right with beer in hand*) is surrounded by Harry Sinden (*right*) and Johnny Esaw of CTV and John Ferguson (*left*). Back row from left is Alan Eagleson, Oliver Babirad of CTV and Bobby Haggert. *Laurielle Chabeaux*

(Top right) Amateur Status Threatened? Stars of Soviet national team goalie Vladislav Tretiak, defenceman Alexander Ragulin and forward Valeri Kharlamov (*left to right*) pose before the series with hockey equipment donated by Cooper Canada. Moscow, August 1972. *V. Cherushkov, Izvestia*

(Above) Friendship Series: Prime Minister Pierre Elliott Trudeau drops the ceremonial first puck at the Montreal Forum between Team Canada's Phil Esposito (*right*) and Vladimir Vikulov of the USSR. September 2, 1972. *Peter Bregg, Canadian Press*

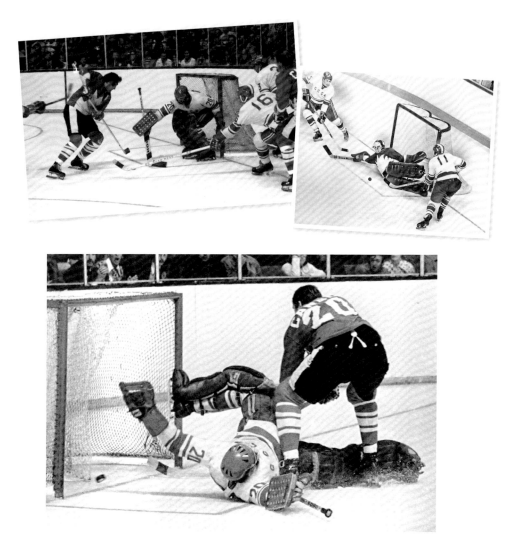

(Top left) Leadership: Team Canada's Phil Esposito scores the initial goal for the second straight game against the Soviet netminder, Vladislav Tretiak. Unlike in Montreal, Team Canada pulls out the win at Maple Leaf Gardens (4–1). Toronto, September 4, 1972. *Barry Davis,* Globe and Mail *via Canadian Press*

(Top right) Big Save: Team Canada's Ken Dryden blocks Evgeni Zimin (11) and Alexander Yakushev (15) during the early stage of Game One. The USSR would score seven goals in a stunning upset victory (7–3) over heavily favoured Team Canada. Montreal, September 2, 1972. *Frank Lennon/*Toronto Star/*Library and Archives Canada/* MIKAN 5677502

(Above) Deked Out: Team Canada's Peter Mahovlich scores a magnificent short-handed goal in the third period of Game Two at Maple Leaf Gardens, leaving Soviet netminder Vladislav Tretiak in a heap. Toronto, September 4, 1972. *Canadian Press*

(Top) Six on One: Team Canada players led by Phil Esposito all turn toward Soviet forward Alexander Maltsev (10), as goalie Tony Esposito awaits a backhand shot during Game Three. USSR's flashy forward, Valeri Kharlamov (17), circles behind the net. Winnipeg, September 6, 1972. *Peter Bregg/Canadian Press*

(Above left) Moscow Nights: Iconic Red Square with the Kremlin (*right*) and St. Basil's Cathedral (*left*). Moscow, September 1972. *Frank Lennon/Toronto Star/Library and Archives Canada/MIKAN 5677503*

(Above right) Soviet Priorities: The new 2,500-room Rossiya Hotel looms over a dilapidated Orthodox church in Moscow, September 1972. *Frank Lennon/Toronto Star/Library and Archives Canada/MIKAN 5677504*

Moscow Bells: Team Canada's Brian Glennie, Ron Ellis and Paul Henderson and their wives pose during an anglophone tour of the Soviet capital. September 25, 1972. *Frank Lennon/ Toronto Star/Library and Archives Canada/*MIKAN 5677505

Day Off: Team Canada's Jean Ratelle (*foreground*), Marcel Dionne (*back right*) and Guy Lapointe (*back left*) and their wives are seen during a francophone tour of Moscow. September 25, 1972. *Frank Lennon/Toronto Star/Library and Archives Canada/*MIKAN 5677506

Mission Possible: Canadian fans ready for action in front of their Intourist bus with a beaver sign in the window. Moscow, September 28, 1972. *Frank Lennon/*Toronto Star/ *Library and Archives Canada/*MIKAN 5677507

Showmanship: Team Canada's Phil Esposito takes a spill during the opening ceremonies before Game Five at the Palace of Sports and follows it up with a sweeping bow to the amusement of all. Moscow, September 22, 1972. *Credit:* CP *Photo/*AP/TASS

Standing Out: Alan Eagleson, on his feet among the crowd, expressing his views. Moscow, September 1972. *Frank Lennon/Toronto Star/Library and Archives Canada/ MIKAN 5677508.*

Fan Mail: Canadian Ambassador Robert Ford (*left*) inspects telegrams and postcards on the walls near the Team Canada dressing room at the Palace of Sports. With him are embassy number two Pierre Trottier (*centre*) and Alan Eagleson (*right*). Moscow, September 26, 1972. *Frank Lennon/Toronto Star/Library and Archives Canada/ MIKAN 5677509.*

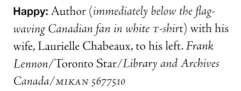

Happy: Author (*immediately below the flag-waving Canadian fan in white т-shirt*) with his wife, Laurielle Chabeaux, to his left. *Frank Lennon/*Toronto Star/*Library and Archives Canada/*MIKAN 5677510

Glum: Soviet fans follow the series through highs and lows. *Frank Lennon/*Toronto Star/ *Library and Archives Canada/*MIKAN 5677511

Choked: Team Canada's Phil Esposito, sitting on the penalty bench, expresses his displeasure with the referees. *Frank Lennon/*Toronto Star/ *Library and Archives Canada/*MIKAN 5677512

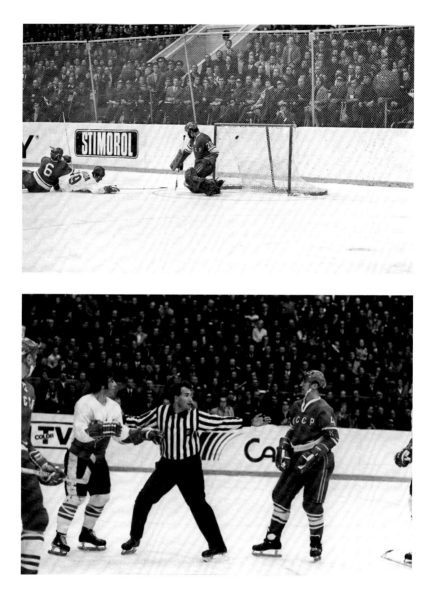

Winner: Soviet defenceman Valeri Vasiliev drags down Team Canada's Paul Henderson, but not before the Canadian winger fires the puck past goaltender Vladislav Tretiak for the winning goal (4–3) with two minutes and six seconds left in the third period of Game Seven in Moscow on September 26, 1972. Henderson, in a remarkable achievement, would score the winning goal in Games Six, Seven and Eight, as well as the last Canadian goal in Games Three and Five. *Frank Lennon/*Toronto Star*/Library and Archives Canada/e010933340.*

Shall We Dance? Team Canada's Jean-Paul Parisé (left) is separated from the USSR's Victor Kuzkin (right) by Swedish referee Ove Dahlberg during Game Seven in Moscow. September 26, 1972. *Frank Lennon/*Toronto Star*/Library and Archives Canada/ MIKAN 5677513.*

Sin Bin: Team Canada's Dennis Hull sits on the penalty bench late during Game Eight in Moscow, September 28, 1972, as shoulder-to-shoulder Soviet militia monitor the hockey crowd. *Frank Lennon/Library and Archives Canada/*MIKAN 5677514

Victory: The Palace of Sports scoreboard shows 34 seconds left after Paul Henderson's goal put Team Canada ahead 6–5 in the eighth and deciding game of the series. Moscow, September 28, 1972. *Frank Lennon/Toronto Star/Library and Archives Canada/* MIKAN 5677800

Hooliganism: Illustrations in a Soviet newspaper, focusing on the physical violence Team Canada used against its opponents.

Hockey Bridge: Russian President Vladimir Putin hosts players from Team Canada and the USSR at the Sochi Olympic Arena on September 12, 2017, during the 45th anniversary celebrations of the Summit Series. Among those pictured are Pat Stapleton, Dennis Hull and Frank and Peter Mahovlich of Team Canada and Alexander Yakushev, Vladislav Tretiak, Vladimir Shadrin, Boris Mikhailov and Alexander Maltsev of the Soviet Team. RT *Media*

Buddies Now: Team Canada and Team USSR players attend the 45th anniversary celebration in Moscow at the Russian Hockey Museum, September 2017. *Helen Parker, Diamond Films*

Giving Back: Paul Henderson (*second from left*) puts on the gloves with the author Gary Smith (*centre*) during a donation ceremony at the Hockey Hall of Fame. Ron Ellis (*left*), Rod Seiling (*second from right*) and Ken Dryden (*right*) look on. Hockey equipment left behind in Moscow by a departing player was donated by Smith, as well as a hockey stick signed by various players from both teams. Toronto, October 10, 2000. *David Cooper/ Toronto Star via Getty Images*

That speed came in the shape of the three young players from the not-well-known "Wings of the Soviets," the home club of assistant coach Boris Kulagin. The "University Line" or "Kids Line," as they were called in the USSR, consisted of Yuri Lebedev, Alexander Bodunov and Vlacheslav Anisin—all twenty-one years old. Bobrov also switched out two of his six defencemen, putting in Yuri Shatalov and the rising twenty-three-year-old star Valeri Vasiliev for Yuri Liapkin and Evgeni Paladiev (the latter had let Peter Mahovlich undress him in Game Two). Sinden, as Bobrov had done after Game One, largely stuck with his winning combination, making only one change, bringing Ratelle back in for Goldsworthy.

There had been an on-again, off-again discussion for a few weeks about the perceived need for a security briefing for the Canadian players to ensure they and their wives were aware of what to expect in Moscow. Winnipeg seemed like an odd place and time for this to occur, but Alan Eagleson had wanted me to join the RCMP to provide a fresh Russia-based assessment. Not everyone was present, but Eagleson undertook to reiterate the main points to the missing players at a later opportunity. Mine was a basic presentation for important visitors—that they should expect their hotel rooms to be bugged, possible surveillance if they wandered off on their own, the standard of food and hotels would not be as they were in North America, and they should absolutely avoid any temptation to exchange currency on the streets or anywhere other than at an authorized site. Single players were warned to be alert to possible Russian swallows mixed in among adoring fans.[120]

After lunch, the two senior Soviet officials, Ragulsky and Romesky, indicated they wanted to go for a walk to get some fresh air and to look in the store windows. My role, as official government escort officer, naturally called for me to go along.

We strolled along without any obvious police escort or close-by bodyguards. There were no notable demonstrations, even though we were in a city with sizable Ukrainian and Jewish populations. Only eleven months previous, both communities had been among the many thousands of Canadians who had publicly protested the visit to Canada by Soviet Premier Kosygin and had made it so unpleasant for him. This was another case where the world of hockey made the difference. Politics could incite demonstrations; hockey normally elicited admiration.

We walked for a while. I asked if there was something in particular they wished to see or to purchase. Romesky finally chirped up and indicated he would like to visit a veterinarian. My eyebrows went up. A veterinarian? Romesky explained he had a very large dog, a wolfhound, and needed some medicine not available in the USSR.

OK. Once that mission was accomplished, Ragulsky, the titular head of the delegation, wanted to go back to the hotel, which we did. Romesky was keen to go on to something else.

The CAHA had advanced me a hundred dollars for incidental purposes. My only charge against it during the entire Canadian trip was for seven dollars to cover the cost of two movie tickets. Romesky had heard about the film *The Godfather* and wanted to see it. Escort duty meant keeping the visitor happy, so along we went. Romesky wasn't interested in any popcorn or other snacks but watched the film with considerable intensity. It wasn't clear whether he got all the subtleties of the dialogue, but he greatly appreciated the acting and story line and remarked on the ability of the Corleone family to obtain what it wanted, by whatever means. Perhaps it was familiar territory for him as a member of the Communist Party and the KGB.

The Soviet players were taken to another movie, one of less substance, a western, and relished Cokes and hot dogs and more Cokes and more hot dogs.

ON GAME DAY, September 6, there was another luncheon, this time at the Fort Garry Hotel, where we were staying. There were smiles all around with the hockey fans who had been invited, but a dark shadow had been cast around the world with the horrific news from Munich that eleven Israeli athletes, coaches and trainers had been killed in a terrorist attack in the Olympic Village. A chilling example of the increasing international intertwining of sports and politics. It was a terrible incident that caused me to reflect on its meaning and the impact it would have on the always troubled field of Middle Eastern diplomacy. I distracted myself after a while with thoughts of Game Three.

The big hockey surprise for me was that Evgeni Zimin was not in the line-up for the Soviets. Standing only five foot eight, like Kharlamov, the flashy twenty-five-year-old winger had led all scorers on the USSR team through the first two games with three points (two goals and an assist). He had been inducted into the Soviet Ice Hockey Hall of Fame in 1968, at the precocious age of twenty-one, and had won Olympic gold in 1968 and again in 1972. He was nowhere to be seen in Winnipeg and there was no news about him. I hadn't noticed his absence on the flight from Toronto. And he didn't appear in any further games—even those in Moscow. It was strange. It wasn't clear whether this was a medical or a political illness. He had performed so well on the ice and was so ready to ask questions.

The opening ceremonies in Winnipeg included the standard individual introduction of the two teams and the playing of the two national anthems. A minute of silence was observed for the victims of the Munich massacre.

Father David Bauer, a Catholic priest and amateur hockey coach from Ontario, was honoured at centre ice for his creation and mentoring of the Canadian national team experiment, beginning with the 1964 Olympics, of a permanent team of student athletes combined with players from the men's senior leagues. The team primarily had been based in Winnipeg, and the national experiment ended in 1970. Bauer handed out commemorative medallions to the players and coaches.

When the puck dropped, Tony Esposito was again in net for Team Canada. Sinden originally had intended to rotate goalies each match but stuck with the hot hand from the Toronto game. As in Game Two, Team Canada came hard out of the gate—determined this time to avoid the penalty box. There was immediate success after only one minute and fifty-four seconds, when Jean-Paul Parisé opened the scoring. It looked like Canada would be off to the races, particularly when Vasiliev took an elbowing penalty for the USSR just over a minute later. But the Soviets could play as well short-handed as at full strength or on the power play. Vladimir Petrov had demonstrated that ability in Game One, and he demonstrated it again with his second short-handed goal in three games—this time with a long shot from the Canadian blue line. It tied the game. Two Canadian penalties passed in a row without any damage before Jean Ratelle rewarded Sinden's trust with a go-ahead goal late in the period to put Team Canada up 2–1.

It was a fast-paced game; back and forth, up and down the ice. Phil Esposito, who else, added to the Canadian lead at 4:19 of the second period to make it 3–1. Once again Canada had the opportunity to bust things wide open when Lebedev took a penalty at 11:00 minutes of the frame. Stars will be stars, and Kharlamov, on a breakaway, scored the second Soviet short-handed goal at 12:56 to reduce the Canadian lead to 3–2.

Paul Henderson returned Canada to a two-goal lead less than a minute later. It would be Canada's final goal of the game but the beginning of a phenomenal chapter in Canadian hockey history. Henderson would score four more final goals for Canada; all of them in Moscow.

The enhanced stamina and speed of the Soviet team became evident with two straight goals by the "Kids Line" (at 14:59 by Lebedev from Vasiliev and Anisin, and at 18:28 by Bodunov from Anisin). The score was back to even, at 4–4, by the end of the second period.

Team Canada had blasted thirty-two shots on Tretiak in the first two periods, almost double the Soviets' total of seventeen. It was a different story in the third period, with the USSR outshooting Canada by the low, tight margin of eight to six. Although there was no scoring in the third, the battle on the ice continued, with White and Mishakov being sent off together for slashing early on. Wayne Cashman would receive not only a slashing penalty halfway through the period but also a ten-minute misconduct for questioning the ancestry of a referee.

Hockey fans everywhere had seen another excellent example of the fastest game in sport. Team Canada though had to be disappointed. Despite greatly outshooting the USSR, and having twice had two-goal leads, they couldn't hang on and had to settle for a 4–4 tie; there being no provision in the Prague Agreement between the two countries for overtime.

Vladislav Tretiak would be chosen as the top Soviet performer for the second game in a row, while the distinction for the best Canadian went to Paul Henderson.

Coach Bobrov and the other members of the Soviet delegation and team were happy enough. They had withstood the anticipated Canadian onslaught. There was an air of contentment and satisfaction on our Air Canada ride to Vancouver, which was made merrier by a stopover in Edmonton for an enthusiastic greeting and gift-giving from Mayor Ivor Dent.[121]

No one thought it necessary to split the Soviet team into two for air travel purposes, but Clarence Campbell did for Team Canada. He and his insurance advisors didn't like the risk of the elite of the NHL going down all together over the skies of Canada or the Atlantic, and so they were assigned two separate aircraft for each journey.

OUR RECEPTION IN Vancouver proved once again that hockey is not only good politics but also good business. The federal government held another gala luncheon, on this occasion at the Hotel Vancouver. Five hundred more guests. The federal election campaign was picking up steam, and Trudeau's Liberals were trailing Robert Stanfield and his Progressive Conservative party in the polls. The Liberals were trying to make up lost ground by increasingly attaching themselves to this widely popular, nationalistic hockey series.

On the business front, the big money to be obtained from the series wasn't from gate receipts or the national lottery, it came from the commercial advertising associated with the broadcast rights that had been obtained by Eagleson through the company he had helped create: Ballard-Orr Enterprises. Television ratings were going through the roof, far exceeding the expectations of those Canadian companies who had been bold enough to pay the high sign-up fees.

The Soviet delegation leaders, and particularly Starovoitov, also grasped both the political and commercial aspects of all this, and he was ready to open talks for a second, follow-up series with Eagleson and me right here in Vancouver, before the Canadian part of the series was over.

The whole Soviet team was impressed with the extremely warm welcome they had received from governmental authorities as well as the Canadian public. Indeed, Rogulsky and Romesky implied they had gone to their equivalent of bureaucratic heaven, sitting at the head tables, as they were, with the prime minister, cabinet ministers, premiers and mayors in a manner normally reserved for only heads of state. Rogulsky wasn't even a full minister, just a vice minister, and here he was being feted by them all and given free rein to speak at each event, where the audiences favourably hung on his every word about friendship between the two countries. Premier Kosygin would have been most envious.

The Soviet team, for its part, had been assigned another luxury bus and had a most enjoyable time with an outing to the Vancouver Aquarium to see the Orca whales, followed by a tour around Stanley Park. They were noticing that capitalist life had its pleasures and that the standard of living of the average person they had encountered appeared to be better than they had been informed back home.

Within a mere week the Soviet stars had morphed from strange and unknown Men from Mars to household names in Canada. Autograph-seekers materialized everywhere. It hit a crescendo in Vancouver with airline attendants and pilots, union workers at the airport, drivers, chefs and waiters in dining rooms, front-hall hotel staff and of course those fortunate enough to have been invited to the official functions. The Soviet players remained neat, prim and proper, keeping any emotions they might be feeling in check.

One subject that had been the matter of discussion during the early days of negotiations in Moscow was the question of gifts. Official visits by heads of state or heads of government called for an expensive, prestigious "National Gift"; but this wasn't the case here, in spite of the Canadian adoration of Rogulsky. However, there would be an exchange of gifts from the Soviet Sports Committee and Soviet Ice Hockey Federation to Hockey Canada, the CAHA and to the Canadian players.

Alexander Gresko had been coy about the identity of their gift. All he would say to me weeks earlier when we first discussed it was it would be "big" and he wouldn't rule out it might be "alive." My initial thoughts had drifted to one or two Russian dancing bears, but Gresko had retorted that if it were to be a bear, he would ensure it came from the Moscow circus and could play hockey.

There were no animals of any kind from the USSR waiting in Vancouver.

As part of the pregame ceremonies on the ice, each Soviet official, coach and player had a different-sized Matryoshka nesting doll, which they individually presented to their Canadian counterparts. Together, they made up one "big," impressive doll.

NORMALLY AND NATURALLY, the conversations of residents of and visitors to Vancouver would turn to the beauty of the mountains and the sparkling ocean, but on this Friday in September it was hockey that was the talk of the town. The Pacific Coliseum filled up early for this final match in Canada, which would determine who had the advantage after the first four games. Excitement was palpable as the early game time of five p.m. approached. Which Team Canada would show up? The fans were abuzz. Some were confident; many less so. Most had sweaty palms.

Coach Bobrov stuck with his most recent formula of eleven forwards and six defencemen, matching the deployment of Sinden. The energy of the games was starting to flag as the series wore on, and the extra body up front helped share the offensive load. Bobrov also was less worried about defence than he had been in Montreal, His defence-men were holding up pretty well, though he decided to rest Alexander Gusev and Vyacheslav Solodukhin and replaced them with Alexander Ragulin and Evgeni Paladiev. He also made two changes among his forwards: Yuri Blinov and Vladimir Vikulov would replace Yuri Shatalov and Evgeni Mishakov. Counting this game, Bobrov had utilized all his twenty-seven players with the exception of his two backup goalies, Viktor Zinger and Alexander Sidelnikov. Tretiak had carried the entire goaltending load. Six of his forwards played all four games (Maltsev, Mikhailov, Kharlamov, Petrov, Shadrin, Yakushev) and three of his defencemen (Tsygankov, Kuzkin and Lutchenko).

Sinden made more extensive changes than Bobrov—seven in all—starting with rotating Ken Dryden back into the net. Serge Savard had a nasty ankle injury, and Sinden would decide it was best to take out his defensive partner, Guy Lapointe, at the same time and replace them with the duo of Don Awrey and Rod Seiling from Game One. Forwards Gilbert Perreault and Dennis Hull would see their first action, replacing Peter Mahovlich and Stan Mikita. Bill Goldsworthy and Rod Gilbert would take over from J.P. Parisé and Jean Ratelle.

Sinden was struggling with how he could equate his earlier promise to the players that they all would see some action with the need to reward those who were performing well and giving the team the best chance to win. Forwards Marcel Dionne and Rick Martin, as well as defencemen Dave Tallon, Brian Glennie and Jocelyn Guevremont, did not see action in Canada. Nor did goalie Eddie Johnston. Only six Canadian forwards were on the ice for each game (Phil Esposito, Cournoyer, Henderson, Clarke, Ellis and Frank Mahovlich), and just two defencemen (Bergman and Park).

With the game underway it only took one minute and twenty-four seconds before Bill Goldsworthy was sent off for cross-checking. Less than a minute later Boris Mikhailov, standing to the side of Dryden, tipped in a Lutchenko shot from the point, with Petrov also assisting. It was the first time in the series that the USSR had scored first. Less than four minutes later, the same scenario repeated itself: Goldsworthy was sent off again, this time for elbowing. Another tip-in by Mikhailov from another point shot from Lutchenko, assisted by Petrov. USSR 2–Canada 0 in the first six minutes.

First period over. No change in scoring.

The confident fans were beginning to have doubts. Didn't Team Canada know the potency of the Soviet power play and the need to avoid unnecessary penalties? The worries of the doubters increased palpably. I could feel the restlessness around me intensify.

Gilbert Perreault, in a stunning individual effort, skated the length of the ice around and through several Soviet players and put Canada on the scoreboard at 5:37 of the second frame. It gave the anxious fans something to cheer about. But not for long. Less than a minute later, at 6:34, Blinov, from Petrov and Mikhailov, restored the Soviet two-goal lead. For Petrov it was his third assist and for Mikhailov his third point—and the game was less than half over. The Soviet attack was clearly multi-faceted. Then, at 13:52, Vikulov scored, from Kharlamov and Maltsev, which upped the count to 4–1.

Shots on goal after two periods: USSR: 25, Team Canada: 18. The fans were left shaking their heads during the second intermission. Now they knew what their compatriots in Montreal had experienced: astonishment at the skills of the Soviets and frustration at what was happening with Team Canada. Booing had begun, but not widely and not full-throated.

There was still a period to go.

Team Canada increased the pace, and the shot count jumped at a rate of almost 4 to 1 for Canada. Tretiak stood tall. Goldsworthy, in a redemptive move, got a goal back at 6:54 of the third, from Esposito and Bergman, but that was wiped out when Shadrin, at 11:05, restored the three-goal Soviet lead with help from Yakushev and Vasiliev.

With less than ten minutes to go, the crowd's discontent began to grow, with pass after Canadian pass missing its target. What had been initial murmuring boos from high up in the arena spread and then broke out all over the stands when Goldsworthy started shoving the head of one of the Soviet players. The boos reached a crescendo after Tretiak dropped to the ice outside of the crease to stop a pass and Frank Mahovlich straddled the prone goalie, holding him down—not just for a few passing seconds but a lengthy, very noticeable amount of time. There was no penalty, and Mahovlich wasn't known for unsportsmanlike conduct, but the action seemed to represent everything that had gone wrong for Team Canada. The fans could hold back no longer, and they let the Canadian players know it.

Dennis Hull's last-minute goal at 19:38, from Esposito and Goldsworthy, did nothing to remove the sour taste from the 5–3 loss. The team could have used his brother, Bobby Hull, who it was said was in Vancouver at the time.

Then came a remarkable moment in Canadian sports. It wasn't witnessed by Phil Esposito's teammates, nor by his coaches, nor by the vast majority of the fans in the arena, most of whom had departed in the dying seconds of the game. Nor did I see it or listen to it at the time—but millions of Canadians did, watching on television across the country.

Boris Mikhailov and Phil Esposito, selected as the best Soviet and Canadian players that evening, had skated to one area of the rink, after the post-game team handshakes. Mikhailov accepted his award with a nod and departed. Esposito remained to be interviewed by CTV's Johnny Esaw. Sweating profusely, physically exhausted and exasperated, he became emotional: "To the people across Canada, we tried, we gave it our best, and to the people that booed us, geez. I'm really, all of us guys are really disheartened, and we're disillusioned and we're disappointed at some of the people. We cannot believe the bad press we've got, the booing we've gotten in our own buildings. If the Russians boo their players, the fans...Russians boo their players...Some of the Canadian fans...I'm not saying all of them, some of them booed us, then I'll come back and I'll apologize to each one of the Canadians, but I don't think they will. I'm really, really...I'm really disappointed. I'm completely disappointed. I cannot believe it. Some of our guys are really, really down in the dumps, we know, we're trying like hell. I mean, we're doing the best we can, and they got a good team, and let's face facts. But it doesn't mean that we're not giving it our 150 per cent, because we certainly are. I mean, the more every one of us guys, thirty-five guys that came out and played for Team Canada. We did it because we love our country, and not for any other reason, no other reason. They can throw the money, uh, for the pension fund out the window. They can throw anything they want out the window. We came here because we love Canada. And even though we play in the United States, and we earn money in the United States, Canada is still our home, and that's the only reason we came. And I don't think it's fair that we should be booed."

"The Speech" would become one of the hallmarks of the series and would eventually be held as one of the great moments in Canadian sports history. One journalist subsequently equated it with Lincoln's Gettysburg Address. Another would compare it to John F. Kennedy's inaugural address. In an interview years later with the *Vancouver Sun*, Esposito himself would relate he had just had a phone conversation in which the caller said his Vancouver speech was Canada's equivalent to Winston Churchill's 1940 "defiance speech" against the Nazis.

Esposito laughed off his own story. Probably best he did because this was very exalted company. Nevertheless, Esposito had the advantage of a massive coast-to-coast television audience, and he was talking about Canada's national game, which to many Canadians was more tangible and immediate than politics and mattered to most Canadians more than politics. The Russians also, as a perceived enemy, had to stir Canadian blood as much or more so than the political foes of Laurier, Diefenbaker or Levesque.

So perhaps the "sweaty hockey player" does merit consideration in this august grouping. But on this night, September 8, 1972, Esposito would leave the ice to more catcalls and shouts by a few fans that the results of the matches in Canada proved the communists had produced better hockey players and perhaps even a better political system. It was then, Esposito would say, he realized this was no longer a game: but a war.

The renowned Canadian hockey journalist and writer Roy MacGregor would observe "what had happened in Vancouver was akin to a country booing its own army."

As far as I was concerned, as a diplomat, Esposito's invoking of the word "war" as a rallying cry for his teammates and Canadians ran directly counter to the Canadian government's diplomatic goal of reducing the risk of "war" with the USSR. No one wanted to replace a stick and a puck with a steel helmet and a bayonet.

The Soviet team, on the other hand, was in a state of euphoria. There were big, broad grins on every face. They had come to Canada as vast underdogs, and with much scepticism in their own country, but they were now leaving with a strong 2–1–1 advantage and victory on Canadian ice.

Red Fisher of the *Montreal Star* had asked to interview Soviet goalie Vladislav Tretiak, and I went along to do the interpreting. In seven short days Tretiak had gone from a nobody to a golden boy. Fisher wanted to know how he did it. How had he played all four games in a pressure-packed situation when his Canadian opponents had divided the burden? How had he allowed only six goals in two games in head-to-head competition with Ken Dryden, compared to twelve by the Stanley Cup champion and MVP in the 1971 NHL playoffs? While he had allowed more goals than Tony Esposito in their two head-to-head contests (8–5), how had he been able to deal with seventy-four shots on goal compared to only forty-six by Esposito? Indeed, Team Canada had outshot the Soviet team in all four games by a combined total of 147 to 107: a forty-shot differential.

Fisher had to look up at Tretiak, who stood just over six feet, and a few inches more with his skates on. Tretiak was remarkably calm and composed for someone who was only twenty years old and in such an intense situation. He appeared fresh-faced and rather handsome. There was no swagger to him. He explained that he trained and worked hard, and his success was as a result of the team's efforts in front of him. This explanation would have pleased any coach, general manager or owner and was sure to be well received by his teammates and particularly by the Party bosses in the Kremlin.

Tretiak at the same time became one notable communist who was well liked and even admired by most Canadians. In this sense he was exactly what Prime Minister Pierre Trudeau was seeking to achieve in his goal "to put a human face on communism."

NOW IT WAS on to Moscow, or back to Moscow in my case. The Soviet team wished to avoid having to pay hard currency and so connected with an Aeroflot flight out of New York. My route took me via Ottawa to check in with External Affairs and then back to the USSR with Air Canada.

I was eager to reconnect with Laurielle. In this era before internet and cellphones, I had not been in touch with her since first arriving in Canada. She was now in her sixth month of her first pregnancy—by herself in our apartment in Moscow.

Looking back on one aspect of the ten days, it was pleasing to learn my momentary sympathy for the Soviet team, after the first two Canadian goals in Montreal, had been echoed by a comment recorded from Bobby Orr. He was quoted as saying, while watching them practice in Montreal a week before: "We were going to beat them so bad I actually felt sorry for them."

There was no need for anyone, including myself, to feel sorry for them any longer. The Soviet team was returning to Moscow as conquering heroes.

CHAPTER TWELVE

IN MOSCOW WITH TEAM CANADA

I T WAS TIME for me to change teams. In Canada I had spent all my time with the Soviet delegation and team as liaison officer. We had stayed in different hotels and flown on different aircraft than Team Canada, and there had been very little mingling between them and no substantive occasion for me to interact with the Canadian players beyond the security briefing. Now I got to revert to being the Canadian embassy point man in Moscow for Team Canada as it prepared to arrive for the second half of the eight-game home-and-home series beginning on September 22.

Team Canada had started the series in the role of Goliath—at this point it was in the position of David.

After finishing his Vancouver interview with Vladislav Tretiak, Red Fisher had wanted to know from me what everyone should expect in the USSR.

"A profound difference," was my reply.

The Canadian players would be on big ice, with European referees. There was wire netting around the end boards rather than glass. All the games would be in the same arena in Moscow. They would have their spouses with them, unlike the Soviet team in Canada. Whether that would prove to provide comfort or be a distraction remained to be determined. The hotels, food and drink would be different and not up to the North American standards taken for granted by NHL players and fans. There were no Hilton Hotels, not even Holiday Inns. Then there was the Soviet authoritarian system of control on travel and contact with and among its citizens. All in all, it would be a major challenge.

Fisher was one of Canada's top hockey writers, but like most other sportswriters, he had at first predicted a complete Canadian sweep. Now he was in a negative, defeatist mode, referring to Team Canada as "Cream Canada."

Fisher knew he would be facing challenges of his own. As a print reporter, he would be competing with the expected one hundred or so other Canadian media representatives, plus another hundred or so European journalists, who were all seeking press accreditation. Then there were the approximate two hundred home-based Soviet journalists looking for their first in-person exposure to the hockey series.

The big unknown, and major difference between the games in Canada and those in Moscow, was the number of travelling fans. Not one Soviet fan had made the trip to Canada, whereas the number of Canadians had ballooned beyond twenty-five hundred on its way toward three thousand. Hundreds, or even a thousand more, could have been added, given the demand, were it not for the lack of game tickets and hotel accommodation. Canadian travel agents and airline personnel were passing along the initial message, or warning, to the embassy that those Canadians and Americans buying their travel packages were "super excited, emotional and intending to party."

The information brochure that Air Canada had prepared for the "Canadian Pilgrims," a term employed by External Affairs given "hockey is a religion" connotation, contained much useful material but read in parts like the Ten Commandments. There were a lot of passages beginning with "thou shalt not."[122] No selling of clothing (read blue jeans) or other personal items. No bringing in or taking out of letters or packages for others. No distribution of religious objects or publications. No distribution of unauthorized foreign literature. No taking out of art that might be considered a national treasure. No importing or exporting Soviet roubles. No exchanging dollars or other foreign currency through "private channels" (read individuals). No taking of photographs from aircraft, and a long list of other photographic prohibitions.

Then there was a paragraph about how "meticulous Soviet citizens were in observing even the most minor rules and regulations." They "did not jay-walk, drop cigarette butts on the ground, arrive late for the theatre or throw objects on the ice surface if they are displeased with the officiating at hockey games." (Harry Sinden obviously did not read that final point.)

The paragraph continued with the admonition that "tourists who break the rules in the Soviet Union quickly stand out" and everyone "should heed the advice of their Intourist guides at all times and when in doubt ask for their assistance."

There was even a paragraph about chewing gum. It noted that wherever tourists went they would be approached by Russian children asking for a stick of gum, as it was unavailable locally and seen as a favourite treat. The point was then made: "Russian parents generally discourage their children from its use."

One thing that was not discouraged in the brochure was drinking. There was mention of the availability of Russian beer (*peevo*) at meals and "the ever-present, excellent Russian vodka." It added, "prepare to learn to drink vodka without a mix, as western soft drinks are not available in Russia."[123]

The public affairs people at External Affairs, due to the publication rush, had missed out on adding another message: "a lot of Russians will make judgments about Canada on the basis of the behaviour and demeanour of the Canadians they see or hear about in Moscow."[124]

Ambassador Ford, Peter Hancock and other colleagues at the embassy had been working long hours during my absence in Canada, as we all prepared for the multi-faceted onslaught. The consular, administrative and commercial sections were particularly hard pressed.

Ford, at the helm, had given us pretty much free rein to get on with matters while he kept his eye firmly fixed on the official delegation, which would be led by Senator Laing and assisted by Ed Ritchie.

Most importantly, the ambassador had gone back to the Foreign Ministry several more times to raise the potentially combustible issue of interaction between the Canadian fans and the Soviet militia. Finally, Ford received the welcome word that the Soviet leadership had instructed the security apparatus to "go easy" on our fans provided there were no major altercations. Their security focus remained on "ethnic Canadians," particularly of Ukrainian, Baltic or other East European origins, stirring up political trouble.

The Canadian reinforcements began to arrive, none too soon, with John Alexander back from Canada to resume his yeoman efforts in sorting out the priorities for Hockey Canada, and Patrick Reid, from External, assuming command of the information centres. We had been looking for additional Russian speakers and those with experience in the USSR, but few were available to assist. The next best were highly competent administrative and consular officers, like Herb Knox from our embassy in Helsinki, who was a massive sports enthusiast and who had been in charge of shipping food, furniture and all sorts of other matter from Finland to the embassy in Moscow.

On the top of my to-do list following my return was settling the issue of securing the embassy's tickets and reconfirming those for all the other Canadians. The hockey tickets seemed to be approaching the value of gold. They had been printed up in their standard flimsy paper form (unlike the sturdy cardstock of the tickets in Canada) and were at the box office at the Sports Palace but "not yet available." The embassy called every day but got the same response. After days went by, we received an unsettling message: the demand for tickets was so large and the supply of tickets so small, more time was needed to work out matters. All tickets would be allotted to interested parties and none would go up for public sale.

Another day went by. The first game was less than a week away. Finally, a call came through telling the embassy representative to show up at the arena box office that day at two p.m.

The box office was small and accessible only from a single outside door. The lone ticket window was secured with iron bars. I approached the ticket window and identified myself to the attendant, asking for the embassy's allotment of two hundred and fifty tickets per game. "You will have to wait. Go and stand with the other two." I was more than happy to find out that one of the two was from Intourist and waiting for the tickets destined for Hockey Canada and the Canadian fans. As the Intourist tickets were being paid for in much-needed hard currency, I assumed they had to be a continuing priority. The second fellow was from the Sports Committee, looking for the ministry's tickets, which he said, in communist bureaucratic fashion, would go to "deserving factories, norm-breakers and others."

The three of us waited and waited and finally a young man came through the door to the street wearing an expensive suit and foreign-bought shoes. Both were easy to spot in unfashionable Moscow. He briskly walked straight to the counter and without a word unclicked locks and opened his attractive, good-sized leather briefcase. The attendant filled it to the brim with sheets of tickets, and when he finished I heard him say, "Twenty-five hundred, right?" There was a slight nod of the head in reply, a locking of the briefcase, and the stranger turned and breezed past us for the second time without a glance.

"Who was that?" I asked the other two.

"Central Committee of the Communist Party of the Soviet Union." No need to say more. I had just witnessed the power and the privilege in the USSR. Sure, Hockey Canada, the NHL and Canadian government creamed off the best tickets in Canada, but the USSR claimed to be a country based on the principle of egalitarianism.

AS WE ALL were working away in Moscow, Canadian news reports began arriving from Sweden, along with diplomatic cables from our embassy in Stockholm. They weren't pretty. Team Canada had gone there to acclimatize itself to European conditions, pull itself together after the great disappointment in Canada, and to play two friendly warm-up games with the Swedes. Instead, there were prominent headlines about

Canadian misconduct and numerous pictures of bloodied faces. It was seen as a failure of sports diplomacy—of diplomacy in general. Instead of hockey drawing the two countries and peoples together, it was pushing them apart.

There was nothing we, in Moscow, could do about the situation in Sweden, aside from worry some more about what was going to happen once the extravaganza arrived in the USSR.

The Soviet team, in the interim, had come back to Moscow in a state of adulation and had taken its foot off the gas. Instead of immediately returning to the training barracks at Arkhangelskoye Park, Soviet players were granted time off for gatherings with family, friends and well-wishers of all kinds. As the astute Russian hockey writer Vsevolod Kukushkin put it, the Soviet players were "nationwide heroes" in great demand and invited by "cosmonauts, composers, writers, and movie makers."[125] Everyone longed to mix with them. Coach Bobrov had his own friends to meet, and the rigid camp discipline was forgotten.

Kukushkin would add the observation, "The dolce vita and prolonged basking in glory are incompatible with maintaining sports form at all times."[126] Bobrov and the Soviet players apparently had never read the story of the hare and the tortoise.[127]

SCOTIABANK'S "GO CANADA" and "Vas-Y Canada" airmail postcards, which had been distributed throughout its vast network of branches across Canada, began to arrive in Moscow in droves, expressing love and support for the team. The front side read "GO CANADA!" and depicted a Canadian player at close quarters attempting to slide a backhand shot past an out-stretched Soviet netminder. The illustration resembled Peter Mahovlich's Game Two goal in many respects, except the artist had used a Canadian fibreglass goalie mask rather than the Soviet bird-cage model.

The left side of the back had an admonition to mail the card by September 25 to ensure delivery before the series ended, a "to" line where you were supposed to add a player's name, room for a short message, and lines to add your own name and your address. The right side had the typed-in address "Palace of Sports, Moscow, USSR."

Initially, the Soviet Post Office delivered the postcards to the embassy, together with dozens and dozens of letters, many of which were simply addressed to "Team Canada, Moscow, USSR." The same happened with inbound telegrams using the Soviet telegraphic office. They were added to our growing collection of telegrams sent direct via the embassy telex system. The matter of what to do with all the bags of mail was put on the pending list awaiting the arrival of the team.

The Royal Bank of Canada took a different approach. Working with Hancock of the embassy, Royal's representatives were able to place an ad in Russian in the newspaper *Sovetsky Sport* saying, "We Wish Team Canada Success." It was believed to have been the first time a foreign company had achieved such a goal in the USSR.

The first two Air Canada, and two Aeroflot charter flights, arrived in Moscow on September 19. It was obvious the partying had gotten underway as soon as the planes full of Canadians had their wheels up after departing from Montreal and Toronto for the long overnight journey. There were reports of continuous singing, including multiple renditions of the national anthem, and of numerous alcohol-fueled toasts. The initial contingent of seven hundred and twenty fans were already decked out in flags and pins, and while most were uncertain whether Team Canada could mount a comeback on foreign ice, they were determined to enjoy their own ten-day sports holiday.

Team Canada's entourage arrived in Moscow on September 20 at seven p.m. but was less festive than the Canadian fans. The break in Sweden had not gone as planned and dissension was building in the ranks. They were buoyed nonetheless to find the lobby and street outside the Intourist hotel jammed with Canadian fans and to see their wives, whose assignment to the same hotel was an on-again, off-again adventure. Some of the players' mothers and mothers-in-law also had made the trip. It was a melee sorting out everyone and everything, but for some, as Peter Mahovlich would say, the supporting presence of family members provided a "homey feeling in an inhospitable place."[128]

The Soviets had expedited matters at the airport, reciprocating what we had done in Montreal, and the separate team dining room and private meeting area in the hotel had been pre-inspected by the embassy and Patrick Reid and were as promised. The team had its first steak dinner that night, prepared by special Russian chefs to everyone's satisfaction. So far, so good.

When Team Canada arrived at the facilities at the Palace of Sports the following morning for their first practice, they were met with a double surprise. Not only were there young figure skaters on the ice, but the boards were covered in advertising. Not Russian advertising, but in English, with some major Canadian, American and international brands, including CCM, Electrolux, Turtle-Wax, Hitachi-TV, Heineken beer, and Stimorol, a popular chewing gum produced in Denmark. A five-metre Gillette ad at centre ice was the largest of the fourteen signs. The estimated total cost for all of them was in the range of $175,000. A flash of Soviet capitalism. The IIHF had permitted ads on the boards in previous years at the World Championships, but there had been no such advertising in the four Canadian rinks during the series.

It wasn't immediately evident who had organized these ads, or who would profit from them, as there was nothing in the text of our bilateral agreement and the matter had never been discussed between Canada and the USSR. Further queries appeared to point to Via Arena Advertising, with the proceeds apparently shared between the IIHF and the Soviet Ice Hockey Federation. As Canada was not a fully participating member of the IIHF at the time, this may have prevented a similar arrangement in Canada.[129]

Coach Sinden was less concerned with the advertising and more with the thickness of the ice (three inches here compared to less than one inch in Canada), which he thought would lead to ice chips and slowing down the puck. Nor was he pleased with the mesh netting behind the goals, with their strange non-glasslike tendency to catapult the puck back into play. As he looked up into the bleachers, Sinden could see numerous Russian coaches watching the proceedings.

There were also complaints about the colour of the ice, this time by Canadian television producers, who thought it was too grey in colour and would impede proper lighting. What to do on short notice? After much head-scratching someone came up with the idea to use powdered milk, and so the Soviet rink attendants were instructed by their bosses to carry in hundreds and hundreds of bags and to mix it in with the water used to make the ice. Ice-cleaning and flooding was performed by two old Zamboni-like machines left behind by a French ice follies troupe.

The practice had barely gotten underway when the first fractious moment occurred. Sinden said he inadvertently had forgotten to include Vic Hadfield on any of the practice lines. Hadfield, in a sulk, left the ice to sit on the bench and picked up something to read. Sinden said there was an unhappy exchange between the two of them about lack of ice time versus poor play. Hadfield headed to the dressing room, informing Eagleson along the way that he was quitting the team and returning to North America.

It didn't take long for the news to spread among the players, and at the end of practice, Rick Martin, who had not played in any games to this point, signalled he would be better off training with his team in Buffalo and was going to leave as well. Jocelyn Guevremont, the only Vancouver Canuck on the team, had joined the exodus by the time the team bus arrived back at the hotel. All three flew out of Moscow the next morning, September 22—the day the series would resume with its first game in the USSR.

For Game Five, Coach Bobrov stuck with the format he had ended with in Canada: eleven forwards and six defencemen. There were some minor adjustments: Gusev and Liapkin re-joined the defence corps, replacing the less experienced Vasiliev and Paladiev. Bobrov also made two changes up front, replacing Lebedev and Bodunov with the more rugged Mishakov and drawing in Martyniuk for his very first game from the additional numbers permitted. Tretiak remained in goal, even as a fourth netminder, Alexander Pashkov, was added to the team. Strange as it seemed after his performance in Canada, Bobrov still had lingering doubts about Tretiak's ability to play well in all eight games.

Anatoli Firsov, once again, did not suit up for the Soviet team and would not do so at all in Moscow. He was either still injured or still in Bobrov's doghouse. Perhaps Bobrov, like Sinden, wanted to rid himself of disgruntled players, fearing their corrosive effect on the cohesion of the team.

Harry Sinden, more or less stuck to the line-up he used in Vancouver. Bergman and Park, Stapleton and White had now become fixtures on defence. Savard was still injured, but instead of sitting his partner, Guy Lapointe, as had been done in Vancouver (the only game he did not play in the series), Sinden dressed Lapointe and paired him with Rod Seiling. Don Awrey sat out and did not appear in Moscow. Up front, Sinden replaced the penalty-prone Goldsworthy with J.P. Parisé, and Dennis Hull with Peter Mahovlich. Jean Ratelle was reinserted in place of his fellow Rangers line-mate Hadfield, while Gilbert Perreault was tagged to play his second consecutive game. Unlike Bobrov, Sinden continued to juggle goaltenders. Ken Dryden had played in the Vancouver game and Tony Esposito the first match in Sweden. The third Canadian goalie, Eddie Johnstone, needed some work, and Sinden used him in the second Stockholm game in place of Dryden. Now it was Esposito's turn again. He would be in net for the first game in Moscow.

FOR ME, THE most important diplomatic event of these games, in terms of its impact on Soviet citizens, was not the final outcome of the series but something that happened before the first puck was even dropped in Moscow for Game Five.

The 13,700-seat Palace of Sports was packed to the rafters. Not a ticket to be begged, borrowed or stolen any longer. Nationally revered poet Yevgeny Yevtushenko had to be satisfied with a seat high up in the stands. Here was the clash of cultures in microcosm: silent, unsmiling, dark-suited high-level male and female members of the Communist Party had come to Moscow from around the USSR for a party conference and melded with equally glum local apparatchiks. For many, it was their first hockey game. The party brass was out in force, seated in a covered tribune at centre ice: Brezhnev, Kosygin and Podgorny, keen to demonstrate to the communist faithful the prowess of Soviet Man, which had been so amply displayed in Canada. Senator Laing and Ed Ritchie sat with them—Ambassador Ford unable to do so due to his physical impediment, but he was glued to the television set. Opposite the tribune, on the other side of the ice, in sections nine, ten and eleven, between the red and goal lines and bulging upward behind, were the twenty-eight hundred or so visiting Canadian fans, reinforced by Canadian embassy personnel and their diplomatic contacts. The non-dressed Canadian players, like Orr and Dryden,[130] were front and centre in section ten. The Canadians numbered less than a quarter of the contingent from the USSR, but were considerably more dominant in voice, colour, flags and enthusiasm. It was no contest on that front.

At eight p.m. Moscow time, the proceedings began. Soviet television came on the air and began its broadcast to approximately a hundred and fifty million viewers across the eleven time zones of the USSR. This was something TV viewers really wanted to watch—not an endless recounting of Soviet agricultural and manufacturing achievements, which nobody really believed and yet had to endure. Sports provided much-welcomed relief.

The Canadian players by now had become accustomed to lining up on opposite blue lines, followed by the playing of the two national anthems. But instead of having politicians and various other dignitaries on the ice to drop the puck, as had occurred in Montreal, out skated Olga Baranova of the Moscow Ice Ballet. Her princess-like costume featured a pearl-coloured tiara, white blouse and a sleeveless patterned dress of purple, black and green. In her outstretched hands was a round loaf of bread, with a small container of salt upon it—a traditional Slavic gesture of welcome. With a wide smile she presented the bread to alternative captain Jean Ratelle. After Baranova came young figure skaters, mainly female, in colourful outfits, who fanned out and presented all thirty-eight players on the ice with cellophane-wrapped clutches of carnations. Then came the introduction of the visiting Canadians, wearing their white sweaters and black pants, lined up in order of jersey number: Gary Bergman (2), Pat Stapleton (3), Brad Park (5), Ron Ellis (6).

And number seven, Phil Esposito. In a brief forward movement his skate caught a dropped carnation petal, sending his feet out from under him and his backside down onto the ice with his legs splayed upwards in front of him. Shock and surprise, followed instantaneously by laughter and smiles all around, even from hardened militiamen, as from one knee Esposito performed a sweeping bow directed at the state box. Phil would later claim he made direct eye contact with Brezhnev—"the guy with the hairy eyebrows"—but it didn't matter; in that brief, very human moment, he had captured the hearts and admiration of millions of Soviet hockey fans.

If it had been one of the Soviet players who had fallen to the ice in the same manner in front of the party leadership, they likely would have immediately scampered back into line full of humiliation and concerned their playing career could come to a quick end.

Here was a showman, an individual not afraid to make fun of himself, and that rare individual who could turn an almost certain embarrassment into a prize pratfall. This was an unscripted moment. Canadian individualism, sense of humour, and freedom of action was on full display for all to see.

FOR THE CANADIAN fans, the game itself was another emotional roller-coaster. It started with unbounded excitement, accelerating to the noisy celebration of a 1–0 lead after the first period, on a goal from J.P. Parisé. After the second stanza, following goals from Clarke and Henderson, a joyous crescendo of flag-waving and boisterous cheers rose from the Canadian sections of the crowd. The score was now 3–0. Team Canada was checking well, largely avoiding the penalty box, and outshooting the USSR 25–22. The Soviets were missing their passes and appeared off their game. Perhaps hometown jitters. Perhaps the after-effects of la dolce vita that Kukushkin had written about. The Soviet crowd was quiet—but then it always was. Nobody wanted to stand out, particularly with the party boss, Premier Kosygin, and other members of the leadership in attendance.

Team Canada's play in Game Five resembled that of Game Two, their victory in Toronto. But this game would have a different ending.

Standing in the hallway between both dressing rooms as the players jointly prepared to return to the ice for the start of the third period, there was nothing I could see in either team's demeanour or in their eyes to suggest what was about to happen. No rah-rah on either side.

So what if Blinov scored for the USSR at 3:34? If Henderson, with another marker at 4:56, restored the three-goal Canadian lead?

Sinden continued to pace behind the bench like a caged wolf, as he had all game, all nerves, shouting out encouragement and touching the players' backs and shoulders as he moved.

Action continued, with equal shots on net at both ends. Then the Soviet passing game started to click and move into high gear. Anisin scored at 9:05, and just six seconds later he passed to Shadrin for another shot, which beat Tony Esposito. With sudden speed, the Canadian lead had been cut to only one. The Canadian fans started to chew their nails. The Soviet fans started to show some form of life.

Clarke was sent off for holding at 10:25, but at the same time Tsygankov was called for high-sticking. They played on, at even strength, until the fleet-footed Kharlamov passed to Ragulin, who sent the puck on to Gusev for another Soviet goal at 11:41. The game was tied. Three goals in just over two minutes. It took only three more minutes before Kharlamov was at it again, with a pass to Vikulov, for what turned out to be the winning goal at 14:46.

Final score: USSR 5, Canada 4. Five Soviet goals on only eleven shots, in the final period, past Tony Esposito, who had played so well in Canada. It should have been a crippling body blow to Team Canada to lose such a game, and now to be behind in the series 3–1–1, with only three must-win games remaining.

While the Canadian fans bit their lips in disappointment, there was no shock at the result, as there had been in Montreal. We all knew by this time that the Soviets were very, very good. There were no boos of any kind either, as had occurred in Vancouver. No, it was as if these die-hard fans who had travelled thousands of miles to watch these guys play hockey recognized their team needed a lift, some real love, and so they showed it with a standing ovation as Team Canada left the ice. The series wasn't over, and the party was just beginning.

Perhaps the Soviet team had had pregame jitters again from all the hype, as had occurred in Montreal, or maybe it had taken them forty minutes to shake off all the rust and party streamers that had built up during the intervening time after their return from Canada. Whatever it was, they were now feeling even more confident about their abilities, and further praise rained down on their heads. It came from Coach Bobrov, and it came from the highest levels of the country and of the Communist Party, who had witnessed it all in person.

In their dressing room, as was Soviet custom after a victory, they arranged a few equipment boxes into a makeshift table, laid out some vodka and drank a toast "to success and to the boys."[131]

This was the pinnacle of the series for the USSR and, as winger Alexander Yakushev would later say, this was the "turning point." The Soviets had read their own game summaries and, in their minds, thought they could now coast to victory, needing only one more win or a tie in three games to clinch the series.

Sinden and Ferguson were in an emotional tailspin immediately after the game, not wanting to talk to anyone and be forced to explain how certain victory had so suddenly turned into another demoralizing defeat.

Rather than select only one player per team as the most valuable players of the game, as was the case in Canada, it was decided there should be two per team. Soviet hockey officials would choose the two

Canadians, while CBC and CTV had worked out an arrangement to choose the two best Soviets. Alexander Yakushev and Vladimir Petrov were picked for the USSR, while Tony Esposito—despite those five third-period goals—and Paul Henderson got the nod for Team Canada.

EARLY IN THE morning the day after the game, Sinden pulled me aside. Phil Esposito had woken up coughing blood. Could I take him for an x-ray without letting anyone know, not even the team doctor, nor the other players, and particularly not the media? Keep it from the Soviet team too? It was a tall order. I told him I would try to do my best, but it would be extremely difficult to prevent Russian officials of some kind from finding out about the health of Canada's top player.

The Canadian embassy relied on Dr. Peter Baxindine at the British embassy. What he couldn't handle himself for medical assistance, and in cases where the patient couldn't be sent outside of the USSR for treatment, he would rely on one local hospital in which he had considerable trust. The good doctor had been at the game the previous evening, compliments of our embassy, and he was only too willing to help with arrangements. It wasn't long before Esposito and I, with an embassy car and driver, were on our way to the hospital and quickly escorted into the x-ray department. The Soviet doctor had been told Esposito was a Canadian hockey player. Two female technicians, clad in white, were there to assist and asked the patient to remove his shirt and gold chain. Esposito was broad-chested, with considerable amounts of body hair, both of which precipitated a round of chuckles and giggles. Another round of giggles ensued when the x-ray machine setting was found to be too small and had to be adjusted sideways and upward to accommodate his large frame.

The doctor examined the x-ray but was quick to state in Russian that he could see nothing wrong—nothing that would keep Esposito from playing the next night. Everyone relaxed. The doctor added one thing that had caught his attention: Esposito had an "abnormally large heart cavity," which, he noted, was a definite asset for a hockey player's stamina. Esposito was rather chuffed when I translated this news for him. (By contrast, Montreal Canadiens legend Jean Beliveau suffered from fatigue at times due to a heart that was too small for his tall frame— or, as one doctor put it in Beliveau's file: "He has an Austin's motor in a Cadillac's chassis.")[132]

All three Russians who attended Esposito indicated they had watched the hockey game the previous night on television and were most pleased they could be of assistance to their important guest. As this was a medical matter, they promised to maintain confidentiality and keep the visit to themselves.

We returned to the Palace of Sports for the team practice and the driver parked outside of the exterior fencing. A militiaman was guarding the pedestrian entrance and, seeing my pass, was about to let us through when a youngster appeared and asked for gum. Esposito was quick to oblige him, digging into his pocket, but the youngster was roughly shoved away by the guard. Esposito raised his voice in objection, saying what kind of system is this when a kid can't receive an offer of gum. He summoned the youngster to return, but the militiaman was having nothing to do with it. The situation became heated. I counselled Esposito to forget about it. This was the way things operated here, and if he persisted, the only one to bear the consequences would not be us, but the kid and his family. Esposito shook his head in disbelief, and we moved on.

While Esposito turned out to be fine from a health perspective, Sinden had another defector on his hands in the form of Gilbert Perreault, Rick Martin's teammate with the Buffalo Sabres. Perreault had dressed and had an assist in the first period the previous evening, but Sinden wasn't happy with his defensive play and hadn't used him for the rest of the game. Perreault used Martin's excuse—if he was not going to play, he needed to get back to his home team to round into shape for the coming NHL season. Sinden was steaming about the four defectors but calmed down after the team had a good practice. When asked what was going to happen to the equipment used by the four, he let out a few expletives. He didn't care as long as the equipment got the hell out of the dressing room, like the players who had worn the gear. Sinden had no trouble with my suggestion that I could use a set for my games with the Moscow Maple Leafs.

The TASS journalist Kukushkin was waiting outside the Intourist hotel when the team returned from practice at midday on September 23. Kukushkin spoke good English and, when he noted Sinden was the last person to leave the bus, asked in a flippant manner whether Sinden felt like the captain on a sinking ship. Maybe because Sinden was feeling more upbeat about the good practice and getting rid of the dissenters, he didn't jump down Kukushkin's throat. He simply retorted that last night was just one game, the boat is still afloat, we have drawn conclusions and we will play the remaining games to win.[133]

That afternoon I was invited to attend the first meeting between Andrei Starovoitov of the Soviet Ice Hockey Federation and NHL president Clarence Campbell, who was accompanied by the club owners of the Detroit Red Wings and Chicago Black Hawks, among others. The purpose was to discuss possible direct collaboration between the two bodies with the goal of club matches and the possible creation of a European professional league, which could become an eastern division of the NHL.[134]

These talks continued the next morning, September 24, even though it was a Sunday and game day again. Later the same day, Eagleson and I met separately with Starovoitov to discuss the ramifications of the NHL proposals for future matches between Team Canada and the USSR national team.[135]

There were a lot of pucks in the air.

On a different matter, the embassy picked up a story that the only downside to the Soviet victory in Game Five, as seen by their leadership, was the enthusiastic screaming and shouting of the Canadian fans, which had overwhelmed the massive majority of Soviet fans. The leadership wanted their fans, instead of their normal silence, to now be as loud or louder than the Canadians. This was a massive break in Soviet mentality and tradition. Alexander Gresko, from the Sports Committee, was charged with making it happen. His counter was to dragoon a number of young female employees from the Sports Committee and have them go up and down the aisles of the rink trying to lead the Soviet crowd in chants of "Shaybu, Shaybu" [We want a goal].[136] But they were no match for the lusty, well-lubricated Canadians.

The Canadian fans had used "Go Canada Go" to great effect and added the clever bilingual English–Russian chant to their arsenal: "Da, Da, Canada. Nyet, Nyet, Soviet."

Not to be outdone by their own compatriots, there were a few Canadians who composed their own words to the opening bars of the Soviet national anthem: "Phil Esposito, Phil Esposito, Phil Esposito; Comes from the Sault."[137]

SINDEN PUT DRYDEN back in net for Game Six that evening on a hunch he would catch fire and come up with a much better effort than his two performances in Canada. Sinden admitted Dryden "didn't play well in either." Sinden's hunch was correct.

On defence, Savard was ready to play again after his ankle injury and took over from Seiling in the pairing with Lapointe. Sinden had been pleased with how his team had performed in the first two periods of Game Five. Accordingly, he only had two minor changes up front: Dennis Hull replaced the departed Gilbert Perreault, and Red Berenson stood in for Frank Mahovlich. Frank's performance had not been up to his usual standards.

On the Soviet side, Bobrov continued to experiment, seemingly not fully satisfied with his defensive and forward combinations—or maybe just looking for fresh legs from his secondary players. Kuzkin and Gusev were replaced once again by the younger Vasiliev and Shatalov on defence. The "Kids Line" suited up while Mishakov, Martyniuk and Blinov watched from the stands.

Sinden and Ferguson wore suits instead of their standard blazers in an attempt to change things up, but what they couldn't change up was their level of emotion. Sinden could have worn a hole in the concrete flooring with his constant pacing back and forth behind the bench, only stopping on occasion to pick up a towel to dry off his sweaty hands. Ferguson, seated right behind the boards adjacent to the gate to the bench, was up and down like a jack-in-the-box with plenty to say.

The Soviets outshot Team Canada in the first period twelve to seven, largely due to having a man advantage for six of the twenty minutes as a result of a tripping penalty to Gary Bergman and later a double minor to Phil Esposito for charging. There were no goals by either side, but the Soviets' smooth-flowing game was disrupted by the heavy Canadian checking, as well as anticipated Canadian hits ("hearing footsteps").

Serge Savard made the presence of his return felt from the very beginning, with his spinning and twirling, often carrying the puck out of the Canadian defensive zone on his own. He and the other five Canadian defencemen (Park, Bergman, White, Stapleton and Lapointe) were jelling and quickly becoming a dominating force, earning the respect of the previously freewheeling Soviet forwards.

Liapkin opened the scoring for the Soviets just after the second period began, at 1:12, on a long, seeing-eye shot from the point, with assists from Yakushev and Shadrin. Dryden was playing deep in his net, in contrast to his approach in his two losing games in Canada. Ragulin went off for interference at 2:09, but no sooner had he returned to play when Team Canada scored three goals in only a minute and twenty-three seconds. Dennis Hull started it off with a close-in shot from Tretiak's right at 5:13, followed by a similar shot from the other side of the net by Yvan Cournoyer at 6:21, and then Paul Henderson caught Tretiak asleep with a slapshot from just inside the Soviet blue line at 6:36, putting Canada ahead by two.

Valeri Vasiliev, the young Soviet defenceman, demonstrated he wasn't afraid of the rough stuff and became involved in several pushing and shoving skirmishes to the side and behind his net. He and Lapointe went off together for one such roughing scrap at 8:29, leaving both teams to play down one skater. Both sides were required to play four on four, even with off-setting penalties.

Then, at 10:12, one of the most significant moments of the entire series occurred. Valeri Kharlamov gathered up the puck at centre ice, broke down the right wing, and crossed over the Canadian blue line. Bobby Clarke caught up to him from the back and side and laid a two-handed wood chop against Kharlamov's ankle. He didn't fall to the ice, but the referee immediately stopped the play and called a two-minute penalty for slashing, as well as a ten-minute misconduct.

It didn't appear that there was much significant damage at the time, as Kharlamov carried on and returned to the ice a number of times until the end of the game. Foster Hewitt and Brian Conacher, the two Canadian television announcers, said during their broadcast that they were uncertain what had happened except for the fact that Clarke had been penalized.

Then, at 17:02, Dennis Hull received a two-minute slashing call. It only took nine seconds, at 17:11, for Yakushev to score in close on the power play with assists from Shadrin and Liapkin. The marker brought the Soviets to within one goal at 3–2.

Ferguson was no longer up and down from his seat—just up, chirping away at the referees for their penalty calls and what he thought were botched offside calls. Ferguson finally had one thing too much to say and was assigned a bench penalty at 17:46. At almost the same time, Phil Esposito drew a penalty for taking a long run at Alexander Ragulin, catching him with a high stick that blooded Ragulin's cheek.

The combined result was a two-minute minor for Ferguson, which Cournoyer served, and a five-minute major for Esposito, with Team Canada having to play two men short for a prolonged time. Surely the Soviets would tie the game before long, as the power play had been a major strength of theirs throughout the series.

But the unravelling stopped. Team Canada bore down. Their three remaining skaters were able to clear the puck several times, and they largely kept the Soviets to the outside perimeter. Dryden made some big saves. Petrov and his teammates claimed to have jammed the puck into the net at one point, but no light came on, there was no signal from the referees, and play continued. Perhaps it was fortunate for Team Canada there was no video review at that time.

After two tense minutes Cournoyer leapt from the penalty box and Team Canada held off the Soviets for the remainder of the second period. Phil Esposito still had two and a half minutes to serve in the third period.

The atmosphere was tense. You could feel it, you could see it, you could smell it.

Sinden was hot—even hotter than usual, if that was possible. At the end of the period, he chased the two West German referees up the corridor to the common dressing room area. Ferguson continued to smoulder, and the Team Canada players were steaming. They weren't alone.

The Soviet coaches and players were livid over the attack against Kharlamov. The Canadian fans were in a lather. A loss in this game would mean a series defeat for Team Canada. The Soviet fans had become very animated, with heavy, shrill whistling that drowned out the referees' calls on more than one occasion.

Strangely, despite all the action and theatrics, each side had managed only eight shots apiece on goal.

If the volcano was going to erupt, I thought it might occur in the corridor that both teams and the referees shared. For some reason the Palace of Sports was designed to put everyone together, rather than having separate entrances to the ice for each team, as in the NHL rinks. The Soviet authorities probably assumed there would be no fighting in the corridors. They might have assumed wrongly on this occasion.

Not that I was going to intervene in any brawl between players on skates and with sticks, but it seemed proper for me to stand in the corridor between the two dressing-room doors, possibly as some form of diplomatic peace symbol.

The two referees emerged, followed by the Soviets, and both groups went onto the ice. That was a good thing. The door to the Team Canada dressing room remained closed. OK, no big deal. They were a few seconds late. Time passed and a Russian official asked me to knock on the door. I refused. There was no sense stepping into a scalding cauldron. Surely, they would return, I thought, and not stage a boycott. They were down one player to start the third period, but up by one goal. All was not lost—yet.

Finally, the door opened and out they came.

Sinden later said he held the players in the dressing room in order to calm them down and collect themselves. He also wanted to send a message to the referees and, by the delay, attempt to throw the Soviet players off their game. The strategy of mind games was at work.

I chose not to go back to my seat. I thought my interpreting ability might be called upon at some point, given the way things were escalating, so I took up a standing position behind the left-hand side of the Canadian bench with Rod Seiling, who was not playing. Frank Mahovlich, also in civvies, stood in a similar position on the right-hand side of the bench. Sinden's pacing area was cut down as a result, but he didn't seem to notice.

The third period was nerve-wracking. More close checking. The shots on net were limited to under ten a side (USSR 9–Canada 7). Team Canada could not afford to lose the game or have it end in a tie. With just over two minutes left in the game, at 17:39, the mild-mannered Ellis, one of Canada's best penalty killers, was sent off for holding. Another man advantage for the Soviet team, and all the Canadian fans held their collective breath. But the Russians could not stage a comeback this evening. Team Canada would live for another day.[138]

Lost in the turmoil was the most valuable players selection: Alexander Yakushev, again, and Vladimir Lutchenko for the USSR; Gary Bergman and Ken Dryden for Team Canada. This was the second game in a row in which a Canadian goaltender had been selected—perhaps Mikhailov's pre-series assessment grid about Canada's advantage in net might have validity.

AFTERWARD, SINDEN, FERGUSON and Eagleson, as well as the Canadian players, would continue to rant about the two West German referees, accusing them of being incompetent and favouring the Soviets.

Meanwhile, Bobrov—and it seemed everyone else in the USSR—now had a public enemy number one in the form of Bobby Clarke, a slashing poster boy for everything that was wrong with "hooliganism" in Canadian hockey. Despite Yakushev's comments after Game Five, many Soviet observers would say the crippling of Kharlamov was the real turning point of the series. The incident stuck in the minds of Russians for decades afterwards. One subsequent Canadian ambassador who served in Moscow in the early 1990s said that in some circles it was equated with dark events like the 900-day German encirclement and siege of Leningrad during the Second World War.[139]

Just to make the evening complete, Eagleson, while seated in the stands, had attracted the attention of a Soviet militiaman[140] when he intervened in a verbal dispute between Joe Kryczka's wife and a Russian in front of her who was blocking her view by jumping up and down. Why Eagleson felt it necessary to become involved physically with a shove wasn't evident, but it would prove not to be his last encounter with the Soviet men in uniform.

The number of militiamen stationed around the rink had increased significantly from the first game in Moscow. Starovoitov would say in the Soviet defence, "There is concern about possible incidents between our citizens and Canadians, both on and off the ice. We are not used to the demonstrations put on by your fans. The militia commanders responsible have issued orders that a senior officer must be called before any action is taken, but we must ensure there will be good order."[141]

THE UNUSUALLY WARM weather in Moscow had continued throughout the series, and the morning of Monday, September 25, brought another fine day and a great one for sightseeing. Today was the chance for the Canadian players and their wives to have time off together by visiting the Kremlin, with its ruby stars along its walls; Red Square with Lenin's Tomb; the golden domes of the Assumption Church; and the candy-cane colours of Saint Basil's Cathedral.

I went along with them to help out, while Alexander Gresko of the Sports Committee escorted Eagleson, Sinden, Ferguson, Cannon and Haggert.

Everyone seemed in good spirits. The players appeared to organize themselves along the lines of their NHL teams (like Henderson, Ellis and Glennie of the Toronto Maple Leafs), but that may simply have been because of the familiarity of their respective spouses with each other. There was much picture-taking and some questioning of the tour guides, led by Ken Dryden's personal interest in history and foreign environments.

We looked just like a group of regular foreign tourists, except for a few, like Brian Glennie, who had worn their white Team Canada wind-breakers with the red sunburst maple leaf (same as their hockey jerseys). This attracted some keen Russian autograph-seekers.

While we were on the bus tour, an undetected political bombshell went off in Premier Kosygin's office in the Kremlin. The Soviet leader had a fifty-minute conversation with Senator Laing, who was accompanied by Under Secretary Ritchie and Ambassador Ford. Hockey initiated the discussion, with Kosygin congratulating Laing on the Canadian victory the previous evening in Game Six. But he also expressed his "concern about the roughness of play." He had attended the first game in Moscow, and watched the second on TV, but was "upset" by Canada's play. Kosygin had expected the professionals to show how to combine a game of strength with beauty, but they were not what he thought they were. He now realized their lives depended on how they play, "unlike our players who are not professional." These were his own views, he added, and not for the ears of the public or the players.

Kosygin acknowledged, however, that the matches were "a great cultural event and brought our peoples closer together." Both teams were benefiting from the games, and he thought there were good relations among the players, though they might be forgotten in the heat of the battle. He wanted Prime Minister Trudeau to know Soviet spectators were shouting "friendship," even when the Soviet team was behind in the first game.

Senator Laing avoided commenting on the nature of Canadian play, but observed the Soviet players were strong and tough themselves, and many of the three thousand Canadian fans already wanted another series the next year. He suggested that planning for this begin before this series was over. Kosygin agreed.

The Soviet premier also spoke generally about how well the bilateral Canada–Soviet relationship was progressing and asked that his pleasure at this be conveyed to the prime minister. Laing mentioned that B.C. Hydro had purchased Soviet turbines and that the appropriate authorities in Manitoba were likely to do so as well. There also was a discussion about the large sales of Canadian wheat to the USSR.

All very interesting, but what really caught my attention in my embassy colleague's report on this meeting was the wrap-up discussion about the Canadian federal election.

Kosygin had said, "We are convinced Prime Minister Trudeau will win the election and if he needs any support, we will send some people to vote for him." Laing remarked that Party leader Brezhnev, during the first game, had already offered to send tapes of support for the prime minister for broadcast in Canada. Senator Laing attempted to forestall this unwanted offer by saying any such tapes would have to wait to be used until after the election on October 30. While the report did not make any explicit mention of it, Senator Laing almost certainly must have also equally rebuffed the premier's offer of election support, whether the premier was kidding or not. Kosygin ended the meeting with the remark, "No other Canadian leader has ever been as well known or popular in the USSR as Prime Minister Pierre Trudeau."[142]

Kosygin's professed enthusiasm for the prime minister was understandable, and a positive development in the context of our stated objective to improve relations with the Soviet Union and reduce the risk of military conflict. But the apparent willingness of Soviet leaders to become involved in Canada's elections, in my view, was a big step too far. Mind you, it should not have been unexpected, as election interference in other countries was not new for the USSR (or Russia in current days), and it is known to be a continuing trait of Great Power international politics.

OF A MUCH more mundane nature, but still an intriguing matter, was the reputed case of the listening device and the chandelier at the Intourist hotel. As the story went, it was either Frank Mahovlich, due to paranoia, or jokesters Phil Esposito and Wayne Cashman,[143] who were the persons involved. Apparently, the bolts on a flat metal box on the floor of a hotel room, a perceived listening device, were unscrewed, sending a chandelier crashing to the floor below. Despite denials it had happened, Patrick Reid would say he saw the remains of a large lighting fixture being carted away by the hotel staff.[144] Years later, the Soviet players, when queried about this incident, would poo-poo it, saying it was all make-believe, and ask what would be achieved by bugging the Canadian players. The fact was there were electronic bugs in the hotel, plenty of them, but maybe not in the iron works of that chandelier.

The most interesting aspect of this affair, though, was that it was reminiscent of an experience Coach Bobrov was said to have had the night he and the Soviet team were preparing to depart for Canada. The coach received a frantic telephone call from his wife advising him their own newly installed apartment chandelier had fallen from the ceiling and shattered on the floor. Bobrov is said to have replied, "It's a good luck sign, we'll win."[145]

For those with a superstitious bent, and following Bobrov's lead, the crashing chandelier at the Intourist hotel may have changed Team Canada's luck in Moscow.

Bugging aside, several Canadian players and fans also reported multiple phone calls in the middle of the night and rooms being entered by people who didn't appear to be hotel staff. A few fans told embassy staff about being followed around Moscow by suspicious Russians in civilian clothing, who also shadowed them at the arena.

Then there was the mysterious case of the "missing" steaks and beer. After the first night's steak dinner for the Canadian players in their hotel, some extremely large steaks disappeared from the refrigerators and were replaced by cuts half their size. Apparently, this wasn't part of a nefarious Soviet plot but the result of a Canadian staffer telling the hotel chefs that portions had to be reduced to ensure the supply lasted until the end of the series. After some hungry players complained, the full-size steaks returned. No doubt there may also have been some pilfering of quality meat, as often happens in hotels around the world. As for the missing beer, no one knows for sure what happened to it. The embassy had lots of backups, though—just not Labatt's.

Kukushkin, the Soviet journalist, would later write that some Soviets believed that all this petty agitation and complaining was simply a ploy by the Canadian officials to rev up their players against the USSR. Maybe, but it didn't take much time in Moscow to make one suspicious about everything. Also noteworthy: the Soviet players had been feted at one gourmet meal after another in Canada, but nothing similar had occurred as yet for the Canadian players in Moscow.

The night of September 26, though, attention shifted back to actual hockey. Game Seven—another do-or-die match for Canada—got underway. The Canadian fans sang the national anthem even louder than before. Telegrams, letters and postcards from across Canada continued to flow into the dressing room, where they were now directed, some with thousands of signatories affixed to them. One was from the HMCS *Yukon*. Another from the Sisters of Charity in Moncton, New Brunswick, with the message: "Use your heads and your legs...we will take care of the knees." There was even one in Russian from a woman and addressed to Phil Esposito: "You have won our Sympathy—Leave good impression of your visit—Don't Fight On Ice." Every message was taped to the walls inside and adjacent to the Canadian dressing room along a seventy-five-foot corridor. The players were hyped by the outpouring of Canadian support. They were still backed into a corner, but at least up off the floor.

Sinden made only two changes to his line-up: Goldsworthy for Berenson up front and, somewhat surprisingly, Tony Esposito in net instead of Dryden, who had played so well in Game Six. Sinden's rotation continued.

The Soviets were without Kharlamov.

Bobrov fell back to the "saving dignity" formula that he used in Montreal, utilizing seven defencemen and ten forwards. The veterans Gusev and Kuzkin would draw in once again, and he would retain the combative Vasiliev. The other defenceman from Game Six, Shatalov, would sit out. Up front, the kids Lebedev and Bodunov would be replaced by Blinov and the other Soviet player who enjoyed the rough stuff, Evgeni Mishakov.

While a number of fans, journalists and hockey people had congratulated Sinden on the Game Six victory, many more of them were telling him how to win Game Seven. Keep hitting them. Knock them out of the rink. Forecheck. Body-check. Be disciplined. Carry the puck. Dump and chase the puck. Shoot from afar. Shoot from close in. Jam the net. Like backseat drivers, only worse, everyone thought they knew the best way forward.

Throwing in my own gratuitous advice, I mentioned to Sinden that he needed to touch the brakes to avoid a parade to the penalty box and having to repeatedly face the now-vaunted Soviet power play. Those brakes would have to include both Ferguson and himself. A bench penalty, like Ferguson had incurred in the Game Six, was just as potentially injurious as a penalty called on a player on the ice.

For Game Seven, Sinden and Ferguson were back to wearing their blazers again. I was in my regular seat with Laurielle and the embassy staff, with most of the non-dressed Canadian players sitting together just in front of us.

There were several line changes on the ice before the puck was even dropped, with both sides trying to establish just the right combinations to best match each other. The game started slowly—no immediate carry over of the zest of the last match. Each player closely marking his opponent. The Swedish referee, Dahlberg, and Bata from Czechoslovakia surprised their Canadian critics by assessing the first penalty to the USSR: Mikhailov, for tripping after only two minutes. He was just back on the ice when Esposito, parked in his customary position fifteen to twenty feet in front of the Soviet net, took a pass from Ellis in the corner, turned and beat Tretiak at 4:09.

Phil Esposito's leadership counterpart on the Soviet team, the rangy number 15, Alexander Yakushev, then scored on Tony Esposito at 10:17 with a long slapshot from just inside the Canadian blue line. The slapshot was a weapon the Soviets weren't supposed to have in their arsenal.

Esposito, who seemed to be everywhere on the ice, found himself in the penalty box at 12:39 for cross-checking the feisty Mikhailov. Esposito sat down but immediately jumped up again and began pointing at Mikhailov. He ran his hand across his throat in a cutting action and displayed his fists, indicating he was ready to fight the Soviet player.

Never one to be shy, Esposito, when he had been penalized in the previous game, had used his hand in a choking motion on his throat to express his displeasure to the referees at their call. Both these gestures were not as well received by the Soviet fans and players as had been his pratfall performance in Game Five.

While Bill White was off for a subsequent penalty for interference, Vladimir Petrov broke in alone at 16:27 and put the Soviets ahead. Their dominant power play was at work once again. The advantage didn't last long when, at 17:34, guess who took another pass in the slot and fired it home past Tretiak.

The first period ended with two goals and three penalties apiece. Shots on goal were limited to nine for Canada and only six for the USSR.

The two referees were functioning well and calling quick whistles behind the nets and along the boards in an effort to forestall dust-ups. There were the usual offside calls but with fewer objections than at the last game. Two-line passes were not permitted in international rules.

The second period brought no scoring but seven penalties—four of them to Canada. The only real man disadvantage, though, came when Gilbert was sent off for hooking at 0:59. Later, at 6:04, Parisé took a slashing call, but he was followed quickly to the penalty box only seven seconds afterwards by Anisin for hooking. Esposito and Kuzkin got into a fencing match at 12:44 and both were penalized for roughing. Kuzkin, showing he wasn't going to be pushed around, took another roughing penalty at 15:14, but that was evened up when Stapleton received two minutes for holding ten seconds later. The referees were evening up their calls. The only problem with the continuing deadlock was that the Soviet team was starting to whirl, outshooting Canada by thirteen to seven.

Both Esposito brothers were performing well—Phil being a stand-out on the penalty kill and Tony, not to be outdone by his older sibling, shedding incoming Soviet shots from all angles. The Canadian defence was rock solid, led this time by White and Stapleton. Bergman seemed to be part of every altercation in the Canadian zone. Twenty more min-utes to go, and Team Canada was again facing the prospect of losing the series. The intense Canadian fans inched forward in their seats.

It didn't take long for Rod Gilbert to break the tie. At 2:13 of the third period, he found himself alone in the corner with the puck and glided out from behind the Soviet net, backhanding a shot past a startled Tretiak. Canada up 3–2.

Bergman took a holding penalty shortly thereafter, at 3: 26, and Yakushev once more made Team Canada pay with another Soviet power-play goal—it was Yakushev's third power-play goal of the six the USSR had scored so far in the series. He was parked by the side of the net and left Tony Esposito with no chance to stop him. Back to a tie at 3–3.

The Soviets stepped up their play and had Team Canada hemmed in its own zone when Gilbert was penalized for charging at 7:25, even though it appeared more like roughing. What the exact call was didn't matter—Team Canada was playing short again and playing with fire. They managed to keep the Soviet shooters at bay, however, and soon, at the ten-minute mark, it was time to change ends (an IIHF practice intended to ensure both teams had absolutely equal time at each end of the rink).

With just over three minutes remaining in the game, and Canada's prospects looking increasingly dim, Bergman and Mikhailov got into a serious battle along the boards behind the Canadian net at 16:26. The Soviet player instigated it by hooking Bergman's waist, throwing a horse collar around his neck from behind, then attempting to pull him down onto the ice. Bergman spun away from Mikhailov and started to land a couple of punches as both men careened into the boards. Mikhailov fought back as reinforcements for both quickly arrived on the scene, pushing and shoving, with even the mild-mannered Cournoyer throwing a few left-handers at Mikhailov. The referees eventually broke up the melee. I had been standing behind the netting at that point and had a good view of the initial proceedings, but Bergman and Mikhailov ended up on the far side of the scuffling, with several players, including Yakushev and Phil Esposito, blocking my view. As a result, I didn't see it, but Bergman and Sinden said Mikhailov had resorted to using the tip of his skates to kick Bergman several times, tearing his stockings and denting his shin pads. Bergman didn't appear to lodge a specific protest with the referees over this non-hockey action, but once in the penalty box pointed his finger at Mikhailov then drew his hand under his throat in a slashing motion. Both players were given five-minute majors for roughing, not fighting, which would have removed them from any further play in the game. The result of the two penalties was more space on the ice, as each side was obliged to play four on four plus netminders.

This alignment might have favoured the fleet-footed Soviet forwards, but Paul Henderson had proved he could skate as fast as the best of them, as well as being a good sniper inside the offensive blue line. With just over two minutes left, Serge Savard fed Henderson a long pass just shy of centre ice, and he broke into the Soviet zone with two Soviet forwards in pursuit and the two defencemen in front of him. In reality a one-on-four situation. Henderson deked this way and that and, just as Vasiliev was bringing him down to the ice, got off a shot that eluded Tretiak at 17:54.

Pretty wasn't the word for it. Tremendous was. The Canadian fans and players erupted.

The game wasn't over yet, though, The Soviets continued to fire from left, right and centre, and it took two big blocked shots just before the game ended to preserve the Canadian victory.

This would prove to be only the second, and final, game in which the USSR outshot Canada (31–25).[146]

For the third game in a row, Yakushev would be chosen as one of the top two Soviet players, along with Boris Mikhailov, while Phil Esposito and Bill White shared the honour for Team Canada.

THE LONG, HOT Moscow summer came to a sudden end that night. There was wet snow as everyone exited the Palace of Sports. The Canadian fans were exuberant, even delirious, with the result of the game. Some of them needed to fasten their coats against the colder weather. Many others were kept warm by the large quantities of alcohol they had consumed during the game. What they all were surprised to see, for the first time, was a ring of Soviet militia, with rifles, standing watch as people boarded their buses back to the hotels.

A message was being sent. Not everybody received it.

I had gone home to our apartment with Laurielle to get some sleep before the dawn of another eventful day. Our embassy reinforcements were down at the hotels to monitor everything. They reported that the fans were flying high, with the bars jammed, hotel-room parties everywhere, lobbies full and people spilling into the streets, but no major incidents. The militia continued to stand by; just watching. So far, no new arrests.

Twenty-three-year-old Canadian water-skiing champion Pierre Plouffe was already in a Soviet jail awaiting his fate. He had been a prominent member of the crowd from the very first game in Moscow, playing his bugle and waving his Canadian flag on the end of a hockey stick.

Plouffe had gone to the Intourist hotel after Game Six on the Sunday, September 24, to celebrate the Canadian victory that night and had more than one drink too many. Apparently, he had become abusive to a server when she cut him off. A number of glasses ended up busted on the floor. According to the subsequent written embassy report, Plouffe continued to be a source of trouble, and the militia were called at five a.m. First on the scene was an undercover police officer, who Plouffe would later describe as "a big guy in a black sweater, built like a brick." They scuffled. Plouffe was hauled away, and a squad of militia descended upon the hotel.

Patrick Reid of External Affairs would say he appeared on the scene, spoke with the militia commander, and after offering to pay all damages, the militia stood down. Reid described the bar as having been smashed.[147] Reid would add that the word quickly circulated among the Canadian fans and was embellished that "the bar wrecker had been scrubbed, tattooed on his heels and had his hair shorn" and the same would happen to anyone else arrested in Moscow.[148]

Plouffe was returned to the University Hotel, where he was staying, at 9:30 the morning of September 25, but was told by the militia that they would be back. So they were, at six p.m., ostensibly for him to sign some documents. Plouffe didn't return to his hotel, and at ten p.m. his parents called the embassy seeking assistance.

It took most of the next day, September 26, in discussions with the Soviet foreign ministry, before the embassy's chief consular officer, Marie Hyndman, secured a meeting at five p.m. at the militia headquarters for herself and Plouffe's parents. What concerned the three of them, and in particular Plouffe himself, who had been brought into the room, was when the Soviet chief investigator stated he could be charged under two articles of the criminal code related to "severe hooliganism" and "resisting arrest." Article 206 had a sentence of one to five years' imprisonment, while Article 191 had provision for one to two years' imprisonment or one year of hard labour or a fine of one hundred roubles. This was no laughing matter.

The consul made a plea for Plouffe, saying all reports we had about him were that he basically was a person of good character. She added, it was unfortunate he had allowed himself to become involved in an unpleasant affair.

The militia captain explained he was just doing his "professional and juridical duty," but in a hopeful sign said he did not want the militia's actions to be "detrimental to present Canadian–Soviet relations."

Plouffe was allowed to speak with his mother for twenty minutes and then taken back to his cell. Unexpectedly, he was allowed to watch Game Seven on television with two of his guards.

Plouffe remained in jail the next day. The cell was as nasty as might be expected. Peter Hancock from the embassy continued to push the political side of the case, and it paid off as we learned the charges would be dropped and Plouffe would be taken direct from custody and put on his scheduled plane on September 29.

Hancock decided to run with the political opening and proposed Plouffe be allowed to attend Game Eight with the embassy providing his necessary militia guards with two tickets to the game. The offer was met with enthusiasm, but before it was accepted the guards pointed out there were really four, and not just two, of them. Hancock dug deeper into his ticket reserve.[149]

Plouffe would end up watching the game in person, in a row with two sets of his guards on either side. He would be returned to jail after the game, then told a half hour later that he was being released.[150]

Needless to say, Plouffe wouldn't break up any more bars.

WHILE HANCOCK WORKED his impressive diplomatic skills leading up to Game Eight, for me the previous twenty-four hours had been all about the bitter quarrel over who would referee the crucial final and deciding game of the series. The combination of the West German Josef Kompalla and Czechoslovak Rudolf Bata had not really pleased anyone, including Bata himself, who said he had only been informed about his participation just before noon and he preferred working with the Swede, Ove Dahlberg.

The atmosphere between Gresko and Romesky, on the one hand, and Eagleson, Sinden and Ferguson, on the other, had soured dramatically following the referee dispute. There was a very bad taste in everyone's mouth. If this was a Soviet ploy to ignite the ever-present emotions of the three Canadians, it was working. Starovoitov was nowhere to be seen in this confrontation, and Soviet coach Bobrov had neither been asked nor wanted to be part of it.

The USSR had come up a goal short in each of the past two encounters, and now everything was on the line. Bobrov had previously made some significant moves in both his defensive corps and forward lines, without success, and his final decision for Game Eight was to go back to the six defencemen and eleven forwards format. He would give up Ragulin on defence for the medically treated Kharlamov up front in order to see what he could get out of the wounded wing of his injured high-flying star.

While Bobrov stuck with Tretiak throughout the series, Sinden continued to flip his goalies, even though Tony Esposito had played so well in Game Seven. Sinden would tell Dryden at practice, "You're going to start" and, to ensure Dryden knew the coach had confidence in him, added, "and finish." The only other change Sinden made was to bring back Frank Mahovlich—someone Sinden said "knew how to play a big game"—in exchange for Bill Goldsworthy, who was in and out of the Canadian line-up.

After seven games, each coach knew what they could expect from their respective players. Dryden was known to have a nervous stomach before games if he thought about them too much, so he distracted himself by touring around Moscow with Bob Lewis, the correspondent of *Time Canada*. Dryden was inquisitive and spent some of his down-time visiting Soviet sporting facilities and institutes to inquire about training and coaching techniques in the USSR.

Before Game Eight even started, our first confrontation with Gresko occurred at the entrance to the ice, near the penalty boxes. We had brought along Canada's sports gift to present to the USSR Sports Committee, reciprocating their Matryoshka dolls in Vancouver. The gift was an attractive, hand-carved and relatively easy to handle five-and-a-half-foot Pacific Coast totem pole. I was there with Eagleson, Charles Hay of Hockey Canada, and Joe Kryczka of the CAHA, who were preparing to take the totem pole onto the ice to present to the president of the Soviet Ice Hockey Federation. All seemingly straightforward enough, except for when Gresko suddenly intervened to say it would not be permitted, as no provision had been made for the ceremony in the Soviet television script.

It was true, we hadn't talked about gifts for some time, and he hadn't been in Vancouver, but he should have known it was an agreed part of the series. We persisted, but Gresko claimed the television transmission would end immediately if something unexpected happened, citing Soviet broadcasting policy. Shaking my head, I encouraged the Canadian presentation party to go ahead. Nothing happened. The sky didn't fall. The Canadian gift was captured on Soviet television for all its viewers to witness.

The players were introduced. Bergman received loud applause from the Canadian fans, and even louder whistles from their Soviet counterparts, for his contentious battle with Mikhailov in Game Seven. Bergman raised his hand in a defiant V for victory sign. Phil Esposito stepped onto the ice, hugging the boards to keep himself from falling again—his new running gag. A wave of piercing whistles swelled up again as Bobby Clarke was introduced. Mikhailov was lustily booed by Canadian fans, while Kharlamov received a rapturous ovation from the Soviet fans.

I took a seat in the Canadian section, next to Bobby Orr. We exchanged a few pleasantries—a few words about our both having grown up on Georgian Bay, and the progress of the series. We hadn't interacted much at all before this, nor really met in any formal sense, and there was no easy spontaneity to the conversation. While he didn't complain about it, Orr naturally greatly preferred to be on the ice helping his teammates rather than sitting in the stands watching the action, but his knee still wasn't up to the task.

The game was underway. The USSR team started fast, buzzing the Canadian net and dispatching a couple of whistling shots at Dryden. Team Canada was back on its heels.

Kompalla didn't waste much time in calling his first penalty, on White at 2:25 for holding, and followed it up with another holding call at 3:01, this time against Peter Mahovlich. Team Canada was down two players before the ice had a chance to dry. The West German referee appeared to be trying hard to live up to his reputation.

Yakushev, who was turning into a giant killer, was parked beside the Canadian net and banged in a rebound for a power-play goal at 3:34—his fourth man-advantage tally.

Ten seconds later, at 3:44, it was time for the Soviets to be penalized, and Petrov went off for hooking. Two dozen seconds later, all hell broke loose.

J.P. Parisé knocked down a Soviet player exiting his zone and was penalized for interference. When Parisé protested too much, he was given a ten-minute misconduct penalty. He was steaming as he entered the penalty box. Then, for some reason, he turned around and skated over to the Canadian bench, which was in full cry itself, with Sinden in the thick of it. Further energized, Parisé skated back to the middle of the ice, did a loop, and then charged at Kompalla with his stick upraised in both his hands. Parisé circled away without touching the referee, but it was a clear, threatening action.

When it was announced Parisé had received a game misconduct and was finished playing for the rest of the match, Sinden threw a stool and then a chair onto the ice from the Canadian bench. A couple of towels came flying after. The Canadian fans started up a new chant of "Let's Go Home, Let's Go Home," echoing Eagleson's public threat about the referees a day earlier. I could see Romesky at the boards, near the penalty box, trying to get the attention of the referees and Eagleson in the middle of the Canadian bench. If Eagleson had said "that's it" at that moment, there was no doubt the Canadian players would have followed him back into the dressing room. But he didn't, likely remembering the conversation the previous evening with Senator Laing and Ambassador Ford.

There was a solid wall of Soviet militia around the Canadian bench to maintain separation between the players and the Soviet fans, in the event either decided to take action against the other.

Players continued to circle, seeking answers from the referees as to penalties, but the temperature began to ease. There was still a game to be played, and Canada was still only down 1–0.

Bata would later say Parisé had yelled out "I'll kill you" when he ran at Kompalla, and that he, Bata, had gone to the timer's bench, in light of the mayhem, to recommend the game be called off. The Soviet officials, led by Romesky, would not oblige him. Kompalla was traumatized though and, according to Bata, largely put his whistle away for the rest of the match.

Foster Hewitt, doing the television broadcast, would say, "The Parisé incident nearly set the place on fire."

It was difficult though to envision what I could do, if anything, in this escalating situation beyond attempting to go to the Canadian bench to try to cool down Sinden. But I was sandwiched in the middle of the row of seats and everyone was packed tight.

Now with something to talk about, Orr and I discussed what had just happened. We had differing opinions. He blamed the referees. He had been manifestly unhappy with the two Germans going back to the games in Sweden. I noted we had spent hours negotiating with the Soviets about the referees, had reached an agreement about them that had got rid of one of the Germans, and even if this was unsatisfactory, we would have to play and win in spite of them. The actions of Parisé and Sinden, I said, weren't helpful; they were disappointing and didn't reflect well on the Canadian team and on Canada. Orr didn't accept this at all, apparently being of the Vince Lombardi school in which "winning isn't everything—it's the only thing." *How* you win is also important, I said, and pointed out that our diplomatic objective in this series was to build bridges with the USSR, not blow them up. "You've been in Moscow too long," he said.[151] We obviously were on completely different wavelengths.

First-period play resumed.

Esposito found himself in front of the Soviet net when Park centred the puck. It went in off Lutchenko, possibly with the Soviet defence-men's help, but that didn't matter: 1–1.

Ellis and Petrov were sent off together at 9:27, followed by another Team Canada penalty, this time to Cournoyer, at 12:51. In the ensuing Soviet power play, Lutchenko redeemed himself with a long shot from the blue line, which beat Dryden, at 13:10. Kharlamov assisted, but then found himself down on the ice near the Canadian bench. He limped off.

The New York Rangers duo of Jean Ratelle and Brad Park combined on a lovely give-and-go at 16:59 to tie the score once again. The first period ended 2–2, with Team Canada, despite receiving the majority of the penalties, holding a fourteen to twelve lead in shots on goal.

Orr and I left the seats separately and went to the dressing room area.

As the second period got underway, I spotted Gresko and moved in to stand beside him. If the place exploded again, it probably was a good idea to know where he was so we could try and resolve matters.

Shadrin scored after only twenty-one seconds, following a shot which catapulted off the netting behind Dryden and landed right on the Soviet winger's stick. Exactly what Sinden had worried about from the first day at the Palace of Sports.

The pace quickened. Kharlamov appeared on the ice but was labouring.

White skated in from the blue line and took a perfect feed from Gilbert for a tip-in at 10:32. Game tied again, 3–3, after the third Canadian comeback.

I initiated a conversation with Gresko about the diplomatic symmetry of a perfectly tied eight-game series (three wins, three losses and two ties). He was no diplomat, though, and pointed out that, under IIHF rules, if a series or tournament is tied in games, the winner is decided by total goals scored. He smiled. The USSR would be the winner. Gresko's smile widened when Yakushev ended up all alone with the puck after a faceoff in the Canadian end and buried it, unassisted, at 11:43. Alexander Yakushev vs Phil Esposito. Phil Esposito vs Alexander Yakushev. Head-to-head as both the points leaders and inspirational leaders of their respective teams.

Gresko brushed off all talk of the consequences of a possible tied series when Vasiliev widened the Soviet lead to 5–3 on yet another power-play goal, at 16:44, with Stapleton off for cross-checking.

Perhaps Gresko hadn't noticed, but Kharlamov had taken a shift on the power play and then never reappeared the rest of the game.

Kuzkin was sent off for elbowing at 18:06, only the second penalty of the fast-paced second period and a marked contrast to the first.

I informed Eagleson of Gresko's comments about the consequences of a tied game. Upon enquiring of Gresko and receiving the same message, Eagleson passed it along to Sinden and the team in the dressing room.

One period to go.

AN UNEXPECTED AND incongruous figure showed up in the hallway outside the Canadian dressing room at intermission. Maya Plisetskaya, the Russian prima ballerina, was here to speak with Phil Esposito. She wished to reciprocate Esposito's enthusiastic applause for her performance at the Bolshoi Ballet the previous night. She referred to him as the "primo ballerino" of hockey and greeted him when the Canadian players came out of the dressing room. She subsequently was criticized by the Moscow cultural elite for urging Esposito on to feats of valour and for what was to transpire in the third period.[152]

Two goals down. It was a hill, or rather a mountain, to climb. The USSR team had never lost an international match when it was ahead by such a margin going into the third period. The Soviet journalists must have been aware of this fact, as Kukushkin would note, as they all would linger at the Press Bar for another round of drinks after the puck was dropped.

But Team Canada had scored three goals in twenty minutes or less twice before in this series: in the third period of Game Two in Toronto and in the second period of Game Six here, in Moscow.

The Soviets started strong, and Dryden was forced to make a big save on a two-on-one rush.

Phil Esposito again took charge, and from his office in the slot scored on a heroic pass from behind the net from Peter Mahovlich, who was pinned by two Soviet players. Time: 2:27 of the third period.

The hill was being climbed, led by the Team Canada's sherpa, Phil Esposito. Perhaps the encouragement of the ballerina had lingered in his mind—or Gresko's challenging comments about the consequences of a tied game.

Gilbert and Mishakov got into a full-fledged fight at 3:41, with the Soviet left winger dripping blood. IIHF rules called for ejection from the game for fighting, but for some reason they were only given five-minute majors.

The two teams were again reduced to four skaters each.

As if to show they were not totally biased, the referees then assigned a two-minute penalty to Vasiliev at 4:27 for tripping. Canada now had a four-on-three advantage for over a minute. But no results. The teams changed ends at the ten-minute mark. The Soviets were checking closely, desperately attempting to hold on to the lead. The momentum though was clearly with Team Canada, who were outshooting the USSR team by a wide margin. Pat Stapleton would say that by this point they could anticipate the Soviets' "set plays," break them up and counter-attack.

From a wild scramble in front of Tretiak, Cournoyer, assisted by Phil Esposito—who else?—and Brad Park, scored the tying goal at 12:56. The Canadian players celebrated. The Soviet players dropped their heads in acknowledgment that it had gone in. Bata would say he saw the puck enter the net and was standing at centre ice—a sign a goal had been scored. The goal light, though, hadn't gone on. It had been late before. I was standing in the corner, beside the boards in the Canadian end, and it was difficult to make out what happened next across the ice, but I could tell it would become another incident.

Patrick Reid, who was in close vicinity, witnessed Alan Eagleson jump to his feet, attempt to leapfrog people in front of him and make his way to the timekeeper's box, all the while yelling and pointing at the goal light. Reid said the goal light came on as Eagleson crashed into a line of militiamen. They decided to remove the unknown disruptor from the arena.[153] There was no evidence they were carrying weapons of any kind.

Reid grabbed a Soviet protocol official and went to Eagleson's aid, but Pat Stapleton and Peter Mahovlich, who noticed Eagleson being hauled away, got there first.[154] Mahovlich, without hesitating, scaled the boards with his stick raised. Everyone from the bench, players in uniform and some not, coaches and trainers alike, arrived like the cavalry, and soon Eagleson was on the ice and being escorted to the Canadian bench. Various hand gestures were made along the way to the crowd in general, most noticeably by Eagleson, his assistant Mike Cannon and Team Canada trainer Joe Skro.

The Soviet crowd was stunned and silent. They had never seen anything like it in their controlled environment. The Canadian fans started up with the "Da, Da, Canada. Nyet, Nyet, Soviet" chant. External Affairs Under Secretary Ed Ritchie buried his head in his hands.

Most of the fracas was captured on Soviet television, the transmission to Canada, and the other international feeds, especially the Team Canada gathering at the boards and the group escorting of Eagleson to the bench. Sure, it was done in the heat of the moment, but it was a stupefying action. What was Eagleson thinking? That the delay in illuminating the goal light was all part of a further communist plot that he alone was going to overcome?

Given the sky-high emotions of everyone else at the time, and an arena ringed with police, it all could have spiralled out of control and gone terribly wrong. Did anyone really believe the Canadian bench at the Palace of Sports, in Moscow, in the USSR, actually provided a safe haven from the Soviet authorities if they had wanted to take action? The government-to-government involvement with the series, and the negotiated understanding that the militia would go easy on Canadians, was what saved the day.

Play finally resumed. Just over seven minutes to go.

Phil Esposito was playing like Hercules on skates. The "best of his life," according to Brian Conacher, the CBC colour commentator. Already a goal and an assist in the third period.

Hull and Petrov accosted each other at 15:24, with the Canadian sent off for high-sticking and the Soviet player for elbowing. Back to playing four-on-four for the next two minutes.

No damage on either side. Two and a half minutes to go. The clock wound down as the Soviet authorities prepared to declare victory.

Then the energy of play shifted.

Henderson replaces Peter Mahovlich. He, Cournoyer and Esposito streak into the Soviet zone. For whatever reason, Liapkin falls to the ice by himself at the Soviet blue line and is out of position. Vasiliev, the other defenceman, fails to clear the puck. Henderson reappears in front of the Soviet net, after falling behind it, and suddenly Esposito swats a pass to him. Henderson shoots. Tretiak saves it. He shoots again.

"Henderson has scored for Canada."

The time: 19:26. Thirty-four seconds remaining on the clock. One last desperate Soviet rush and the puck is cleared. The Canadian fans start the countdown: eight, seven, six, five...

Final score, 6–5 for Canada.

Bedlam among Canadian fans, still able to able to produce full-throated cheers even after several hours, and indeed multiple days, of having done so. Joyous hugging among Team Canada players, coaches and staff. Pat Stapleton quietly makes his way to the Soviet end and picks up the almost forgotten puck.

Before the rink became deserted, Phil Esposito and Bill White were told to stay on the ice to receive souvenir samovars as the best Canadians of the match, while Vladimir Shadrin and Alexander Yakushev—for the fourth straight game—received specially designed Canadian medallions. Vladislav Tretiak had twice been selected for his play in Canada, but not once in Moscow.

The Soviet players were downcast but not glum. Victory had been within their grasp for the last three games but had eluded their ambition. They would need to learn to play the full sixty minutes of a game right to the end. Still, there was pride in having held their own with the professionals. The Soviet fans had slipped quietly into the night, perhaps ruminating on another sporting loss after Boris Spassky's earlier chess defeat and wondering whether it might have something to do with the poetic Slavic soul being destined to suffer.

I didn't join the jubilation of the Canadian players in their dressing room, nor attend the makeshift dinner Gresko had organized at the Metropole hotel for both teams but which had only sparse Soviet attendance. Many of the Canadian fans took their peaceful celebrations to Red Square with conga lines, while militiamen looked on placidly as any excessive Canadian exuberance remained in check. Hotel bars continued to do a brisk business, while hotel-room parties sprouted aplenty. Fast friends had been made these past ten days.

To those Canadians in Moscow who either played in the series or helped with its organization, our life had revolved almost exclusively around the Palace of Sports. There was the feeling of being inside the eye of a hurricane. We were shielded; blinded from the true impact of what was happening outside, back home in Canada. Only later, when the storm had passed, would we learn that the entire country had come to a halt, with all eyes focused on a grainy television transmission from where we had been.

WHAT A TREMENDOUS opportunity and privilege to have been part of it all—to have been behind both benches, in both dressing rooms, to have seen all eight games in person, and to have participated in most of the negotiations as well as the disputes. A diplomatic baptism by fire.

The series had also taken its toll on me, both physically and emotionally. It had been a draining eight months since my first physical encounter with the "Snowman." The work had consumed almost every waking hour—and many sleepless nights.

The hockey train, miraculously, had stayed on the rails till the end, but just barely. On a number of occasions, it seemed certain to be headed for the ditch. There was no doubt I was thrilled with the Canadian come-from-behind victory, proud of the challenges the team had overcome in a strange land, and impressed by the never-ending perseverance of the players, but there was reason to pause and question the incidents involving Clarke, Parisé and Eagleson. These acts of aggression may not have been out of place in the NHL—in an era when the Philadelphia Flyers, AKA the "Broad Street Bullies," would soon dominate the league with rough play and intimidation—but this was international hockey, a so-called friendship series with a diplomatic objective.

I felt a need to just go back to the quiet of our apartment with Laurielle in order to regain some sense of my sanity. To take a complete break and to spend quality time with her for a change. She had booked a week-long package tour out of Helsinki to Tenerife in the Canary Islands, and we were booked to leave the next day. So what if the Finns liked to break out the vodka as soon as wheels were up and to continue drinking throughout the week. We would spend our time together on the black volcanic sand beaches choosing names for our first child, due in December. A Russian name to mark our posting.

Tatiana.

CHAPTER THIRTEEN

TEAM MAGNIFICENT AND TEAM UGLY

T HURSDAY, SEPTEMBER 28, 1972, had been a momentous day for Canadians. While Henderson's goal was scored during the evening in Moscow, it had been midday or earlier in Canada. Workers across the country had laid down their tools, telephones and order books, students put aside their studies, all to gather in front of television sets for the rare shared experience of watching Game Eight. A coming together of national anticipation. Not just a sporting moment, but a defining cultural event of "where were you when" dimensions. Like the US astronauts' moon landing on July 20, 1969.

An estimated sixteen million Canadians were part of that record audience—three-quarters of Canada's population at the time. More than double the viewers of the previous Stanley Cup Finals.

Paul Henderson's heroic last-minute goal sent Canadians pouring into the streets with unbridled joy, in a fashion unseen since the celebrations in May 1945 marking the end of the Second World War in Europe.

Time magazine's Canadian edition of October 9, 1972, ran a story largely featuring Phil Esposito. The cover displayed a full-page photo of him in action with the caption "The Greatest Show on Ice." Inside the magazine was an illustration of Esposito holding a Trudeauesque rose in his hockey glove with the caption "Canada's first Italian Prime Minister."[155] He was no longer just another hockey guy called Phil from the Sault, but now Mr. Philip Anthony Esposito from Sault Ste. Marie, Ontario with his name on an Order of Canada nomination paper being put forward by the Premier of Nova Scotia, Gerald Reagan—a member of the ruling Liberal Party of Canada. Even though there were no Team Canada players from the maritime provinces,[156] another local premier— Frank Moores of Newfoundland, a Progressive Conservative—wanted to get in on the reflected glory as well by offering a free government paid week-long holiday in the province for any team member.

Other politicians of differing stripes were also front and centre- the New Democratic Party Premier of British Columbia, Dave Barrett, from the press gallery in the legislative building in Victoria; James Laxer of the fringe Waffle movement from a smoke-filled bar in Toronto; and former Prime Minister John Diefenbaker and his wife Olive from their home in Prince Albert, Saskatchewan. All four, as well as ordinary people like a fishing family from down east and a waitress from Devon, Alberta were glued to television sets for Game Eight, with a CBC camera recording their every excited reaction for a special program later named "Where were you in 72?". Even so-called highbrow people who had chosen instead to attend a Shakespeare play in Stratford, Ontario, rose to their feet in applause when an actor cleverly slipped in an off-the-cuff line with the final score.

There were a few, small exceptions to the nationwide euphoria.

"Team Ugly" was not a phrase coined by a disgruntled Soviet journalist, but by John (Robbie) Robertson, a sportswriter for the Montreal Star. Robertson had put out a cry-into-the-wind warning before the series about the skill and training of the Soviet team and predicted they might win (his precise call was the USSR would take two games in Canada— which they did—and all four in Moscow—which obviously missed the mark[157]). Now he climbed onto a perch and rhetorically asked how an impartial European might view what had happened in Moscow and then answered his own question with harshly negative comments about the brutish-like deportment of the team and its leadership.

Whether Robertson's aim was to be provocative, to avoid any possible herd mentality among sports journalists, or to simply report the news as he saw it, his views were largely dismissed by his fellow sports and news columnists. Yet Robertson wasn't entirely alone. The City

Council in Victoria, BC, for one, had only reluctantly agreed to send a congratulatory telegram to Team Canada after Mayor Peter Pollen objected to the negative impact the team's poor sportsmanship could have on future generations.

Prime Minister Pierre Trudeau, though, spoke for the nation in a press release issued on September 29, containing the text of a telegram he had sent to Premier Kosygin: "The historic and exciting hockey series just concluded will long be remembered. This great event has not only brought the teams together but millions of people in Canada and the USSR. I congratulate the Soviet players for their skill and stamina which have won our admiration. Canadians hope that we will have many opportunities to watch them play again."[158]

Trudeau came to Dorval airport in Montreal on Sunday, October 1, joining a tumultuous crowd—estimated in the range of 30,000–50,000—to welcome the team back onto Canadian soil. Merriment and joy were everywhere as the players circulated the tarmac aboard a fire truck.

The Montreal Canadiens players, along with Ferguson, deplaned here as they said their emotional goodbyes to their September teammates and returned to the fold of their NHL club. The remaining players, along with Sinden, Eagleson and staff, carried on to Toronto and were greeted at City Hall by a jubilant crowd of eighty thousand in the pouring rain.

Suddenly, Team Canada was no more. There would be no national celebration for all the players—possibly because of the election campaign or the conflicting demands of the NHL schedule, or both.

Premier Kosygin would respond on October 2 with a diplomatic message of his own to the prime minister: "Thank you for your kind message on the occasion of the hockey game series between Canadian and Soviet teams. I share your view that this series generated wide interest everywhere, and became a great event in the sporting life of our countries. To athletes, including hockey players, and to millions of viewers, the masterly efforts toward outstanding athletic achievement is greatly valued. I wish to express my conviction that Soviet-Canadian athletic ties will be further developed."[159]

The last sentence, in particular, was worth noting in terms of further matches.

The Soviet newspapers, however, were full of Kosygin's private criticism of Team Canada, but without mentioning his name. One published a full page of illustrations about "Canadian professionalism" with a variety of images, including: a boxing glove at the end of a Canadian stick; a bus full of players arriving and then the vehicle being repainted into an ambulance during the match, before carting off injured players; a Soviet hockey matador holding up a cape with a puck on it, and being charged, like a bull, by a Canadian player; and a person in both an arm and a leg cast with a chessboard under their arm, being asked, "So how was your chess match with the Canadian professionals?"

On October 4, in a confidential telegram to External Affairs in Ottawa, Ambassador Ford provided his lengthy analysis of what had happened and its impact on Canada's diplomatic relationship with the Soviet Union.[160] His first paragraph captured the essence of the yin and the yang of the series: "I think one can safely say that we have come through the last two harrowing weeks with Soviet-Canadian relations intact, probably improved, and with the Soviet public and official attention focused on Canada to an extent which must be the envy of all other diplomatic missions in Moscow. Although not all of that attention was good, the end result must be to arouse considerable interest in Canada in every sphere and to facilitate our task in other fields of endeavour."

On specifics, Ford wrote: "I do not want to excuse some of the unnecessary behaviour of the Canadian players such as the constant protesting of penalties and particularly threats to referees on several occasions which of course were seized upon by the Russians as examples of Canadian hockey. At the same time the refereeing by the West Germans was incompetent and extremely biased."

He added on the point of the players, "I feel considerable sympathy for a team which was playing in totally unfamiliar surroundings and rules, and tended naturally to adopt the NHL style of play. Furthermore, the Russians did play quite dirty hockey but they were clever at concealing it, their favourite trick being the hard end of the stick during a tussle against the boards and of course they were far more disciplined than our stars."

Regarding Eagleson's ice-crossing affair, Ford stated, "The Soviet militia were nervous and prepared for the worst but the fans, though noisy, were remarkably well-behaved. Incident with police involving Eagleson was well publicized in the Soviet Union but on the same occasion my wife was manhandled by two militiamen when she was consoling Mrs. Eagleson near the players dressing room. Even after she identified herself the police continued to push her roughly. Later I insisted on a Colonel of the militia personally apologizing to Mrs. Ford, which he did."

In summation: "The Soviets were naturally disappointed that they did not win the series and particularly that they lost the final three home games. They should have been delighted that they did so well against Canada's best, but they find it difficult to accept anything but victory. Many viewers no doubt genuinely felt that the Canadians played a rough, tough, dirty game and the Soviet press is still playing up this aspect of the series, but none could have failed to be thrilled by the marvellous display of first-class hockey and most Russians must be happy to see some kind of international hockey competition with Canada starting again. Furthermore, Russians admire toughness and courage and deep down they must respect the skill and bravery of our team. Perhaps the truest reflection of the attitude here towards the games is that Soviet fans, officials and players are already enquiring about the dates for the next series."

As a final point to his report: "I think therefore that the hockey series has helped to improve awareness of Canada in this country, indeed there must be few countries of our size in the world now so well known in the USSR as Canada. I would hope at the same time that the thousands of Canadian fans have profited from their exposure to the USSR to get a clearer idea of this country and what it means to the future of the western world."

A week later, on October 11, a senior official in External Affairs wrote to the ambassador asking for his comments on an enclosed newspaper column from Ted Blackman of the Montreal *Gazette*. Blackman had quoted Eagleson as saying he had received a letter from the ambassador.

Blackman's quote of Eagleson read: "[Ford's] letter, more or less said, 'No matter what anyone says, you did the right thing—that's the only language these people understand.'"

The ambassador wrote back to the senior official on October 20: "I suppose it is pointless to say that I never wrote to Alan Eagleson and, having enough experience of him, I would not even have said such a thing in his company. How he could have invented that he received such a letter from me is simply beyond my comprehension. The damage, however, has been done and I see no way in which it can be repaired."[161]

Ford, who was a master of language and phrasing, did write a carefully crafted letter to Eagleson, on December 15. It was addressed to Mr. Eagleson—no crossing out of the formal salutation and replacing it with the more personal Alan.

I was about to send you a Christmas card when I received your letter of November 23. So I take this opportunity to send you and your wife all the very best for next year. Whether that will include another hockey series in Moscow is, I presume, in the hands of the Gods.

In retrospect I think we can consider the hockey series a great success and I have so assessed it in my report to the Governement. In spite of the many snide remarks made by Soviet officials and the press about our type of hockey I think the important thing is that maybe as many as 150 million Russians saw the games and were able to appreciate the high standard of Canadian hockey.

I don't need to say how much of the success was due to your unstinting efforts. You know it much better than I do but I got pretty angry when I began to receive the Canadian papers and saw some of the unfair comments made about your role. However I have no doubt about your ability to defend yourself.

All in all, it was a great experience and we do hope we can see you and your wife again sometime.

With very best wishes, Robert.[162]

Ford ended the letter less formally than he began.

This contretemps involving Ford and Eagleson passed.

ON OCTOBER 24, TASS news agency carried an English-language translation of an interview with Coach Bobrov in the newspaper *Trud* (Labour/Work), which was intended for foreign audiences and particularly Canada. It contained the official criticisms expressed by the Soviet Sports Ministry but also some hockey insights about the players.[163]

The article began with a declaration that the Soviet national team would not play again in matches with teams that "show the worst sides of professional ice hockey, that respect neither their rivals nor the spectators." At the same time, Bobrov added, Canadians needed to realize that the Soviets were ready to play against professionals if the games were what he described as being "real and noble hockey, requiring courage." The USSR national team was not inferior in any way to Canadian professionals, and there were things the professionals could learn from the Soviet players, such as "thorough physical training."

Bobrov then stated that the Canadians played a rough game in an attempt to intimidate the Soviet players, and when they failed, they started a "hunt" for the best player, Kharlamov, and inflicted "serious injuries" on others. This was because they had come up against a team of "effective and masterful performance."

At same time, Bobrov acknowledged the "high class" of the Canadians, their good technique, that they skated well and were good at forechecking. He noted Canadians "fight with determination until the last second and that is an example for us to follow." Yet, when asked to compare Canadian professionals to European "amateurs," Bobrov expressed the opinion that Europeans are "stronger" and more promising in some respects, such as "tactics."

He was no longer satisfied that "some members" of the Soviet team played as well as the professional stars: "all our players must be better than the professionals." Finding such "replacements" to make this happen would be his main task. The last comment was obviously said with his future job prospects, and the Party bosses, in mind.

A month later, a Soviet documentary film of the series emerged, called *Hockey against Hockey* and directed by B. Rychkov of the Central Documentary Film Studio in Moscow. As the title suggests, its purpose was to demonstrate the differences between the two hockey systems and to make the point that "we do not like such hockey" when referring to the Canadian brand. This was a phrase often used by the Soviet television broadcaster Nikolai Ozerov during the series.

One of Moscow's evening papers, *Vechernaya Moskva*, ran a review of the film, written by M, Gavrilov.[164] He reminded his readers that Soviet sports fans had heard long before the series had started about the "fantastic masterly techniques of the Canadian professionals and their uncompromising toughness." During the series millions had witnessed their skills with a puck—their courageous game all over the ice and their great will to win. But Gavrilov added, the series had "shattered the invincibility of the Canadians" and shown them to be "brawlers and hooligans"—showed how they "knocked down those players of greatest danger to them; organized scuffles and even threatened referees."

Gavrilov described the early moments of the film, during which small Russian boys are playing hockey when two of them, imitating the professionals, enter into a scuffle. The film, he says, proceeds to show the "hooligan tricks of the bully Cashman; the nasty behaviour of Phil Esposito and the really gangster attacks of Gary Bergman on the Soviet players." Slow motion and freeze frame are used in the film to demonstrate. Gavrilov notes much of the film repeats shots that were highlighted by the Soviet TV crew during the actual series—including Esposito showing he was ready to cut somebody's throat—but adds that the film shows all this in a more dynamic and emphatic fashion.

Gavrilov then goes on to criticize the filmmaker for focusing too much on the games themselves and not enough on the higher context of class structure and communism versus capitalism. In Gavrilov's view, Rybakov missed the opportunity to show the life of "unemployed Canadian professionals" or the "inexorable laws of western competition which make such famous sportsmen like Orr, Esposito, Clarke, Bergman and others fight for their places in the sun with all means possible." The film, in Gavrilov's view, could have been a "meditation and a publicist documentary."

It would have been more accurate of Gavrilov to have said it could have been a communist propaganda film, which it already was.

In her January 1973 review of the film in the journal *Ogonek* (Little Flame),[165] N. Kojevnikova is more lyrical, describing the majesty of the two teams lined up side by side and then arriving on the ice together, largely expressionless and without apparent malice toward one another. She identifies Valeri Kharlamov, Alexander Yakushev, Phil and Tony Esposito, Vladislav Tretiak and Ken Dryden as being names "well known around the world." She writes that this film allows the viewer to see them, and others up close and personal in a manner far better than that provided by the best seats in the arena. It paints portraits of their characteristics.

Kojevnikova describes Tretiak as so attentive and serious that one has the impression he is not in the rink at all, but somewhere else in the midst of trying to solve a difficult mathematical question. On the other hand, she sees Phil Esposito in the film as someone who has an "explosive and imperious character," with a temperament which is both "furious and overwhelming." Describing Kharlamov's skating ability, she calls him a "whirlwind." Wayne Cashman appears, in her view, to be like a gentle "cherub," but rather is a "battling boy."

She also considers the film's comparison of the two head coaches. Bobrov is seen as composed, serious, to one side of the bench, but full of thoughts and nerves about the importance of the struggle on the ice. Then Sinden, energetically moving back and forth behind the bench with his blazer wide open, never taking his eyes off the rink, but crying out in a loud voice. Each in their own manner according to their respective temperaments, she says.

While the film does not mention the scores of the games, she asks whether these differing personal traits really matter to the outcome. She answers her own question that indeed it is very important and mentions the attack against Kharlamov and the stick work against Yakushev. She wonders whether this action is all "childishness" but says no, as the film demonstrates that it becomes "more dangerous and relentless."

Kojevnikova concludes that the film makes it clear there are two elements at play here: the sporting one, as well as morals and ethics. They cannot be separated. "We highly appreciate the skills of the Canadian professionals, but at the same time we cannot accept nor understand their attitude toward their sporting adversaries."

The intent of the writings of Gavrilov and Kojevnikova, about the film, and of other communist commentators who continued to bang the drum of "Canadian hooliganism," was twofold: firstly, to distract the general public in the USSR from the fact the Soviet side lost the series; secondly, and perhaps more importantly, to ensure the Soviet public did not try to emulate the individualism of the long-haired Canadians and their challenge to convention and authority.

As time passed, some of the Soviet press, particularly sports publications, began to put aside all the negative hyperbole and propaganda about Team Canada and to cover the positive hockey lessons learned from the play of the Canadians. *Sports Games*, for instance, ran a lengthy article entitled "Way to The Goal," by Konstantin Loktev, a coach and "Honoured Master of Sports."[166] Loktev's question was: Which way should players approach the net? Direct, with defencemen awaiting, or along the boards to the corner and behind the net with what, he said, were practically no obstacles in the way. In his analysis, the second way was more harmless, as there was less risk of losing the puck. But this method played into the hands of the defence, as they can block the way to the goal and wait for the forward to make a move. Coaches advise, he said, "go straight, don't go aside," but often players ignore this and go the roundabout way. Unfortunately, Loktev said, this also is what the Soviet national team does, as demonstrated in the Summit Series. Only Kharlamov and Yakushev went straight to the net. It wasn't easy, but they did it.

Almost all the Canadians, on the other hand, went straight. Henderson's last-minute goals were achieved with Soviet defencemen in front of him. The Soviet players would hesitate in such a situation, trying to determine whether to go forward or not, or to wait for additional partners to appear. This hesitation worked against them. Henderson didn't wait—he attacked without delay. Loktev believed Henderson would have done the same thing, even if there were three opponents in front of him. The determination to press forward leads to the highest reward—a goal.

Loktev stressed he did not want his readers to think the Canadians were brave and the Soviet players were not. Courage is a component of the game—perhaps not the most important but certainly not the least; "courage is useless if a player remains without the puck." Canadians learn to play this way from childhood. Soviet teams though—especially the junior ones—are not reprimanded for this type of play as long as they can score goals. There are very few Soviet defencemen who are skilled at body-checking and so players have little experience dealing with it. In his opinion, this creates a weakness among forwards at the national level.

Some coaches tolerate the low skills of a forward who is ready to play rough, but the purpose of rough play should be to get the puck. Canadian players forget about their rivals as soon as they get control of the puck and continue to play. Soviet players, after pressing someone to the boards, continue fighting and forget about the puck.

Some commentators in the USSR, Loktev said, criticized the Canadians for their individualism and for not being team players. But when the coach asked it of them, the Canadian players could change tactics easily and often several times during a game: "The Canadians were not repetitious."

In looking at the Team Canada line-up and what was written about it, Loktev said one detail in particular struck him—how many times hard work was mentioned: "Clarke is one of the most hard-working players of the club..."; "Parisé works very hard on the ice; he can do everything even if he is not notable for anything special." In other words,

Sinden included, not only "stars" but also players who spare no effort on the ice.

Loktev praised Sinden for putting Clarke rather than Esposito with Henderson and Ellis, as Esposito and Henderson might feud over who should feed whom. Putting Esposito with the hardworking Parisé and quick Cournoyer took some of the backchecking burden off Esposito and allowed him to do what he does best—play in the forward zone "where he was really indispensable."

The area in front of the net is the most dangerous but, he noted, Soviet forwards often just skate through it. When asked about this trait, the Soviet players say, "I have been there," but Loktev asks what sort of "there" can that be if a forward skates through it once or twice and stops there for less than a second.

This is where Esposito shines. He stays in front of the net but doesn't just stand still. He is always manoeuvring, trying to get into a position where he can receive a clean pass from his teammates. He doesn't worry that the Soviet defence is between him and the goal or breathing down his neck. He bends forward with his stick far in front of him and cannot be moved. As soon as a puck lands on his stick, he shoots. A short, hard shot.

Soviet centres usually stand straight waiting for a pass, making it easy for the Canadian defence to push them around or lift their sticks. Short, hard shots were how most of the goals were scored in the series. Not from long slapshots or lengthy wristers.

Loktev concluded his analysis on a positive note for the USSR. He recalled how Soviet teams had learned many lessons early on from Canadian amateur teams and then overtook and surpassed them. There is no need to overtake Canadian professionals now because, he said, the series showed "we are already on equal ground." But in order to surpass Canadian professionals, it is necessary to learn lessons from them.

The article by Loktev was a breath of fresh air—an effort to get away from communist ideology and back onto the merits of how best to play the game of hockey. That was what the true Russian hockey fan desired.

CHAPTER FOURTEEN

NHL TORPEDOES TEAM CANADA

A LAN EAGLESON MAY have been the first to realize that the series was a money-making opportunity, but it did not take long for the Soviet officials to catch on as well, once they arrived in Canada and saw the tremendous reaction not only of the public but of all levels of government and, most importantly, the avid desire of the Canadian business community to become involved. Hockey is good business, and international hockey at the professional level, particularly for the first time, proved to be exceptional business.

As good businessmen themselves, several NHL owners showed up in Moscow, along with league president Clarence Campbell, anxious not just to witness the games in person, but to play a more direct role in the action going forward. They did not want to play second fiddle to the CAHA, Hockey Canada, the Canadian government, nor the NHL Players' Association, and certainly not the rival World Hockey Association. It was not surprising therefore that there were a variety of formal and informal discussions about a future series and future games even while this series was still underway. I found myself part of them.

In all the encounters, the general secretary of the Soviet Ice Hockey Federation, Andrei Starovoitov, laid out three main points in describing the USSR position: 1) that games of some sort should continue (they had proven to themselves, and particularly to the Party bosses, that they could beat the "professionals"); 2) they wanted to deal with a Canadian organization or persons who could make the games happen with the least amount of trouble (Starovoitov was well aware of the Canadian infighting); and perhaps the key point, 3) that the Soviet side would get an increased share of the large amount of revenue generated in Canada. The first person out of the gate had been Eagleson, who, in Vancouver on game day, September 8, had asked me to join him for a discussion with Starovoitov about the "next series." The latter was accompanied by the ubiquitous Viktor Khotochkin. After some preliminary to-ing and fro-ing, an understanding was reached that the same format would be used as the Summit Series, with two important exceptions: there would be four games played in the USSR and six in North America; and the Soviet side would share the gate and TV revenue from the extra two games. As well, several of the six North American games would be held in the USA. Eagleson believed this arrangement would enable him to more easily persuade the American owners to let their players become involved in another series between Canada and the USSR. (Eagleson did not say why he thought the American owners would agree to having Team Canada marketed in their US arenas, but presumably he believed financial rewards and Players' Association's leverage would do the trick.) While several dates were bandied about for the next series, nothing was agreed upon at the Vancouver meeting.

Harold Ballard, the majority owner of the Toronto Maple Leafs, was present when the series shifted to Moscow, even though he had been convicted a few weeks earlier in Canada on forty-seven of forty-nine counts of fraud, theft and tax evasion and would shortly be sentenced to three consecutive three-year terms in a federal penitentiary. Ballard was known to be staunchly anti-communist and was reported to have called the Soviets "parasites and barnacles who steal our money."[167] With those views, it was surprising he showed up in the communist capital, as well as having allowed Team Canada to practise in Maple Leaf Gardens, hosted the second Canadian game at the Gardens, and permitted three Leafs (Paul Henderson, Ron Ellis and Brian Glennie) to join the team. My only encounter with him was to witness the tail end of an expletive-laden shouting match he had with the IIHF's Bunny Ahearne—the subject matter of the dispute was not clear.

ON SEPTEMBER 23, THE day after the first game in Moscow, NHL president Clarence Campbell, along with owners Bill Wirtz of the Chicago Black Hawks and Bruce Norris and John Ziegler of the Detroit Red Wings, had sought a meeting with Starovoitov. Both Wirtz and Norris served as chair of the NHL board that year. Campbell asked Aggie Kukulowicz and me to attend as advisors, observers and interpreters, which was agreed to by Starovoitov, who had Viktor Khotochkin at his side as usual.

I listened with rapt attention as Campbell began the meeting by outlining the various hockey organizations operating in Canada and then going on to express the NHL's displeasure with "organizational aspects" of the current series. He said, in his opinion, a series like this would never take place again. Before September, the NHL was unsure about the strength of the Soviet team, but this strength had been amply demonstrated in Canada, and he now wanted to discuss future games between the NHL and the USSR. He mentioned that John Ziegler had been travelling around Europe attempting to set up a European Professional League, with teams from Sweden, Finland, West Germany, Switzerland, Czechoslovakia, and with one in London, and he hoped the Soviet Union would join in. The idea was that the winner of the European Professional League would meet the winner of the Stanley Cup for the "World Cup." When asked for his views on this possibility, Starovoitov replied that the Soviet Union was interested in such an idea but its experience, particularly with Czechoslovakia (with whom the USSR currently had major political problems), was that European countries talked a lot but were not prepared to act. In any event, a European Professional League could not start operations for several years and they needed to talk about present possibilities.

Campbell pressed forward, asking if the USSR was prepared to deal directly with the NHL for a series between club teams. The response was yes. Campbell then asked if there would be any problems with the IIHF. Starovoitov wryly answered he was confident Campbell would take all the necessary steps in North America to arrange such games and he himself would look after the IIHF president, adding for good measure, that he foresaw no difficulties with Ahearne.

Starovoitov concluded the meeting by expressing his wish that all future communications should be done through me. This was not totally surprising. We had worked together for many months now and Starovoitov trusted me to be professional and accurate. I also had been involved in the Eagleson talks in Vancouver about another series. Moreover, using me as the go-between with the NHL meant the Canadian government would be in the loop, and Starovoitov was well aware that the current series was the result of an agreement at the highest political levels of both countries. He did not want to get himself offside with his own political bosses in this regard.

The next day, September 24, the day of Game Two in Moscow, Starovoitov had called early to tell me he was ready to meet again with the NHL. The only participants this time were Campbell and Wirtz, with Starovoitov on the Soviet side, accompanied as usual by Khotochkin. Aggie and I again sat in. Starovoitov reported he had spoken with the chairman of the Soviet Sports Committee, Sergei Pavlov, and had received his approval for a series of games between NHL and Soviet teams. This decision, which was made remarkably quickly by Soviet standards, perked up the discussion. In short order an oral agreement was reached for three or four games to take place January 18–30 of 1973 (the coming year) between Central Red Army and "senior NHL club teams." Chicago, New York, Boston and Montreal were mentioned (Norris and the Red Wings for some reason dropped out of the equation, perhaps reflecting Norris's no-show at the second meeting). There also was no reference to Toronto, presumably because Ballard was not onboard with the idea or was not a welcome participant. Financing was discussed, but Starovoitov was unable to decide between a substantial flat fee or a sharing of the gate and TV revenues without specific figures being available from Campbell. These were promised.

Campbell, Wirtz and Starovoitov also reached an oral agreement for a ten-game series to be held during the 1973–74 season. Six games would be held in North America around Christmastime with two Soviet teams, each playing three NHL teams. In return, two NHL teams would come to the USSR in the spring of 1974 for two games each. The Soviet side would share revenue from the extra two games in North America. Campbell, Wirtz and Starovoitov shook hands. Campbell said he would discuss the proposals at the NHL board of governors meeting at the end of October and, following what he believed would be a favourable decision, he would send a formal written proposal to Starovoitov for signature.

The NHL train was getting ready to move out of the station on its own track, leaving Team Canada on a siding. I sought out Eagleson after the NHL meeting and urgently advised him to have his own discussion with Starovoitov to clarify what was happening, particularly in relationship to the earlier conversation in Vancouver. Eagleson agreed and the two of us saw Starovoitov later that afternoon. Starovoitov summarized matters but most importantly said he had no objection to a second USSR–Canada national series "if the Canadians wished it that way." Eagleson indicated that was his preference and suggested a possible ten-game series between the two national teams in March 1974.

While it was satisfying to have the confidence of all sides, I was being put in a difficult jam. Ziegler had made me an offer to work for him and the NHL in developing and carrying out their plans for a European Professional League and separate international matches with the USSR, the Jewel in the European Crown. He had been impressed with what I had done in helping organize the Summit Series, my Russian language skills, knowledge of hockey and ability to operate at a high level with all concerned, particularly in Moscow. He offered a large salary and benefits and said I would work out of their current offices in Montreal. It was an attractive proposal, and I asked for a day or two to think about it. I enjoyed my position as a diplomat. Representing your country and fellow citizens was a privilege and an honour, and it held more value for me than representing a large business enterprise, however exciting that might have been. It was why I had joined the government in the first place. Hockey was great but diplomacy offered so much more of real significance, as well as endless variety. Besides, I was just twenty-eight years old and had only just started my diplomatic career; who knew how far it might take me.

Following the second meeting with Campbell and Wirtz, and after turning down the employment offer and then seeing him again with Eagleson, I told Starovoitov I could not act as a go-between with the NHL and USSR unless I was so instructed by the Canadian government. The NHL was a private entity, and while it represented three Canadian cities at the time, it was primarily USA-oriented. What would happen if an agreement was made for an American team to play a Soviet team, with TV and other arrangements handled by a US company. How would the Canadian government, and by extension myself, be involved? Perturbing also were the remarks of Clarence Campbell about there being no further Team Canada series involving NHL players. I mentioned to Starovoitov that there were other parties to be considered in discussing future games, including Hockey Canada, the CAHA and the Canadian government, and I was sure none of them would be too pleased to learn of Campbell's remarks.

Starovoitov replied that the Soviet government wanted good relations with Canada and that he would pass along my observations to chairman Pavlov.[168] There were no follow-up discussions with Starovoitov, in which I was involved, prior to the end of the series. Aggie did, however, see it in his own best interests to pursue the hockey path, and he became a well-recognized figure on the international circuit, culminating in a major IIHF award in 2004 for the extraordinary manner in which he promoted the sport of hockey worldwide.

Following the series and my return from the one-week holiday, on October 11, I met with Alexander Gresko of the Sports Committee to run over the various options in play and asked him to describe the Soviet position. Gresko said, as I would know, there was interest in holding future games. However, there had been no written formal proposal from the Canadian government as of yet. When pressed, he stated that the current Soviet preference was to play with club teams. Starovoitov was a tough, professional straight-shooter, but Gresko, with his KGB background, often preferred to be more ideological and to take the low road where required. He emphasized there had been unpaid bills at the hotel, for international phone calls and considerable champagne, when Team Canada departed, and that the team had been very undisciplined. The Canadian team leaders, he went on, who were supposed to discipline the players, "were the very people who needed the most discipline, judging from their actions." He believed a club team would be more disciplined, because the owners who paid the players' salaries could control them better.[169]

So much for the professed Soviet belief in the value of workers and unions over that of their bosses.

Gresko was venting, but he was right on the essential point about there being no formal written proposal from the Canadian side. Eagleson, in all likelihood, was playing both sides of the street. The NHLPA would be involved one way or another in either a club or national format, though he likely would have a greater role in pulling the strings with the renewal of the national option. Hockey Canada and the CAHA, on the other hand, would be excluded in a club-vs-club format run by the NHL and would be back to square one on a country-vs-country series without NHL participation. How could there be a formal Canadian proposal in this situation?

My good friend Aggie was keeping me informed on the quiet about the state of the NHL negotiations, and this information was passed back to External Affairs. Starovoitov met in Montreal on December 13, 1972, with Clarence Campbell. The proposed January 1973 matches had been dropped due to a lack of organization by both sides and particularly the requirement to get all relevant secondary parties on board. Starovoitov and Campbell identified November 26–December 9, 1973, as the window for two Soviet teams (Central Army and either Spartak or Dynamo) to play four games each in North America. Starovoitov managed to ratchet up the fee to be paid to the Soviet Ice Hockey Federation to a whopping $135,000, based on a percentage of gate and television receipts as well as compensation in hard currency for transportation costs.[170]

The NHL wanted to firm this up by mid-January of 1973, but Starovoitov later begged off, saying the key decision-makers in Moscow were "sick" (that old political illness again). Despite the enhanced money and the chance to further deflate North American hockey egos in mid-season, Starovoitov was running into trouble at higher levels with the continuing Soviet bugaboo of Olympic and World Championships eligibility.

In late January and early February, I exchanged correspondence via diplomatic bag with Alan Eagleson, who was seeking travel guidance about attending the World Championships in Moscow in March and participating in any further meetings with the Soviet Ice Hockey Federation. He noted that nothing was going to happen on the NHL front without the approval of the Players' Association.

There was no clarity about the extent to which the NHL was discussing its plans with him. In my response I suggested he co-ordinate his efforts with the NHL reps in Canada before arriving in Moscow so there would be a united front in dealing with the Soviets. Additionally, I noted it was no secret that he was not the most popular man in Moscow these days. However, popularity was not the most important factor to the Russians when they wanted to talk business. The decision on when to come to Moscow was his to make. For whatever reason, he chose not to make the trip.

The NHL proposal for club games later that year collapsed when the Soviet leadership decided gold medals had a higher attraction for the USSR. Starovoitov could not finesse his way around Bunny Ahearne on this project. The CAHA also had been reiterating its position as the Canadian conduit to the IIHF and through it to the Soviet Ice Hockey Federation.

The same fate awaited the proposed European Professional League. Bruce Norris and John Ziegler of the Detroit Red Wings had led the NHL charge. To get the ball rolling, they reputedly spent in the vicinity of three hundred thousand dollars to finance and launch the London Lions hockey team in the autumn of 1973. Made up largely of Canadian players, its home games were held at Wembley Stadium in the British capital, and the team travelled around Europe playing various local squads in exhibition matches, much as the Harlem Globetrotters did with basketball. There had been three close games held against Dynamo in London, another in Stockholm, and a 4-4 tie versus Spartak in Geneva. The USSR and Czechoslovakia however refused to join the proposed professional league because of the Olympic eligibility question, and it never got off the ground. The Lions, having played seventy-two games, folded after one year.[171]

All this cleared the ice and, in due course, Starovoitov rekindled his relationship with the CAHA (and by extension, with Hockey Canada). With the blessing of the two governments and the IIHF, agreement was reached on a second nation to nation series to be held in September/October of 1974. This time Team Canada would be made up of WHA stars.

The WHA had only materialized in 1971 and was a thorn in the side of the NHL from the beginning with its new franchises in Canada and the USA, large salaries, ending of the infamous "reserve clause," and the hiring of European players and heretofore "underage players" between eighteen and twenty. Participating in an international series of its own gave instant global credibility to the WHA and allowed it to show off its stars who had been excluded from Team Canada '72: Bobby Hull, Gerry Cheevers and J.C. Tremblay. A few of the famous players from the '72 team (Paul Henderson, Frank Mahovlich and Pat Stapleton) played for the '74 team as well after joining the WHA in the interim period. Gordie Howe had come out of retirement to sign with the WHA and suited up in 1974 against the USSR. The Soviet players were finally given the chance to play against Hull and Howe, as they had wanted two years earlier.

The NHL's desire for club play only materialized after Bunny Ahearne's departure from the IIHF presidency in 1975. Dubbed the "Super Series" it was held during the Christmas/New Year's holiday period of 1975–76 with all but one of its eight games being held in the United States: Chicago, Boston, Philadelphia, Pittsburgh, Buffalo and two in New York (against the Rangers and the Islanders). The one Canadian match, a thriller, took place in Montreal on New Year's Eve 1975. The Central Red Army team and the Wings of the Soviet played four each of the eight games.

The USSR got the money (hard currency dollars) it was looking for and new bragging rights. Using the same 1972 formula of an initial four games in Canada and then four games in Moscow played under international rules, the USSR team beat Team Canada '74 by the count of four wins, one loss and three ties (4–1–3) in a close series. Meanwhile the two Soviet teams sent to play NHL teams in North America came home with a record of five wins, two losses and a tie. To the NHL's partial credit, it was noted that the Soviet teams were unable to beat the top three teams at the time: Philadelphia, Montreal or Buffalo.

The NHL club games scheduled for the USSR did not materialize. The money to be made at the time was not in Russia but in North America, and the Soviet authorities did not welcome games outside of Moscow for both security and logistical reasons. No NHL club team played in the USSR until 1989, when the Soviet Union was opening up and the Calgary Flames and Washington Capitals appeared.

While Eagleson and the NHLPA were excluded from the 1974 series, given the emergence of the WHA, he was acutely aware of the growing demand for international hockey at the highest level between national teams. He and Doug Fisher of Hockey Canada combined to set in motion the very successful "Canada Cup" series beginning in September 1976, which involved national teams from six countries (Canada, USSR, Sweden, USA, Czechoslovakia and Finland) with the blessing of the IIHF, the NHL, Hockey Canada and the USSR. While five such Canada Cup tournaments were held over fifteen years, from 1976 until 1991, all the games were held in North America, where the money was to be found.

AS THE SUMMIT Series aftermath cooled down and the 1973 World Championships ended, my attention turned toward other duties under the General Exchanges Agreement, including visits to the USSR by the Stratford Festival and the National Arts Centre Orchestra. An embassy colleague took on the responsibility for the 1974 series, as I was due to be transferred back to External Affairs headquarters in June of that year. My colleague also played for the Moscow Maple Leafs hockey team and had learned Russian as I had. My counsel to him was to prepare for an exciting but demanding time and to develop a professional, frank and trustworthy working relationship with whomever would be calling the shots in the evolving world of Soviet hockey. By the time of our departure, Laurielle and I had spent forty months in the USSR—twice the length of the normal assignment and twenty-one months after Bobby Orr's comment that I had been in the Soviet Union too long.

AFTER MOSCOW, MY career was on an upward trajectory. Three years later, with son Eric now a member of the family, I was assigned to be Canada's representative to the Political Committee at NATO headquarters in Brussels, where ongoing assessments were made of the political situation in the USSR and Eastern Europe. In 1981 it was off to be second in command at the Canadian embassy in Israel—a turbulent land in an even larger turbulent area, and my assignment occurred during the highly contentious Israeli invasion of Lebanon in June 1982, as part of Israel's continuous conflict with the Palestine Liberation Organization.

The Cold War was heating up in Europe though, and the Israel posting was cut short when I was returned to External Affairs headquarters, to take over as director of the Arms Control and Disarmament Division. In that capacity, in 1983–84, I found myself working again in close proximity to Prime Minister Pierre Trudeau as he launched his International Peace Initiative to help cool the heated rhetoric coming out of Moscow and Washington and to suggest specific measures to reduce the risk of military conflict. A handful of advisors, including me, accompanied the prime minister to sixteen countries, meeting, among other national leaders, British Prime Minister Margaret Thatcher, French

President François Mitterrand, US President Ronald Reagan, Soviet Foreign Minister Andrei Gromyko, Chinese leader Deng Xiaoping, and Pope John Paul II.

In June 1985, Canada suffered its worst ever terrorist incident with the bombing of Air India flight 182 over the Atlantic, resulting in the death of three hundred and twenty-eight persons, of whom two hundred and eighty were Canadian citizens. I found myself a year later in New Delhi as deputy high commissioner, helping out with the ongoing political and personal ramifications. The summer of 1989 saw my transfer to West Germany as minister at the Canadian embassy, just in time to witness the fall of the Berlin Wall, assist with two visits by Prime Minister Brian Mulroney, and help deal with the subsequent withdrawal of all Canadian military units from the newly reunited Germany. A return to Ottawa as director general for Asian Affairs, in 1993, led me to play a significant organizational and advisory role in Prime Minister Jean Chrétien's initial Trade Team Canada visit to China, in 1994, with nine Canadian premiers and over four hundred Canadian businesspeople. External Affairs then sent me for a full academic year to Harvard University's Centre for International Affairs to do research and lead seminars prior to being appointed Canadian ambassador to Indonesia in the summer of 1996. On the agenda there was handling the economic and political fallout from the notorious Canadian gold-mining scandal (Bre-X) and the need to evacuate all Canadians from the country in May 1998 when the Suharto government collapsed and law and order broke down.

When my time as a career diplomat ended, in the summer of 1998, it was easy to conclude, looking back, that diplomacy had been a great professional career choice.

Through all these other diverse situations, hockey never again played the major role it did in Moscow. The reasons were obvious where it was largely an unknown game with few followers, as in India and Indonesia. In countries where it was a national sport—like Czechoslovakia, when Pierre Trudeau was there in January 1984 as part of his Peace

Mission—the topic of hockey was a helpful ice-breaker and a common point of reference for broader issues. For my part, I routinely followed the hockey scores, even from afar, and always had the hockey experience in the back of my mind as an example of how sports of any kind could help the diplomatic process. As for Canadians, if the subject of conversation ever turned to my foreign postings, it would invariably gravitate to Russia and the 1972 Summit Series.

CHAPTER FIFTEEN

RETURN TO MOSCOW

"HEY GARY, PAT Stapleton here, calling from Hockey Heaven, Strathroy Division."

He didn't have to say any more. I knew immediately who he was and about Strathroy, a smallish town not far from London, Ontario, where a good friend of mine once lived. It was early 2016. My time as a career diplomat and Canadian ambassador was behind me.

Pat, who had been born in not-too-distant Sarnia and was now seventy-six years old, was one of those guys who loved to tell stories and anecdotes, as well as to layer on the blarney. Always positive on the outside, he would continually say he was "perfect" when one enquired about his health, or that he was "perfect" because he had just met you. He always carried a pocket full of Life Savers, which he dispensed to everyone with a friendly "stay sweet" remark. An excellent companion, whether over a cup of coffee or a beer.

I hadn't really engaged with Pat personally during the Summit Series but was a big fan of his stellar defensive skills against the Soviets and his plus-minus record of plus six, which was one of the best on Team Canada. He was small in stature, at only five foot eight, but was a giant of determination and bodily strength, acquired from his farming background. His defensive partner Bill White and he had not been on the ice for Game One in Montreal but, together, had played all seven remaining games.

Pat's telephone call came out of the blue.

I had had no direct contact with Team Canada members since November 2000, when I donated a stick autographed by players from both teams, a Team Canada hockey bag and Gilbert Perreault's hockey equipment to the Hockey Hall of Fame in Toronto. Paul Henderson, Ken Dryden, Rod Seiling and Ron Ellis had been on hand for that occasion, which coincided with the announcement of the monument being installed outside of the Hall to honour Team Canada.

Pat explained that he and a high-school historian from St. Catharine's, where Pat had played junior hockey with the Teepees, were attempting to cobble together a book of reminiscences about the Summit Series. They had gone to Manulife looking for funding. The company executive, in saying their proposal would be considered, added that her father, Peter Hancock, had been at the embassy in Moscow and was well worth talking with.

This opened a window for Pat. He knew the series had not materialized out of thin air, but he hadn't given much thought to the off-ice political and international dimensions until he'd spoken with Hancock. Peter had taken out a piece of paper and sketched out a number of concentric circles, with the Summit Series at the inner core. Around it was the state of Canadian hockey and its various participants. Next came the state of Canadian politics, then Soviet politics, and then the state of bilateral relations between Canada and the USSR. A final circle was the state of international affairs. All five outer circles, he explained, had to be in close symmetry with each other to create the right conditions for the Summit Series to occur. Pat had been impressed. Peter then put Pat onto me.

Pat was a persistent and persuasive guy. It was essential, he said, that Peter and I contribute to the book. He went into his blandishment phase of saying people like us had made a major contribution to the success of the series. We should be considered as builders in the Sports Hall of Fame in Calgary and be recognized just like Team Canada players and coaches had been. I knew it was all blarney, but he liked to gild the lily.

Calls from Pat multiplied.

Pat brought me up to date on recent history. Members of Team Canada had scattered with the four winds after the series finished at the end of September 1972. There had been the airport celebration in Montreal and a larger gathering and parade in Toronto, but no national celebration for the entire team. Everyone went back to their respective NHL teams and carried on, renewing old rivalries against their recently bonded teammates. Boston disliked Montreal, and vice versa. The Black Hawks were no friends of the Rangers or the Leafs, and so on.

There had been a modest celebration of the twenty-fifth anniversary in 1997 at the Civic Centre in Ottawa, in which Prime Minister Jean Chrétien had participated. Canada Post had issued a special stamp and the Royal Canadian Mint produced a commemorative coin.

The Russians on the other hand were always happy to celebrate a positive occasion, and they considered 1972 not as a defeat but as a spectacular event in which "both sides won." "Hockey itself was the victor" went the claim, often stated by Vladislav Tretiak, who at this point was the president of the Russian Ice Hockey Federation.

Russian President Vladimir Putin, though himself diminutive in stature, liked to demonstrate his strength and courage as defender of the Russian nation and was more than happy to take off his shirt in front of the cameras and ride a horse through a creek or climb a mountain. Hockey suited him to a tee, with its broad sporting appeal across Russia and with its unofficial national anthem "Cowards Don't Play Hockey."

Putin and the Russian Ice Hockey Federation invited several Team Canada members to Moscow in February of 2012. The president hosted a lunch for them and several Soviet players, and there was a demonstration game on a newly created outdoor rink in Red Square. The whole Canadian team was invited again in September of the same year to mark the fortieth anniversary of the Summit Series. The Canadian government's celebratory policy, on the other hand, only called for marking the twenty-fifth, fiftieth and hundredth anniversary of significant historic events, and so the fortieth would have come and gone in Canada without any official involvement. Up stepped a private Canadian land developer from London, Ontario, who had a love for hockey and a good business sense for hockey connections. He organized and paid for a gala dinner and, through his involvement with the Conservative Party, was able to secure the attendance of Prime Minister Stephen Harper. The story goes that the prime minister, through no fault of his own, was roundly chastised from the podium by Phil Esposito for the lack of Canadian governmental recognition of the Summit Series, compared to what the Russian government had undertaken.

Over time, Pat explained, there were numerous celebrity golf tournaments that involved a number of individual players. There was a recognition by some, however, about the need not just to celebrate or reminisce about the past but to examine how the team's legacy might be carried forward into the future via involvement with Canadian schools and communities.

Equally important was the cohesion of the team itself. Not everyone had played in the series, as had been originally expected. Four members had left early. Some played in only a few games, while others felt it had not been their finest hour compared to their achievements in the NHL. The spotlight had shone on some players, but not others, and subsequent financial reward from advertisers and marketers had been uneven.

The contentious question was what to do about Alan Eagleson. He had been the key architect in the construction and management of the team. The head honcho. The lead organizer of the series, or at least that was how it had been portrayed in the media. The one who commanded the room and all the oxygen therein. He had captured almost all of the off-ice attention and acclaim. He was the gravitational pull for Team Canada for two decades or more, until the revelations of his financial transgressions with the NHL Players' Association fund and with some of his personal clients, particularly Bobby Orr. Then came his eighteen-month prison sentence in 1998 for fraud and embezzlement of Canada Cup proceeds from 1984, 1987 and 1991; his immediate disbarment as a lawyer from the Ontario Bar Association as a result of the sentencing; his resignation from the Hockey Hall of Fame, into which he had been inducted in the builder category in 1989; and his unprecedented removal from the Order of Canada. It was a spectacular fall from fame and fortune.

There were strong arguments by some players that the past was the past and that previous achievements shouldn't be sullied by subsequent events, but in the end Eagleson was not invited to the gala dinner for the fortieth anniversary. Nor was he invited to be part of the new organization being put together by Pat Stapleton and others: the 1972 Summit Series Hockey Team Inc (SSHTI). The decision of the organizers was to limit membership to the thirty-five players and two coaches (or their heirs) of the Summit Series hockey team and no more. An elected board of directors was set up to include Harry Sinden, Phil Esposito, Serge Savard, Ken Dryden, Brad Park, John Ferguson Jr. (in place of his father), with Pat Stapleton as chair. The organization was legally incorporated, and a close personal contact of Stapleton's, Chad Dawson, was installed as a voluntary general manager. A business plan was sought, as well as clarification of who actually owned the commercial rights to the Team Canada name, logo, films, sweater design, and other aspects of this glorious history.

The overriding theme of the organization was "the power of teamwork," which had manifested itself through eight games, four hundred and eighty minutes, twenty-eight thousand seconds; not just one brief second of time. As it was described in their literature, "In 1972, thirty-five players and two coaches from ten different NHL teams had put aside innate, fierce animosities and came together and gelled as a team that captivated the nation for an entire month."

The group's stated mission was threefold: protect the heritage and legacy of Team Canada 1972 for all Canadians; nurture and enhance the emotional connection Canadians of all ages have to Team Canada 1972; and leverage the Team Canada 1972 legacy to give back to the country, particularly its youth.

Pat and I continued to chat about the history of the series. How did it really come about? Who were all the people involved behind the scenes? What were the politics? How could this story be told?

He wanted me to engage more fully with his efforts, such as the four-city re-enactment tour in September 2016. An organizer arranged to have some members of Team Canada travel to Montreal, Toronto, Winnipeg and Vancouver for informal reminiscences and banter with the audiences. Pat thought it important that the broader story be told as an introduction to the on-ice saga.

But the timing was not good. Laurielle was failing badly after a gallant eleven-year battle with stage-four ovarian cancer. The medical specialists were amazed that she had got so much quality time out of life after the initial diagnosis in December 2005 had given her only six months to live. In the ensuing years she had battled through abdominal surgery, breast surgery, brain surgery, brain radiation, twenty-four rounds of chemotherapy and experimental drugs. Interspersed were happy times of seeing our granddaughter, Maya, born to Tatiana, golf trips to Hilton Head, two Caribbean and Central American cruises and a getaway to Las Vegas, as well as numerous family gatherings and a boatload of flower and scrub plantings in our gardens.

Pat called again to see if I could attend the Toronto event on September 10 (the Toronto game in 1972 had been on September 4, but this date was the best available). I thought about it for only a brief second before declining. As fate would have it, that very night I was obliged to call an ambulance, and Laurielle died the next day in the Ottawa General hospital.

One tries to keep busy and find new purpose after a devastating personal loss—out of the house to visit friends in Canada and the US—and throwing myself into the work of the board of directors of the Retired Heads of Mission Association (RHOMA), an Ottawa-based organization of former Canadian ambassadors, high commissioners and consuls general.[172] Pat informed me that the Team Canada board of directors had agreed to make a donation in Laurielle's name to the Cancer Centre of Eastern Ontario, in Kingston, where she had received the majority of her treatments.

As winter ebbed and spring arrived in 2017, I let Pat know I would be travelling in his neck of the woods. He was quick to invite me and my lifelong friend Hal Stoyles to lunch at the Stapletons' modest home in

Strathroy. What a welcome. Stories and laughs leapt from our lips. Pat had plenty to say, naturally, and brought all sorts of memorabilia and gear out of his basement. There were jackets and sweatshirts recently acquired from a manufacturer from the tour to Winnipeg, and two of his most prized possessions: his Number 3 Team Canada jersey from 1972, and captain's jersey from the 1974 WHA version of Team Canada.

Pat's wife, Jackie, was a much quieter personality. As we sat down for a casual lunch, we talked about their hard-working farming background and the demands that constant moving had placed on them as a hockey family with six children. Laurielle's passing came up, but I grew silent as Jackie mentioned the loss of two of their daughters to cancer. Saying goodbye to a long-time spouse is one thing, having to do it to two of your children is infinitely worse. Their strong faith helped them cope.

Jackie was quick to bring out her own souvenirs, in a meticulously well-organized binder. Prime among them being a letter that had been sent to the spouses of all the players advising them what to expect in Moscow. Bugs were mentioned, not the spying kind but the large local cockroaches. The letter also spoke about expected deportment and suggestions of clothing and personal items to bring along with them.

Her photographs of her time in Moscow were of a high quality thanks, she said, to having sat next to the president of Kodak Canada on her return flight to Toronto. Just before dessert, Pat jumped up from the table to say Hal and I had to see something special. Down he went into the basement again, re-emerging to say he had the famous puck with which Paul Henderson had scored the winning goal with thirty-four seconds remaining in Game Eight. Out from behind his back, with his right hand, came a nondescript black puck with a hole in the middle, threaded through with a rope, much like the cord through a bar of soap-on-a-rope.

My eyes widened and my jaw almost hit the floor.

"Nooooooooo, Pat, you didn't," I gasped.

"Ha. Ha. Ha. Got you, didn't I?" he laughed. Pat was a well-known trickster—he sure fooled me.

Then out from behind his back came his left hand, holding what he said was "*the* puck." The most famous puck in the world, historically linked with "the goal." It didn't have a hole in it, thank God, but was no more distinctive than the puck which did. There were no identifying crests or markings of any kind. Just a plain black rubber puck.

Many individuals and organizations would like to acquire the puck, Pat explained, but he wanted to keep it for the benefit of the team as a whole. It would be an issue we would discuss on and off for over a year.

My first point to Pat was, regardless of the puck's ultimate disposition, he should make a formal declaration and have it certified by a lawyer that it was the original puck. That declaration, together with the TV footage showing him plucking a puck from the net at the end of Game Eight and skating off the rink with it, would be strong evidence of its authenticity. Besides, there were no other serious claimants of ownership.

My second point was that the team could benefit from the puck if it were to be donated to a place where *all* Canadians could see it. The Hockey Hall of Fame was open to the public and could provide charitable receipts for donations if requested, but apparently did not pay for mementos. On the other hand, the Canadian Museum of History in Gatineau, across the river from Ottawa, could propose either option if the proposed items fit their acquisitions criteria. Moreover, the museum was busy assembling its own sports collection. Such an arrangement could suit his objectives.

Pat could be stubborn. He dug in his heels. It became a back-burner issue for him.

Before we left their house that afternoon, Pat mentioned he had just received word from Moscow, not from the Russian government, but a private individual, about a forty-fifth anniversary celebration in Russia. The Russian organizers wanted Team Canada members to attend. Pat wanted me to come along.

In the good old days of the Cold War, the Soviet government controlled everything. Now Russian oligarchs, the new capitalist bosses, were the major players, having secured personal ownership, legitimately or otherwise, of the main elements of the former USSR state economy. This era came with some shoots of democracy. They had gotten too big for their britches though by the early 2000s. Vladimir Putin, with his KGB background, turned the tables on them by shipping their leading member, Siberian oil magnate Mikhail Khodorkovsky, off to jail and reminding everyone else who was really in charge of Russia.

Pat and Chad's Moscow contact was a certain Dimitry, who worked for an undisclosed oligarch involved in, among other things, the Russian hockey world, and who of course had direct connections to the Russian president.

The preliminary plan was to assemble the former Soviet and Canadian players of '72 and their spouses in Moscow in early September 2017 to highlight the opening of the new Russian Museum of Hockey. Honoured guests would attend a gala dinner and have an encounter of some kind with the president. Dimitry's boss would pay for individual appearance fees, business-class return airfare, deluxe hotel accommodation and all associated costs in Moscow.

There was a lot of haggling via transatlantic telephone calls over the summer months about terms and conditions of the visit, and Pat sought my advice several times about how best to deal with the Russians. A key matter was which Team Canada players were available and interested in going. We dropped the idea of bringing spouses. Those among them who had wanted to return to Russia after 1972 had done so already in 2012 and that proved sufficient. Some players had never returned to Russia, like Bobby Clarke, who wished to avoid having a Russian audience replay the contentious collision between his stick and Valeri Kharlamov's ankle.

Appearance fees (given we were dealing with a Russian businessman) were finally settled, though the Russians were prepared to pay two to three times more for the presence of Phil Esposito. In Russian eyes, Esposito, not Paul Henderson, was the star of Team Canada. Russian audiences loved how he handled his pratfall at centre ice to begin the series Game Five Moscow opener. They loved his grit and tenacity in front of the Soviet net and the multiple goals he scored as a result. They loved his outsized personality. Certainly, no Soviet player had a personality that large—if they were permitted to develop a personality at all. Esposito was ready to participate, as were Brad Park, Dennis Hull, Mahovlich brothers Frank and Peter, Red Berenson, Dave Tallon, Wayne Cashman, Don Awrey and Jocelyn Guevremont, as well as Pat Stapleton himself.

Other players, including Ken Dryden, as well as Coach Harry Sinden, wanted to attend but had other commitments, ongoing health issues or were simply not up to the gruelling ten-hour flight each way, with only three nights in a Russian hotel bed in between. Assembling everybody was also complicated by the fact their homes were scattered across Canada and approximately half the team had taken up residence in the United States.

The most significant bone of contention was Pat's desire to include a number of non-players in the delegation, myself included. There was Barry Wright, the Brock University professor who had developed the team's business plan; Mario Siciliano, the curator/CEO of the Sports Hall of Fame in Calgary; David Morris, a media expert; Wendy Thompson, a management guru; Ron Bremner, an advertising expert; Vito Feija, who had funded the fortieth anniversary dinner; and a two-person film crew of Helen Parker (of Diamond Films) and Colleen Hixenbaugh. We became the self-styled "gang of nine."

Pat believed that exposing this grouping to Moscow and the hockey encounter would be of great assistance in forward planning for the new Team Canada enterprise. Dimitry, and more particularly his boss, had no interest in funding this motley crew. But I counselled Pat to hold out. We were all part of the Canadian team, the Russians were the demanders in this exercise, they had the president involved and, as a result, would bend.

A compromise was reached. The Russians agreed to pay for all expenses for the nine non-players in Moscow, while Pat would cover international airfare. Chad Dawson, the general manager, would be included with the player contingent.

Just when everything seemed to be falling into place, Dimitry called to say President Putin was going to receive a last-minute high-level visitor and our dates would have to be changed. Moreover, the encounter with the president would no longer be in Moscow but at his summer retreat in Sochi, on the Black Sea; an additional flight, two hours from the Russian capital.

Lift-off from Toronto was now set for the evening of September 11, 2017. The majority of the players flew business class on Lufthansa via Vienna, while the rest of us took economy class with Air Canada to London and then by Aeroflot to Moscow. The plan was to meet there. But like most plans, this one had a hitch or two.

Hurricane Irma, at the time the third-largest Atlantic hurricane at landfall ever recorded, struck the Florida coast. Airports were closed, roads flooded, and Florida residents were ordered to stay home, Esposito, Awrey and Tallon were stranded and were unable to make the trip.

Pat also had arranged to have seven dozen Team Canada sweaters made up, in both the home red and away white colours. The gang of nine's job was to pack them into our suitcases, have them autographed by the players of both teams, gift one each to the Soviet players, and bring the rest back to Canada for publicity and charity purposes. I was the designated carrier of the "special sweater," Number 11, destined for President Putin. It was his favourite hockey number and the number he used on his own sweater when playing the game. A Russian journalist told me that while the president was obviously the number-one person in the country, he respected hockey tradition that only goalies wore that number. Hence Number 11—double one.[173]

The gang of nine arrived at London's Heathrow Airport prepared for the transfer to the Russian airline. The British authorities, however, were still indignant about Russia's annexation of Crimea in 2014 and its ongoing military support for ethnic Russians in Eastern Ukraine. One way the British had decided to show their displeasure was to assign Aeroflot to the farthest part of the airport.

It had been thirty years since my last Aeroflot flight. What a change. New foreign aircraft. Much better food and service. Plus, flight attendants of the kind seen in the early days of air travel— uniformly young and attractive, all attired in bold red jackets and skirts with matching pillbox hats. Gone were the old, ill-fitting blue Aeroflot uniforms. Still around though, was a hulking, stern male attendant to whom you would not wish to cause offence, let alone engage in a tangle.

The aircraft set down three hours later at Sheremetyevo, the main international airport in Moscow. The sun was just rising. Here again a revelation: a completely new airport building brimming with international shops and goodies, just like its worldwide counterparts. We cleared the still-unsmiling passport control officers and were greeted by a pleasant young man who had been hired uniquely for the occasion to take us to the hotel. He volunteered few details.

"When are the players landing?" He didn't know, but it would not be here.

"Where then?" Probably Vnukovo. The opposite side of Moscow to where we were.

"Are they going to the hotel where we can meet them?" Probably not today or tonight.

"When then?" He didn't know.

"What's happening?" The players are likely going to immediately transfer to a special flight to Sochi.

"I need to meet with Pat Stapleton before they depart." Can't help you, not my job.

My Russian experience encouraged me to invoke higher authority.

"Look, I have a special sweater for President Putin that needs to be hand delivered to Mr. Stapleton. If this doesn't happen, you can explain it to the president."

His tune quickly changed. "I'll get someone to call you."

Our trip into the city in our new Mercedes van was eye-popping. The city had grown out to meet the airport and had populated what were once fields. The grey doom and gloom of the Soviet-era city was gone. Fresh pastel paint in blue, yellow and pink had been applied to stucco-sided centuries-old buildings. Residential and commercial skyscrapers, with digital signage, were everywhere, many of the latter touting German products and companies. The roads were jammed with what seemed to be thousands of high-end German vehicles. I looked for the x-shaped Soviet tank traps from the Second World War, which had been so prominent on the airport highway in 1971. With some intent searching, I finally spotted them, but they were surrounded with other modern aspects of city life. They could now easily be missed by passing motorists, which was not previously the case.

One was left with the general impression that German commerce had succeeded where the German army had failed.

Equally manifest was that Eastern Orthodox churches were back in vogue. Abandoned or destroyed by the communist regime, one could now readily see that they had been refurbished or built afresh—by the thousands, I was later told. An intertwining of church and state in protection of "traditional values"—a favourite Vladimir Putin theme.

Our hotel, the Lotte, part of a South Korean chain and a member of the "Leading Hotels of the World," lived up to its deluxe billing with its internationally designed decor. In fact, it was five stars—on par with the Moscow Four Seasons, Ritz-Carlton and Kempinski. Top-notch lobby, restaurants, spas and pool. The room I shared with Ron Bremner was luxurious, with its fine Egyptian-cotton linens, as well as outstanding French toiletries and marble fixtures in the washroom and separate shower areas, spacious enough to host a mini-convention. The hotel claimed to have the largest and most expensive royal suite in Russia. The absolute highlight for me, though, was opening the curtains to see the sun reflecting off the golden towers and bells of the Kremlin and nearby churches.

The Soviet hotels that Canadian fans were crammed into in 1972 were the best of the bunch at the time, but they could not match this world-class lodging. There was no comparison between then and now.

Still, you couldn't forget where you were. There was a heavy security presence on the street and in the immediate approaches to the hotel. The driver of our van had to navigate through several metal police gates, and there was a mirror check under the vehicle. Plain-clothes security operatives were at the front door and in the lobby. Exchanging foreign currency was the same tiresome and lengthy procedure, involving the signing of multiple documents.

Then there was my cellphone. It didn't work any longer, despite my having paid for a supplementary Russia package before we left Canada. Nobody's cellphone worked. No texting or anything. It was pretty clear they were being blocked by someone.

Ron and I were just getting acclimatized when the room telephone rang. The plane with the players would be arriving in two and a half hours. There were two options for me to deliver the president's sweater to Pat. I could get to Vnukovo airport under my own steam or, if I could get to Legends Park within half an hour, I could ride with the former Soviet players in their bus.

The choice was easy.

Helen Parker, our photographer, desperately wanted to ensure she could interview some of the players from the USSR team. I called her room on the seventh floor. She was just coming out of the shower. "If you can be in the lobby in five minutes with your camera," I urged, "you can have your wish." Down she flew with her wet hair.

Napoleon once said he preferred a lucky general to a good general. I was lucky. No taxi would have made our rendezvous on time in Moscow's heavy traffic. The hotel concierge did however have a driver with a loaded M-series BMW sedan. The price naturally would be considerably higher than an ordinary cab. This was no time to haggle, so I agreed to the hefty charge, and we jumped into the speedmobile. The driver knew his business and his car. We arrived early. More security gates. No problem. Cars of this kind were seldom stopped, and if they were, it usually was only for a cursory look or a passing question.

Situated on the sprawling site of a former ZIL (Lenin) automobile factory, Legends Park was billed as a "sports and entertainment district." We were invited into the arena's dressing room, where several of the Soviet players were finishing up after a morning workout and swim. Vladimir Lutchenko, the big Soviet defenceman, was quick to smile and approached with some faint glimmer of recollection. He had been hired as a scout for the New York Rangers back in the 2004–05 season and continued to perform that function.

We chatted in a mix of Russian and English and then walked out and boarded a full-size Mercedes bus. Some of the other ten to twelve players on the bus were not in as good condition as Lutchenko, and I had difficulty putting names to faces—expanded waists and broader faces did that to many people, even athletes, after forty-five years. The players were somewhat leery of Helen and her camera at first and asked questions about who she was, while at the same time looking around, as they were wont to do, for a Russian official to bless this encounter. Seeing none, they came to the conclusion that if we were on board the bus it must be approved by somebody in authority.

The big stars, like Tretiak and Yakushev, who now occupied senior positions in the Russian hockey world, must have made their own way to the airport via separate means, but we stopped along the highway to pick up Alexander Maltsev. He had parked his Range Rover nearby. The players were obviously doing much better financially now than in the dying days of the Soviet Union, when several were reported to have been in dire financial straits. Maltsev was in good shape himself but remained as standoffish and sullen as I remembered him to be from 1972. The talented former scoring leader, in 1970–71, in the top Soviet club leagues, who had tied Valeri Kharlamov for league MVP in 1971–72, was now a politician with the "A Just Russia" party.[174] The party was on the left wing of the Russian political spectrum, but still supported President Putin and his "United Russia" party.

The bus doors opened as we pulled up in front of the airport terminal, and we were met by a small greeting party. I advised Helen to stay close to the players, and we marched off through one side door and then another, finally arriving in the VIP lounge. Not a pause, nor a question, nor a check. The players were persons of importance and so, obviously, were those with them.

We had just turned around in the VIP lounge when Pat, the Mahovlich brothers, Red Berenson, Dennis Hull and Chad Dawson burst through another door, setting off a noisy round of greetings, hugs and handshakes with the assembled Soviet players. Brad Park, Wayne Cashman and Jocelyn Guevremont, who were on another flight and had connection problems, were nowhere to be seen. Pat and company looked beat but were highly presentable in their blue blazers with Team Canada crests on the breast pockets. While they were no longer the strapping young athletes from 1972, they remained robust. Berenson, in particular, was in great shape, having just ended a thirty-three-year head coaching job with the University of Michigan Wolverines men's hockey team. Then, a brief few minutes later, passengers on the special military flight to Sochi were told it was boarding. Helen and I were not on the manifest. Our little escapade had come to an end, and with that Pat was handed the sweater for the president. Mission accomplished.

Park, Cashman and Guevremont missed the flight. The other six flew off with the Soviet players. Helen and I were escorted to the airport taxi station and told this was how we were to get back to our hotel. This was a different world from the Mercedes bus. There was one big taxi boss and several minor bosses who hung on his every word. A gaggle of drivers waited patiently, caps off, for a crumb of a fare to be directed their way. The asking fare was highway robbery. When I refused to pay the grossly inflated rouble price, the boss switched over to a reduced rate of American dollars. Still too high. We haggled. He wasn't impressed by my mention of the name Putin. "What does that matter," he retorted, "we're here to make money." I reverted to speaking Russian and mentioned we were here with Canadian hockey players. He dropped the price into an acceptable range. We had no more leverage, nor alternatives, so accepted, and were finally off in a cab back to the hotel.

PAT STAPLETON WAS no stranger to Vladimir Putin.

Pat had been among the seven members of Team Canada (Phil Esposito, J.P. Parisé, Marcel Dionne, Jocelyn Guevremont, Brad Park and Don Awrey) who, along with NHLPA president Don Fehr, had been invited by President Putin to a small luncheon at the presidential mansion at Novo-Ogareva during the February 2012 visit. The Canadian players had been impressed by the gesture and the attention paid to them. Putin had related how he and his parents had watched all the games on TV in 1972, when he was still a teenager. Of course, they all had rooted for the USSR Team. The Soviet players were treated like "national heroes," he said. The Canadian players were no less popular, he admitted, and he "personally remembered them all by their names."[175]

Now Pat was in Sochi as head of the Canadian group of players. He found himself seated to the immediate right of the president as they watched a junior squad of Russian boys scrimmage on the Sochi Olympic rink. Dennis Hull sat beside Pat, and the Mahovlich brothers were directly in front of Putin. Alexander Yakushev was to the president's immediate left, followed by Vladislav Tretiak. An interpreter sat in the row behind as they exchanged small talk. The remaining Canadian players and their Soviet counterparts were clustered around them.

The Canadians praised the quality of the scrimmage and the arena. Frank Mahovlich later observed that it "was impressive to see the beautiful rinks and to witness how much hockey had influenced [Russia]." Dennis Hull was taken by the noise and yelling of the players and fans, which, he observed, was something new.

When the scrimmage ended, the president and his entourage des-cended to the ice for a chat with the young players. He was quoted, in an English translation, as saying: "We have brought here today the most legendary players in the entire history of hockey. The people who have done an awful lot for the development of hockey. Both the Soviet and Canadian hockey players who took part in this outstanding series in 1972 and pushed the development of hockey forward. Thanks to this series, the interest in hockey grew worldwide."

Russian national television captured every word and image.

Stapleton would later mention that in the stands Putin had been equally positive and enthusiastic about hockey and the series. New facili-ties and improved youth training were important, Putin had said. The president related how he enjoyed hockey and would like to play every day if he could. The series had created friendship between Canada and the USSR during the Cold War, and he would like to follow up on it. For his part, Pat would refer to his concept of looking at the series as a whole, from beginning to end, not just parts of what had happened. Current politics were not raised by either party. Following the game, it was back to the presidential residence and dinner. The day was growing long. Three flights, starting from Canada, and then an hour bus ride from the Sochi airport to the Olympic rink. Tough travelling for any-body, but when an encounter with the Russian president awaited you at the end, it only added to the stress level.

The Number 11 sweater was presented, but not put on by President Putin. His security detail wanted to check it out first, lest it be infested with some foreign substance, or perhaps because it was just a matter of protocol when dealing with international gifts.

It was no secret the president only learned to skate and play hockey when he was sixty years old; just five years previously. Nonetheless, there were glowing reports in the Russian media about his goal-scoring prow-ess. Multiple goals a game. Rumour had it that when he played with the national or other star-studded teams, the players were advised to "part like the Red Sea" to provide him with an unobstructed path to the net. The goalies were no impediment either. How could it be otherwise?

Several months later, on January 1, 2018, the main Russian evening TV news program, *Vremya*, celebrated its fiftieth anniversary. When asked to comment on this occasion, the president was quoted as saying he recalled two major events as a boy watching the news program over the years. The first was the inaugural flight of the Soviet supersonic passenger aircraft, the Tupolev TU-144, in December 1968. The other was the Canada-Soviet hockey series of 1972. Putin was but part of a vast Soviet TV audience who witnessed both events at the time, but he also knew what subjects resonated with the public. Both were events of national pride in the USSR, and he wanted to be associated with them. After all, national elections in Russia were only two months away, in March 2018, and the president was seeking a fourth six-year term.

No officials were invited to the September gathering in Sochi, not even the Canadian ambassador; likely a reflection of the very cool official relationship between Canada and Russia at the time.

Those of us who remained in Moscow were treated to dinner and a hockey game at the Dynamo arena, in the owner's box at the end of the rink. Long gone were the days of dim lights and silent men seated with their fedoras and cloth overcoats, fresh from work and eating salami, cheese, onion and bread from their leather briefcases. Those Soviet days of no entertainment except for the game on the ice were past. Now there were bright lights, fresh paint, comfortable seating, laughter, cheering, singing, yelling, drum-beating, music, decent food, lively announcements, big screens. Cheerleaders in revealing outfits led the merrymaking and then swept the ice between periods, blowing kisses to the crowd when they finished. There was even a good-sized remote-controlled blimp, which circled the ice at the start of the game. The uniforms were more colourful than in the early Soviet days, and sponsors' names and ads were splashed everywhere. The Russians had cottoned on to the idea that, for fans, hockey was as much about entertainment as it was about sport.

As for the game, Dynamo Moscow was playing Tractor from Chelyabinsk, a large city in west-central Russia, close to the Ural Mountains. Known for its tractor production, the city's nickname during the Second World War was Tankograd.

The hockey itself was hard and fast, exhibiting the classic Russian preference for stick-handling and passing rather than dump-ins, though the players were not shy about going into the corners if need be. Stiff body-checking was in evidence, particularly around the nets. Although this was Dynamo's home rink at the time, and they had the vast majority of the fans on their side, Tractor won the game 4–1.

What hadn't changed was the Russians' apparent love of drinking—male Russians, I should add. Our hosts had plenty of vodka and cognac toasts to propose: to hockey, to Canada, to Russia, to the Soviet Union. And when those topics had been repeated and exhausted, toasts to whatever else popped into their minds. My reliable old game plan was to eat before drinking—fish, preferably herring. Its oils provide a good coating on your throat and intestines to ward off the astringent impact of multiple vodka shots.

Much of the non-1972 discussions between the Canadians and Russians, in between toasts, focused on the state of the KHL (Kontinental Hockey League). It was no longer just a Russian league but now included teams from seven countries: Finland, Latvia, Belarus, Slovakia, Kazakhstan, Russia and China; the latter added in 2017. Its geographic reach was enormous, stretching from Bratislava, Slovakia, in Central Europe, all the way east to Vladivostok and Khabarovsk, on the Pacific Ocean; a distance of 10,963 kilometres.

The equivalent of Lord Stanley's Cup, the Gagarin Cup was awarded to the winner of the KHL playoffs. Named after Yuri Gagarin, the first human in space, it was no shabby vase but made of sterling silver with gold-plate overlay on the upper half.

There were similar individual player awards (top goal scorer, etc.), but unlike in the NHL, there also was a trophy for the person judged top referee throughout the season. Appropriately, it was called the "golden whistle." Named after Andrei Starovoitov, it was not so much in deference to his leading role with the Soviet Ice Hockey Federation and the Summit Series, but more in recognition of his long service as a referee at eight IIHF championships (1955–66), when the USSR first appeared on the international hockey scene.

The KHL itself was made up of twenty-seven teams at that moment. Our hosts at the Dynamo–Tractor game thought there were too many. Too many teams strung out over great distances, some with funding issues and some light on star or top-notch players. All three issues being interrelated, of course. (By the 2020–21 season, four had dropped out: Admiral, Lada, Slovan and Ugra.)

The overall quality of the league, though, was very good in their opinion, not all that far behind the NHL. KHL players originated from fifteen countries, including Russia, Canada, Czech Republic, Sweden, the US, Finland, Kazakhstan and Latvia were the top talent suppliers, in that order. Many went back and forth from the NHL. This also applied in the KHL's previous incarnation as the Russian Superleague (1999–2008). In the 2004–05 season, for example, the AK Bars from Kazan, the fifth-largest Russian city, located on the Volga River southeast of Moscow, had stars like Dany Heatley, Vincent Lecavalier, Ilya Kovalchuk and Alexi Kovalev on its team at one point or another of the season.

Ownership of the KHL teams was a murky question. Nobody really seemed to know or, if they did, they were reluctant to state it. In the days of the USSR, it had been clear. The communist government owned everything. State agencies like the Army, Air Force or Security Services had teams, as did major state-owned enterprises, such as those in the oil and gas, chemical, farm implement, railroad and automobile industries.

Now, large conglomerates run by oligarchs controlled the teams. For example, the AK Bars Snow Leopards, who had won the Gagarin Cup three times already (2009, 2010 and 2018), listed its ownership as Tatneft, an oil and gas company.

There were other examples of financial and resource conglomerates owning hockey teams, not because there was money in it, but reputedly because Putin believed hockey was a matter of national prestige and had a personal interest in the sport. A one-time Canadian coach in the KHL suggested the reason there was a Chinese team in the league was due to the insistence of the president in making participation a part of a Russia–China oil and gas deal.

The Sports Club Army team in St. Petersburg began to assemble high-quality players (critics said they were "funnelled" there) and won the Gagarin Cup in 2016 and again in 2017, when the team made up most of the Russian national team that won gold at the 2018 Winter Olympics in PyeongChang, South Korea. (St. Petersburg is the president's hometown.)

BY THURSDAY AFTERNOON, September 14, everyone was back from Sochi, and we all reassembled at Legends Park. The joke in our group that day was that Pat Stapleton and Vladimir Putin could see eye to eye with each other on issues because they were both five feet eight inches tall.

In addition to the sports building and a large asphalt parking lot in between, Legends Park contained a temporary one-storey modern tubular structure used for various large hospitality gatherings, including the gala hockey dinner planned for that evening.

Next to it, and completely incongruent in style, was the Russian Hockey Museum and Hall of Fame with its red-brick sides, green roof and numerous white-cladded windows. Architecturally, it could be described as "Stalinist Gothic," the same style used by Soviet dictator Joseph Stalin from the mid-1940s to mid-1950s, when he erected seven wedding-cake-like buildings around Moscow nicknamed "The Seven Sisters." The museum was to be the location for the official celebration of the forty-fifth anniversary.

Parked in front of the museum building were two grey BMW SUVs that had been driven around Moscow and used for advertising the event. On the back door of one vehicle was a rendition of Phil Esposito against the backdrop of Team Canada's starburst maple leaf. On the front door was Vladislav Tretiak in his goalie crouch, with the Soviet hammer and sickle emblem nearby, preparing to fend off the oncoming Esposito. The second BMW featured on the front door a full-length depiction of Bobby Clarke on the ice, while the rear door had a close-up picture of now-deceased Valeri Kharlamov. Not a provocative act, perhaps, but a clear linking of the two.

The space in front of the museum was often the site for picture-taking by Russian NHL hockey players who brought the Stanley Cup to Moscow, as Evgeni Malkin did in 2016 and 2017, and Alexander Ovechkin in 2018. The display area was not as large as that of the Hall of Fame building in Toronto and there was only one interactive activity—playing the role of a goaltender—but it was very nicely done and provided the visitor with a comprehensive history of the start of bandy and ice hockey in the USSR and its many achievements over the years. Particularly impressive was a multicoloured floor-to-ceiling mural of three of the greats (Tretiak, Kharlamov and then-reigning NHL Vezina Trophy winner, goaltender Sergei Bobrovsky) looking down from a height at the viewers. There was also a display of the 1972 series, with photos and sticks, skates and gloves, and on a nearby pillar a listing in gold paint of all the players and coaches of both teams in both Cyrillic and Roman script, which had been specially prepared for this event.

After mingling around the displays, drinks in hand, members of both teams and invited guests crowded into the all-white presentation room with its impressive glass etchings of the hundred and forty-three inductees to the Russian Hall of Fame. The Soviet players, dressed in their red CCCP sweaters, sat up front on the right-hand side and the Canadians to the left of the aisle in white Team Canada sweaters, which had been given to them on the spot to pull on over their dress shirts and ties. There was much laughter as a few of the Canadians struggled to get them on, claiming it was a Russian trick to have given them sweaters that had shrunk. I had to lend a hand to Stapleton and Park, who had put on an extra kilogram or two.

The ceremony itself was warm and light-hearted, with many laughs, and it was easy to tell that the intense rivalry of 1972 had given way to genuine respect in 2017. Tretiak and Park were the respective spokespersons. The word which both sides used most frequently to describe each other was "great." The series was "great," your team was "great," you were "great." Hockey and hockey fans were the winners. Even Boris Mikhailov, who infamously kicked Gary Bergman with his skates, was made fun of for his transgression and embraced by the Canadian players. All of the players received rather expensive commemorative rings with multiple gems, funded by the unmentioned businessman organizer of the event and given out by the staff of the museum. Many group pictures were taken.

Throughout the ceremony, two large flat screens embedded in the front wall ran video scenes of the series games. High definition had not yet been invented in 1972. At one point there was an "In Memoriam" tribute to those players who had passed away, and the audience was asked to stand as their images were displayed on two screens. To me, this was the most poignant part of the ceremony: to realize so many young and vital players and coaches were already gone. At that moment, this included six Canadians (Gary Bergman, Bill Goldsworthy, Richard Martin, Jean-Paul Parisé, Bill White and assistant coach John Ferguson Sr.), and almost double the number from the Soviet team.

The overall life expectancy of the Russian population during that period was significantly below that of Canadians. Russian men on average also lived ten years less than Russian women, partly due to war-related injuries but also because of widespread heavy drinking and associated health problems.

Galina Ragulin, the wife of the former all-star defenceman, was present throughout the ceremony and mingled extensively with the audience, distributing photos of her husband on the ice in a face-to-face confrontation with Phil Esposito, each exchanging expletives unknown to the other. She had an obvious enduring love for her husband and also recognized the importance of the event he had participated in against Team Canada.

One Soviet player who was badly ailing and whose medical issues prevented him from making the Sochi trip to be with President Putin was Evgeni Zimin, the top Soviet point scorer after the first two games in Canada, and someone who had subsequently disappeared from the roster. I had a few quiet moments with him to finally ask what had really happened. Zimin explained that he had developed appendicitis right after the game in Toronto and had been immediately hospitalized and unable to make the trip with the team to Winnipeg. The matter was kept quiet, perhaps as Harry Sinden had wanted with Phil Esposito's blood-coughing episode in Moscow. Zimin said he eventually made it back to Moscow and could only resume playing hockey for Spartak at the end of the 1972–1973 season. He went on to coach the Soviet national under-18 club (1981–83) and to be general manager of Spartak for two years (1998–2000). And after the USSR opened itself to the NHL, in 1989–90, the Philadelphia Flyers hired him as a scout in Moscow in 1992, a position he held for twenty years, many of which overlapped with his old Team Canada rival Bobby Clarke's tenure as the Flyers' general manager. If there were any lingering doubts in Canada about a political cloud having been over Zimin's head, they were completely dispelled when he passed away in 2018 and received an effusive tribute from President Putin.

Of all the encounters that afternoon, the one that stood out in terms of personal bonding and respect for the other's skills took place between Brad Park and Alexander Yakushev after the official ceremony. Park did all the talking, in English, with Yakushev standing beside him, just smiling. They were both being filmed by Helen Parker. After pointing out the height difference between the two (Yakushev was three inches taller) and saying he had to defend against this big guy, Park grabbed Yakushev's hands and held them reverently up to the camera. These hands, Park said, were capable of scoring small goals and big goals. There was "no one better from the top of the circle to the net." Yakushev responded with an "aw shucks" shake of the head.

BOTH TEAMS PROCEEDED to sign sweater after sweater after sweater and to have their individual hands imprinted in plaster moulds. Russian cameras swirled, as did Helen Parker's.

The Russian organizers had gone to great effort to celebrate the occasion, including designing a forty-fifth anniversary circular logo with two faceless Soviet and Canadian players shadowing each other on the ice, one behind the other. The logo was displayed on variety of mementos: pucks, mugs, booklets.

The event concluded with a gala dinner next door, with strict security and a closely guarded guest list of Russian hockey personalities. Vladislav Tretiak acted as host in his capacity as president of the Russian Ice Hockey Federation and elected member of President Putin's political party, "United Russia," in the Russian Parliament, the Duma. The room was elegantly decorated, and tables groaned with high-quality food and beverages. Videos of the series again were continuously displayed on projection screens, but this time there was the added pleasure of musicians, prime among them being six preteens who danced and sang their way through Stompin' Tom Connors' "The Good Old Hockey Game" and the Russian hymnal equivalent, "Cowards Don't Play Hockey"— all interspersed with the Russian hockey chat of "Shaybu." Dennis Hull described the party and associated events as "fabulous," adding, it was now time for Canadians to offer up reciprocal hospitality to the Russians. Hull stated he would be speaking to the Canadian prime minister about it.

Amidst the gaiety and levity of the party I had a word outside with Canadian Ambassador John Kur. Hockey, he told me, was one of the only threads holding the bilateral Canadian–Russian relationship together. Ever since the Russians took over Crimea and provided military assistance to Eastern Ukraine, Ottawa had protested these events by cutting off contacts with senior Russian officials and forbade a number of them from visiting Canada. The Russians had retaliated by banning visits by senior Canadians, including the Minister of Foreign Affairs Chrystia Freeland. The ambassador couldn't call on anyone senior in Moscow, nor could he receive them at a meal in the official residence. Not that he would anyway, because it was severely run down and under repair. A new embassy building in Moscow had previously been agreed upon, but it too was now on hold as part of the freeze in relations. Canada's trade policy was now "no policy."

The ambassador and staff were working under more stringent bilateral restraints than Ambassador Ford, Peter Hancock and I had in 1972 during the Cold War.

After the gala, with the lengthy preceding events and the impact of jet lag, we should have packed it in and called it a day. Instead, several of us gathered at the hotel bar for a wrap-up and to initiate a discussion on the period ahead, leading to the fiftieth anniversary in 2022. Drinks of various kinds were ordered all round.

Our little gathering produced widespread agreement on a few points: first of all, it was essential all the surviving Russian players be invited to Canada—not just one or two (whether health would permit all to come for the fiftieth anniversary was another matter); secondly, the "Power of Teamwork" was an excellent legacy to build upon but required the participation of all Team Canada players; and thirdly, 2022 should be seen like the date of a space rocket lift-off, a five-year countdown between now and then was required, involving various annual preparations and activities to ensure a successful launch.

THE NEXT MORNING, we awoke to news that overnight there had been a domestic terrorist bomb threat in Russia aimed at hotels. Thirty thousand guests around the country had been forced to evacuate their rooms. Our sleep at the Lotte, no matter how short, had not been disturbed. The official explanation at the front desk was that there was sufficient security around the hotel so a decision had been made that there was no real risk to the guests. A more gregarious employee revealed that the guests at this hotel, including Russians, were not the type of people who would take kindly to being dumped into the streets in the middle of the night. The employee added that there might also be some embarrassing personal relationships which could become public and were best avoided. OK. The episode passed.

Later that day, Friday, September 15, we paid a return visit to the place where all the excitement and glory had happened in 1972: the Palace of Sports. The Russians had said the building was under major repair and was not worth visiting. Team Canada players held a different opinion. They insisted on seeing this venue filled with memories. Tretiak came along as co-host with Yakushev, who carried the largely titular title of president of the Hockey Legends Club. The other Soviet players from 1972 were absent.

The building had been erected in 1956, and its yellow brick and mortar exterior was being stripped away to be reconstructed. There were large piles of rubble everywhere. Peter Mahovlich bent down to pick up a piece for his brother. Frank liked to collect souvenir rocks, stones and even pieces of concrete, Peter confided.

Inside, the seats had been dismantled, a previous renovation in 2002 had reduced seating capacity from the original 13,700 down to 11,500 and the entire interior was in disarray. All was made worse by poor lighting. At first it was difficult to orient ourselves, but then we found the hallway where the players of both teams had lined up, side by side, to come onto the ice. We were reminded where the team benches were. Then we recognized the area in the stands where the cheering Canadian fans had sat. Several of the Canadian players in our group said that was what they remembered most: the cheering Canadian crowds, as well as all the telegrams, letters and postcards which had been put up on the walls of the Canadian dressing room. With those words expressed, it became easy to remember what it was all like then, even if now there was only general silence in the rink. I also thought of the small ante-room and the heated dispute over referees before Game Eight.

Changes were afoot, though. Ambitious Russian plans for the Palace of Sports had an interesting republican twist. No longer was it to be a just a "sports arena" for high-powered athletes, it was to become a "popular public space," with two training rinks for a hundred people each; a five-hundred-seat stadium; a six-lane swimming pool and a spa centre; all "serving the needs of city residents as well as athletes." But with a touch of extravagance, the promotional material announced the two main entrances would have "stained-glass panels with crystal-like embellishments."

The Palace of Sports that had hosted the final four games of the 1972 Summit Series, it seemed, would be no longer.

Back outside we drove over to the huge soccer stadium that was part of the same complex. The stadium, which like the hockey arena had been built around 1956, was now in the final stages of an extensive and impressive rebuild in preparation for the hugely popular World Cup soccer tournament, which Russia would be hosting the following June, in 2018. The running track around the oval had been removed; seating increased from 78,000 to 81,000, and a hundred VIP boxes added. Tretiak and Yakushev were proud to display the stadium. Originally named Central Lenin Stadium, it now carried the title "Grand Sports Arena of the Luzhniki Olympic Complex—or Luzhniki Stadium for short— named after the meadowlands on which it was located.

Not only was Lenin's name gone from the stadium, but the bronze statue of him that had been located on one of the main thoroughfares in the complex was now nowhere to be seen. In its place was a bronze statue of Valeri Kharlamov, stick in hand, leaping over the boards onto the ice. The Canadian players stopped to admire it and posed for pictures with the Soviet hockey legend.

With the embassy's official residence out of commission, the Canadian ambassador, as reciprocal hospitality, invited the Canadian and Soviet players to a Canadian-run pub near Red Square with the straightforward name "Papa's." It was quite popular with the foreign community, and its prime location attracted plenty of tourists looking for an alternative to the standard borscht menu. The proprietor, who was from Nova Scotia, was a big hockey fan and was only too happy to festoon his large pub with Canadian and Russian flags, to go with his existing sports motif, and to run the series video on his television screens.

The news of the presence of the Canadian players, and a small sprinkling of Russians led by Tretiak and Yakushev, had spread on social media and drew a steady if limited number of happy autograph- and photo-seekers. It was an unstructured, informal affair, but the atmosphere of camaraderie was best captured by Tretiak's cheery Russian toast, "May we drink beer and champagne together until we are one hundred and twenty."

Frank Mahovlich slipped out at one point during the afternoon to purchase a few souvenirs at the nearby famous GUM department store abutting Red Square. He returned to tell the story that many Russians had recognized him from the ongoing television coverage of the visit and, indeed, one merchant waved off his attempt to pay, saying he was happy enough just to salute the Canadian players from the famous Summit Series.

SINCE THIS RETURN to Moscow was part of a stroll down memory lane, I decided to seek a personal visit to 23 Old Stable Lane to see the Canadian embassy building during our last evening in the Russian capital. The number-two official at our embassy, Stephane Jobin, was kind enough to extend the courtesy to a former diplomat, made the arrangements and escorted me. The yellow pastel exterior seemed unchanged, but the building was now hemmed in by tall apartment complexes. City infill to be sure, but it also provided optimal views for surveillance. The Russian security guards were still there to check your documents before entry, but now once inside the gates we were immediately greeted by an armed member of the Canadian military police—a new development since 1972—who verified our car and its occupants.

Time had not been kind to the old building. Whatever interior elegance there might have been was now gone. Additional small, unsightly offices filled previous open spaces in order to make room for more needed staff. I immediately felt sorry for the occupants. Moscow was a tough enough assignment without cramped working conditions. The Canadian Club in the basement was still in operation, and its red-painted walls decorated with memorabilia—some of it hockey related—provided the only place of comfort.

Stephane asked if I thought I could find my old office. A door here, a corridor there, followed by a flight of stairs, and there we stood. Full circle. There was the old desk where I had read the Snowman's *Izvestia* article which lit the final fuse to ignite the series.

BACK AT THE hotel, Colleen Hixenbaugh and Helen Parker, our film crew, discovered that while they were out someone had entered their room and had rifled through Colleen's items, leaving Helen's untouched. Nothing seemed to be missing. Perhaps someone wanted to check up on what they were recording. Or maybe these intruders were just sending a warning.

The next morning, Saturday, September 16, the eight Team Canada players and the gang of nine departed Moscow on our respective aircraft. Our cellphones began working again upon arrival in London.

A week after returning to Canada, there was an invitation from the Russian ambassador in Ottawa, Alexandr Darchiev, to attend a hockey game to mark the forty-fifth anniversary of the Summit Series. He was getting in on the sports diplomacy action and had put together a team of players from the Russian embassy, with reinforcements brought in from their offices in Toronto and Washington. The Russian team wore the colours and called themselves "The Red Machine," the nickname of Central Army. Their opponents were "The Commandos," a team with a historic past, made up of personnel from the Royal Canadian Air Force. The result was a spirited game, with the Commandos emerging as the victors, 4–2.

In late November, Pat Stapleton, Frank Mahovlich, Chad Dawson and I set about meeting with politicians and bureaucrats in Ottawa to talk about preparations for the fiftieth anniversary of the Summit Series in 2022. We received a very warm reception. There were discussions about the Royal Canadian Mint producing one or a series of commemorative coins and Canada Post doing likewise with special-issue stamps. Parks Canada, which has responsibility for heritage designations, revealed plans to install trilingual (French, English and Russian) bronze plaques at the sites of all the games, in Montreal, Toronto, Winnipeg, Vancouver and Moscow. The Department of Canadian Heritage and the Canadian Museum of History also manifested considerable interest.

Sadly, the unfortunate passing of Pat Stapleton in April 2020 took much of the inspiration and steam out of the efforts and curtailed his initiative to pass on the personal lessons of Team Canada to a new generation of young Canadian students.

COVID-19 restrictions prevented a proper farewell to Pat, but the City of Sarnia, in a salute to its native son, renamed its municipal hockey arena in his honour. Two of Pat's other admirers, Martin Dupuis and David Honsberger, and I pulled together press clippings and personal messages of his passing into a printed booklet entitled *I'm Perfect Because You're In My Life*—one of Pat's favourite sayings. The booklet was presented to Pat's wife, Jackie, and her family. Fellow Team Canada board members Ken Dryden and Serge Savard picked up the reins from Pat.

CHAPTER SIXTEEN

THE HOCKEY BRIDGE

P AT STAPLETON, RIGHTLY, was seeking to create an enduring legacy for Team Canada with a vision based on the "Power of Teamwork." The Summit Series itself had an almost instantaneous legacy of its own: the internationalization of hockey. From the very first games in Canada, fans were mesmerized by a new brand of hockey: a new Russian and European brand based on speed, passing and puck control. They lapped it up and demanded to see more. The practitioners of this new brand became known overnight—Kharlamov, Yakushev, Mikhailov, Tretiak.

The WHA was looking to expand overseas to live up to the "World" in its name; while the NHL, perhaps out of competition with the WHA, was exploring its own idea of a European Professional League—a sort of eastern division—to play against North American NHL teams for the Stanley or World Cup. There was a second option in play—to draft European players into the NHL. In the 1971–72 season the NHL was made up of 359 Canadian players, 16 Americans and one each from Britain, Sweden and Denmark. A North American league almost entirely manned by Canadians. Following the Summit Series, North American coaches and scouts began showing up in Europe, beginning perhaps at the IIHF World Championships in Moscow from March 31 to April 15, 1973. At that tournament, thirty games were played in a double round robin in Group A, involving the USSR, Sweden, Czechoslovakia, Finland, Poland and West Germany. The Soviet Union won back the World Championship after losing it in Prague in April 1972 to the

Czechoslovakian team. This would be the twelfth Soviet championship. Accolades went to now familiar names: top scorer, Vladimir Petrov; top forward line (Petrov, Boris Mikhailov and Valeri Kharlamov); and among top defencemen Valeri Vasiliev and Alexander Gusev.

The North American coaches and scouts licked their chops at the thoughts of these Soviet stars playing for teams in the NHL or WHA, but despite various financial blandishments and being put on draft lists, it was not going to happen. The Soviet communist system controlled the players' destinies and would do so until the USSR and its hegemony over Eastern Europe began to collapse in 1989 and the early 1990s.

Strangely Vladislav Tretiak was not chosen as the top goaltender in 1973 in his home country, either by the tournament directorate or by the media selectors. Both opted instead for the Czechoslovak netminder Jiri Holecek. Given the communist regime in Prague at the time, Holecek was not going anywhere, either. There was, however, another player selected on the media all-star team at the World Championships. A defenceman, from Sweden, and not under the thumb of a communist government.

Gerry McNamara, a former goalie for the Toronto Maple Leafs, was one of the scouts who had come to the tournament. He had his eye on Swedish left winger Inge Hammarstrom. McNamara and I were seated together for one of the two Swedish games against the USSR, and based on seeing some of the earlier matches, I suggested he watch for the Swedish defenceman. Not long afterwards, the defenceman scooped up the puck in his own end and made a solo dash through the entire Soviet team.

His name was Borje Salming. Salming finished the tournament with ten points—one more than his countryman Hammarstrom. McNamara was most impressed, and based upon his recommendation, Salming was signed as a free agent by the Leafs less than a month later. Hammarstrom would follow suit in June, and both began their NHL careers with Toronto that September. Fellow Swede Tommie Bergman, a year earlier, was the first European to play a full season in the NHL, with the Detroit Red Wings.[176]

Despite withering criticism from commentators such as Don Cherry that the Swedes were "too soft," "chicken," or that they could go into a corner with eggs in their pockets and come out without them cracked, many of the pioneering Swedes had outstanding careers. Salming would go on to be chosen as one of the top 100 NHL players of all time by a blue ribbon panel comprised of distinguished members of the hockey community, including executives, media members and NHL alumni.

In 1974 Anders Hedberg and Ulf Nilsson would form a top scoring line with Bobby Hull of the WHA Winnipeg Jets. Both Swedes would later play for the NHL New York Rangers. Finland got in on the action, and in the early eighties Jari Kurri would form part of the "dynamic duo" with Wayne Gretzky for the Edmonton Oilers. Kurri would also join Gretzky on the NHL's top 100 players list.

The real sign that things had changed in the NHL was in 1989, when a European, Swedish forward Mats Sundin, was chosen first overall by the Quebec Nordiques in the annual draft. The European floodgates would open in that same time frame, led by Jaromir Jagr of Czechoslovakia, Nicklas Lidstrom of Sweden, and Teemu Selanne of Finland.

The Soviet players from 1972, as skilled as they were, were never permitted to join that exodus. Not only would it have severely weakened the Soviet national team's ability to continue winning World Championships and Olympic medals, but it would have exploded the long-held myth of the superiority of "Soviet Man" produced by the communist system. How could the system be superior if everyone wanted to leave it?

The Montreal Canadiens' general manager, Serge Savard, had put his former rival Vladislav Tretiak as number seven on his draft list in 1983, but all it turned out to be was a compliment to the star Soviet goalie.

The 1970s and early '80s passed with no change in Soviet policy, but in the last half of that decade, *glasnost* (openness) and *perestroika* (restructuring) arrived in the USSR, spurred on by new Communist Party General Secretary Mikhail Gorbachev. More information about what was happening in the rest of the world became available. Outstanding national team players like Igor Larionov would learn that players their own age, like Finland's Kurri, were reaping fame and wealth in North America far beyond what they could achieve in the USSR. Larionov and other Soviet players also would chafe at the harsh training camp regime imposed by Coach Viktor Tikhonov, confining every player, even if they were married, to eleven months in the Central Army training facilities— just as his predecessor Anatoli Tarasov had done many years before.

Then a slight crack in the door. Viktor Nechayev played three games for the Los Angeles Kings. Sergei Pryckhin in 1989 was given permission to play in the NHL and in two years suited up for forty-six games. Neither were top-flight players, but Soviet stars soon began to appear on NHL draft lists and political defections started, led by Alexander Mogilny, who boarded a plane in Stockholm after the World Championships there on May 1, 1989, and joined the Buffalo Sabres. Mogilny's line-mate Sergei Federov, with the help of Detroit Red Wings ownership, defected from the 1990 Goodwill Games in the US. The Red Wings also were able to surreptitiously extricate top defenceman Vladimir Konstantinov from the USSR and discharge his army service.

With the prospect of further defections and player pressure building from within, led by Viacheslav (Slava) Fetisov and Igor Larionov, Sovintersport, the governing body of sports at the time, reluctantly agreed to let eight players depart in exchange for cash compensation from their NHL salaries and a guarantee they would continue to play internationally for the Soviet Union.

By 1995, Red Wings management had acquired forwards Sergei Federov, Vyacheslav Kozlov and Igor Larionov as well as defencemen Vyacheslav Fetisov and Vladimir Konstantinov. They hit the ice together on October 27 of that year against the Calgary Flames and instantly became known in the hockey world as 'The Russian Five." Detroit would go on to win three Stanley Cups, in 1997 (with all five), 1998 (minus Konstantinov due to an automobile accident) and 2002 (with Larionov and Federov only). Their stellar play in winning North America's top prize put paid to the idea that the Russians, like other Europeans, were too soft and should not be over-represented on one NHL team. Their puck-control skills were also a discovery for younger players, who had never witnessed firsthand such prowess by their Summit Series predecessors, such as Valeri Kharlamov, Alexander Maltsev and Alexander Yakushev, over two decades earlier.

And just as Canadians had seen "a human face on communism" in the person of Vladislav Tretiak, so too did the Russian Five demonstrate to Americans and Canadians alike that they were not to be feared or hated, but rather admired for their skills and character.

Since then, Russian players have continued to flow into the USA and Canada on NHL rosters and perform in a spectacular manner—stars like Evgeni Malkin of the Pittsburgh Penguins; Alexander Ovechkin of the Washington Capitals, chasing the all-time goal-scoring record; and Nikita Kucherov of the Tampa Bay Lighting, the 2021 Stanley Cup finals MVP. The Stanley Cup itself has been carried to Moscow more than once since Slava Fetisov first did it in 1997.

By the autumn of 2021, seventeen different nationalities were represented in the NHL, led by Canada (44%), USA (26.6%), Sweden (9.5%), Finland (5.6%) and Russia (5.5%). A massive change from the Canadian dominance of 1972.

I WAS FORTUNATE enough to be able to return to Moscow for a second hockey visit in late September 2021—exactly forty-nine years after the Summit Series. Russia was experiencing great challenges in dealing with Covid 19 and it was a journey not without some risk. But the reward was to stand at centre ice with Vladislav Tretiak in the still existing and cleaned-up Palace of Sports; to be with him, Alexander Yakushev, Boris Mikhailov and Igor Larionov at the Russian Hockey Museum; and to stand on the street in front of the now-closed Canadian embassy chancery building on Old Stable Lane, gazing upwards one more time at my former office.

White Pine Pictures of Toronto and Adobe Productions International of Montreal had received partial funding from the

Department of Canadian Heritage to produce a bilingual, full-length documentary about the Summit Series, entitled *IceBreaker*, and the film's director, Robbie Hart, had asked me to accompany him to Moscow and to be part of the storytelling.

My renewed presence in the Russian capital provided considerable opportunity for reflection. To recall the time when Canadian solders first pulled on their skates to play ice hockey in Siberia in the winter of 1918–19; the introduction of the Canadian version of the game to the USSR back in the 1930s; the shocking Canadian defeat when the Soviet team first appeared on the international scene in 1954; the Summit Series itself and the multiple people in both countries who laboured so hard to organize the first-ever encounter of the best vs the best; and above all to recall the players and coaches who took to the ice to play what has since been called "The Series of the Century," providing what the CBC named the "Greatest Moment in Canadian Sport." All of it leading, for decades, to anxious anticipation and excitement whenever Canadians and Russians, at whatever level, face off against each other.

As a former diplomat it was impossible not to think about politics and diplomacy. I was asked as a case in point by the film director, while in front of the Eternal Flame adjacent to Red Square, to talk about the time from 1941 to 1945 when Canada and the USSR were allies in the Second World War. It was a high point in our relationship, but there were many lows over the years. Current bilateral relations seemed to be even frostier at this time than they were only four years earlier, in 2017, when I had last visited Moscow. More Canadian politicians and senior officials had since been added to the list of those persons who could not travel to Russia, reciprocating Western action. As a matter of fact, no Canadians would be issued a Russian visa without "special permission" from the Russian Foreign Ministry. In the bigger picture, Russia was being put back on NATO's enemies list. The only way director Hart and I could obtain a visa was through the intervention of the Russian Hockey Federation, led by Tretiak and the official connections to him by Canadian ambassador Alison LeClaire. Tretiak had been honoured by Canada on April 28,

2006, when presented by Governor General Michaëlle Jean with the Meritorious Service Medal (Civil Division). Now, the new official residence, occupied by Ambassador LeClaire, was to have a room named after him in recognition of his past accomplishments and ongoing role as President of the Canada-Russia Friendship Society.[177]

The past few years have witnessed political disagreements, bitterness, recriminations and military tensions between Canada/the West and Russia. The hockey bridge held nevertheless, and Russian NHL players continued to cross it into North America, as did junior and women's hockey players. Plans called for a celebration of the fiftieth anniversary of the Summit Series in September of 2022 and for the World Junior Championships to be held for the first time in two Siberian cities at the end of the same year.

Then on February 24, 2022, just as this book was sent to the printer, a thick, dark and menacing cloud descended on the international scene with President Putin's decision to use military force to invade democratic Ukraine. The rules-based international system has been severally challenged and almost unthinkably, the spectre of war has returned to Europe. Canada, as it did in 1951, has returned troops to Europe to help protect fellow NATO countries from further aggression by Vladimir Putin.

It is a situation not completely unlike what Pierre Elliott Trudeau faced in the early 1970s when dealing with a nuclear-armed hostile power following the Soviet invasion of Czechoslovakia. Russia cannot be wished away; nor the Russian people blamed in full measure for the actions of its leadership. President Putin has to be dealt with from a position of strength with no illusions, but we continue to need to find common ground to prevent further violence and war, and to encourage change.

Engagement and dialogue remain the foundation of diplomacy. And though diplomacy may falter from time to time, it remains an essential element of foreign policy. Hockey has been, and can again be, part of that process with Russia.

ACKNOWLEDGEMENTS

A LTHOUGH STILL IN diplomatic harness without the requisite time required to write a book, my best friend, Harold (Hal) Stoyles, kept prodding me over the decades to record the unique view I had of what was to become a seminal event in Canadian history. I thank him for his perseverance.

It always was easier to contribute background information, insights and quotations to other people's print accounts, broadcasting and film adaptations of what happened during those exhilarating and gut-wrenching twenty-seven days in September 1972. The downside to this approach was that others got to create the narrative. Often the diplomatic and political lead up to and context of the series was not adequately explained or was entirely missing. In one film re-enactment, the script for which was based in part on lengthy interviews with me, my person was transformed completely into a smoking francophone woman—a "composite character," I was later told.

Robin Higham, of the Retired Heads of Mission Association (RHOMA), led an effort to publish a series of personal essays written by former Canadian ambassadors and generously encouraged me to contribute. This endeavour stimulated the creative literary juices, and I wrote a short story about the Summit Series for the first publication, entitled "Declassified." A second series of essays followed under the title "Not Mentioned in Dispatches," in which I made two contributions, one about travelling abroad with family pets and another, more serious account summarizing the Pierre Elliott Trudeau "Peace Initiative" of 1983/84.

Diplomatic colleague and former Lieutenant-Governor of Ontario James Bartleman, with eight full-length books to his credit, provided valuable insights into the trials and tribulations, but spoke of the great satisfaction of writing longer and more personal stories.

My involvement with Pat Stapleton, Frank Mahovlich and others associated with Team Canada '72 Inc., and our visits to Moscow and Ottawa in 2017, made it abundantly clear there remained large and devoted Summit Series audiences in both Russia and Canada. A big thank you to them and as well to Jackie Stapleton for inviting me into her house to hear her story and to witness what seemed to be "the puck."

Jeffrey Simpson, former national columnist for *The Globe and Mail* and devoted hockey fan, urged me to go forward and introduced me to Roy MacGregor, who is seen by many as Canada's most beloved hockey writer. Both argued that history required an in-depth firsthand account of what transpired diplomatically behind the scenes of the Summit Series. Roy was gracious and magnanimous enough to lead me to Westwood Creative Artists in Toronto, where Chris Casuccio became a guiding light as my literary agent, shaping and bringing sparkle to my initial chapters. Chris was instrumental in negotiating offers from three Canadian publishing companies and in securing an American contract for an audio version of this book. Thank you, Chris.

I feel humbled that Douglas & McIntyre publisher Anna Comfort O'Keeffe took a chance on a first-time author such as myself. She has warmly welcomed me into the fold, been extremely responsive to my various queries, and demonstrated great patience with a rookie in the publishing world. The assignment of substantive editor Derek Fairbridge to work with me was my lucky day. I was thrilled that he loved hockey, was an avid historian and had a soft personal spot for the 1970s to boot. Derek rescued me from going off on multiple tangents, falling into the bad habit of reciting long lists, and writing in places as if I was record-ing the minutes of a meeting rather than telling a narrative to hold the interest of readers. He helped me find my voice on many occasions by asking the right questions and by making adroit suggestions. A hat trick for you, Derek.

Copy-editor Noel Hudson kept me amused with his light touch and professionalism as we waded through the not-so-glamorous but vital work of dealing with various forms of grammar and punctuation, as well as fact-checking. Thanks, Noel, for all those corrections you had to make.

Beth McAulay, owner and senior editor of The Editing Company, was unfailingly prompt, courteous and competent in dealing with the ever-tricky questions of securing permissions to use certain texts and photographs.

My researcher, Sean P. Stoyles, deserves special mention for his uncanny ability to locate relevant files and documents in the vast treasure trove of Library and Archives Canada. These materials have helped refresh my memory and ensure accuracy in telling the diplomatic story. Accessing documents was doubly difficult these past two years as a result of Covid, which shuttered LAC for lengthy periods of time and reduced essential staff. I appreciate in this regard the special efforts of Kayley Kimball and Pascal LeBlond of LAC for exceptional service in ensuring timely access to the photographs of Frank Lennon.

The one person to whom I absolutely owe a deep sense of gratitude is my Embassy Moscow colleague and long-time friend Peter Hancock. Together we experienced the Trudeau and Kosygin visits of 1971 and were front and centre for the 1972 Summit Series. He was a brilliant mentor about East-West relations and the mystery of Russia, and our careers intersected several times later on European affairs. He was a natural go-to on a myriad of issues and personalities when I needed trusted and true advice as I prepared this manuscript. We discussed it for hours on end to capture the right content and balance. This book is in good part yours, Peter. Much appreciated.

At the same time, I should say how fortunate I was to have had Robert A.D. Ford as my first ambassador, one of Canada's most distinguished. He taught me a great deal about what was required to be an effective and respected Canadian representative abroad. I am pleased this book has allowed me to highlight some of his valuable and essential contribution to improving relations between Canada and the Soviet Union and to the making of the Summit Series. The role of the Under Secretary of State for External Affairs Ed Ritchie in dealing with the big diplomatic picture associated with Prime Minister Trudeau's detente mandate also needed to emerge from the shadows.

Thanks to the following External Affairs personnel for providing me with some of the finer details of the history and exploits of the Moscow Maple Leafs: James H. (Si) Taylor, Doug Woods, Les Cundell, Terry Hayes and, of course, "Goal-a-Game" Hancock. Also, a big tip of the hat to Jan and Janice Drent for their able assistance in recalling our time together in Russian-language school and the initial days in Moscow.

Roy MacGregor deserves a second round of applause for introducing me to documentary filmmakers Peter Raymont of White Pine Pictures, in Toronto, and Robbie Hart of Adobe Productions International, in Montreal. The latter two, with an eye on the fiftieth anniversary of the series, were looking for a different optic by which to tell the story of 1972. They optioned this book with the valued assistance of my film agent at Westwood, the astute and highly regarded Michael Levine. Roy, Peter, Robbie and I melded into a formidable team in writing a film proposal, securing financing and arranging unique interviews. While this meant I was riding two horses at once, with a book and film, the experience generated enormous amounts of cross-fertilization, opened unexpected vistas and permitted a second return trip to Moscow. I thank the three of them for their intelligence, energy, enthusiasm and skill. The anticipated success of the film, entitled *IceBreaker*, will be due largely to their efforts.

When the writing and everything surrounding it, including numerous deadlines, became frustrating or seriously challenging, I could count on my immediate neighbours, particularly Val Leavitt, for a sympathetic ear and encouragement. Thanks to them and to Julia Dashkevich of Images Interalia, in Perth, for her help with numerous printings of drafts and uploading of various materials.

My daughter and son, Tatiana and Eric Chabeaux-Smith, were behind me one hundred percent of the way. The storytelling became a family affair, and they supplied lots of love and constant support when I needed it most. When I asked for their advice on an early draft, both were quick to respond not only with certain praise but also valued critical comment on areas for improvement. They didn't hold back on the latter. When my computer appeared to go haywire or text alarmingly disappeared into cyberspace, they were the ones who calmly answered my frantic calls for assistance. Don't worry, Dad, was a constant refrain. Love you both.

Finally, and most importantly, my beloved Laurielle. While she had departed by the time I started this book, she was with me in spirit every step of the way. How could it not be so when I was writing about our life together? She was my love, my wife, my friend and my partner in diplomacy. Every scene I described brought images of her thousand-watt smile, her admirable sense of style, her warm understanding, and her determination when circumstances so dictated. We shared the Moscow experience together, and I would have achieved little without her. I only hope I have captured some of her essence and vitality in this book.

GARY J. SMITH
Perth, Ontario

NOTES

1   Captain W.E. Dunham, "The Canadians in Siberia." *Macleans*, May 1, 1919.

2   Ibid.

3   Twenty-one members of the Canadian force died of illness or accident, with fourteen buried in the local Churkin Naval Cemetery.

4   The bandy net is 11 feet by 7 feet, almost like a field hockey goal, while an ice hockey net is only 6 feet by 4 feet.

5   The USSR was made up of fifteen different republics in the 1970s, of which Russia was the largest.

6   Russia and the USSR are different entities, though many people use them interchangeably, as they do when referring to Russians or Soviets. The Soviet Union/USSR was created in December 1922 and was dissolved in December 1991.

7   Anton Trolanovski, "As Russians Vote Resignation, Anger and Fear of a Post-Putin Unknown. *New York Times*, September 17, 2021. The activist Mikhail Ezhiyev, in noting the unpredictability of Russia, observed that Lenin's prediction in January 1917 that a decisive uprising could be decades away was proven wrong when the revolution began only a month later. Equally, he noted that the USSR in the 1980s seemed like it could last forever but collapsed a few years later.

8   In addition to being a professor of Economics and Political Science, Leacock was said to be the best-known English-speaking humourist in the world during the years from 1915 to 1925. He is perhaps best remembered for his book *Sunshine Sketches of a Little Town*.

9   Sinden's views on the referee situation are extensively spelled out in his book *Hockey Showdown: The Canada-Russia Hockey Series* (Doubleday Canada, 1972).

10   The Department of External Affairs vacated the Langevin Block in 1973 when it consolidated all its operations and personnel in the Lester B. Pearson Building on Sussex Drive. The prime minister and staff and elements of the privy council became the new occupants of the Langevin Block.

11   Ingrid Hall. Female foreign service officers were first hired in 1947, though they had carried out the same functions starting in 1943 as "clerks" during the war. Margaret Meagher became the first female Canadian Ambassador in 1958 when assigned to Israel.

12   See Brendan Kelly's biography *The Good Fight: Marcel Cadieux and Canadian Diplomacy* (UBC Press, 2019).

13   Russian bombers have been intercepted off the Alaskan and Canadian coasts in recent years.

14   Diplomats were not paid overtime, though administrative staff were.

15   Normally the Governor General's Foot Guards.

16   The United States, United Kingdom, Australia, New Zealand and Canada.

17   Romania and Albania did not participate, while troops from the German Democratic Republic were held back by Brezhnev at the last minute out of fear of stoking memories of previous German military intervention.

18   There was an exception for "very little purposes (research, medical, pharmaceutical or protective)."

19   Locations of the language schools had varied over time, as had those responsible for the program. In September 1969, it was under the nominal authority of the Royal Canadian Air Force, even though all three branches of the military (Navy, Air Force and Army) had been unified into the Canadian Armed Forces nineteen months earlier.

20   There were three military attachés at the embassy (Navy, Air Force and Army).

21   German word for "defence power" or military.

22   To be fair, skyjacking had increased around the world, particularly in 1969 and 1970, including an Aeroflot flight from Batumi in October of 1970. Bombing of civilian aircraft had been occurring for decades. Indeed, Joseph-Albert Guay was hung in Canada on January 12, 1951, for the September 9, 1949, bombing of a Canadian Pacific Airlines flight over Quebec which killed all nineteen passengers and four crew members.

23   Any freely traded currency on world markets. The Soviet rouble was considered a soft currency because no one outside of the USSR wanted or needed it.

24   Ford also was a man of letters, having received wide acclaim for his own poetry and translations of Soviet poets. In 1956 he won the Governor General's Award for Poetry or Drama for *Window on the North*. McClelland and Stewart in 1969 published his book *The Solitary City: Toronto*. He was made a Companion of the Order of Canada in 1971.

25   When it was later exported, the name was changed to Lada, which was easier for foreigners to pronounce.

26   Yes, the Leafs' last Stanley Cup.

27   The chancery is the office part of an embassy. The other part being the official residence of the ambassador, which may or may not be collocated.

28   Canada was in the Second European Division, with Britain, Australia and New Zealand, as part of an English-speaking grouping. The First European Division was responsible for all other Western European countries. When Britain joined the European Communities on January 1, 1973, Canada was relocated to a new North American Division with the USA.

29   Lester Pearson had been there in 1955 but as External Affairs Minister, not as PM.

30   Christina Newman, "Our Heroes on the Russian Front," *Macleans*, August 1, 1971.

31   The fact that Gwishiani's husband had a long history as a KGB agent seemed not to have mattered.

32   J.L. Granatstein and Robert Bothwell, *Pirouette: Pierre Trudeau and Canadian Foreign Policy* (University of Toronto Press, 1990), p. 195. The part of the quotation in brackets was not included in the *New York Times* report of the press conference. See "Trudeau Says Pact with Soviet Affirms an Independent Policy," Theodore Shabad, May 21, 1971.

33   External Affairs confidential telegram PDM-174 of May 28, 1971 to Ambassador Washington only and copied to Ambassador Moscow only.

34   This was part of the "Nixon Shock," which also included two other major measures: suspension of the convertibility of the USA dollar and other currencies into gold and a 90-day freeze on US wages and prices to control inflation.

35   Geza Matrai.

36   Retold in an August 8, 2014, *National Post* story by Tristin Hopper: "In 1971, a Canadian rode the Soviet premier like a horse and only spent two months in jail."

37   Confidential briefing note prepared by External Affairs for the prime minister, September 30, 1972.

38   Laing was to lead the official Canadian delegation to the Summit Series games in Moscow.

39   Kosygin was presented with a new pair of skates during his visit to Parliament.

40   Jay Walz, "Hockey Breaks the Ice and Kosygin Smiles," *New York Times*, October 24, 1971.

41   "Metro Morning" broadcast April 7, 2006, Andy Barrie interview with Aggie Kukulowicz, CBC Radio Archives.

42   Ibid.

43   Ibid.

44   Starovoitov never referred to this proposal in my presence, though he did recall Eagleson's reference to being a lawyer for the workers.

45   Contained in a confidential briefing note of April 19, 1971, by D.P. Hicks for Prime Minister Trudeau's visit to Moscow.

46   Ibid.

47   Ibid.

48   Tarasov had been a player-coach until 1954, when he was named the team's head coach. Central Red Army won every national championship from 1955 until 1972 except for four years (57/62/67/69).

49   Told by Murray Williamson, coach of the US national hockey team, to Ambassador Ford and conveyed in embassy numbered letter 535 of August 13, 1971, to External (FAI), entitled "Canada and International Hockey."

50   Contained in embassy restricted telegrams 493, of February 24, 1971, and 606, of March 12, 1971.

51   Embassy dispatch 687 of October 14, 1971. The translation had been held up due to urgent work about family reunification associated with the Kosygin visit to Canada.

52   Report contained in confidential telegram 4021 of December 1, 1971, entitled "CDA-USSR Hockey Relations."

53   Sweden sent a junior squad to the dismay of the Izvestia tournament organizers.

54   The embassy's numbered letter 14 of January 6, 1972, conveyed the interviews of Soviet coach Chernyshev and IIHF president Bunny Ahearne under the title "Izvestia Hockey Tournament."

55   The Soviet gift-giving equivalent of Santa Claus.

56   Films of the Stanley Cup were sent out annually to military staff and embassies by the Department of National Defence.

57   This was not paranoia. The state security apparatus was well known to have its agents located in strategic positions within all Soviet government ministries and particularly within the various elements of the Soviet military.

58   The reports on the Starovoitov/Fedosov meeting and embassy recommendations were contained in dispatch number 80 of February 8, 1972, and restricted telegram 281 of February 9, 1972, entitled "CDA-Soviet Hockey Relations."

59   Contained in embassy numbered letter 116 of February 29, 1972.

60   Moscow classified telegram 645 of March 28, 1972, entitled "Innatl Hockey."

61   Moscow confidential telegram 806 of April 17, 1972, to Embassy Prague. This would have been passed to the Canadian delegation.

62   Ibid.

63   Prague confidential telegram 323 of April 18, 1972, to External (FAP).

64   Accounts of press coverage of the events are contained in Embassy Prague numbered letters 261, of April 21, and 285, of May 4, 1972.

65   Contained in Canadian embassy Prague numbered letter 285 of May 4, 1972.

66   Contained in Moscow telegram 829 of April 19 and numbered letter 350 of April 27, 1972.

67   Ibid.

68   Ibid.

69   Ibid.

70   Moscow confidential telegram 1419 of June 22, 1972, addressed to External (FAP), entitled "CDA-USSR Hockey Series."

71   Contained in a restricted memorandum to file by A.T. Chernushenko of Information Division, entitled "Report On Hockey Negotiations in Moscow, July 19-20, 1972."

72   Ibid.

73   Eagleson later mentioned the number seven plus three for a total of ten out of the thirty-eight; player Pat Stapleton told the author in latter years his speculation was "close to half"—but he provided no specific count nor specific names.

74   Ibid., plus Patrick Reid, *Wild Colonial Boy: A Memoir* (Douglas & McIntyre, 1995), pp. 207–222.

75   Eagleson, Sinden, Ferguson, Haggert and Cannon.

76   Chernushenko, "Report On Hockey Negotiations in Moscow, July 19-20, 1972."

77   Moscow restricted telegram 1651 of July 22, 1972, to External (PDM), reports on the strategy used related to the Prague game. Restricted telegram 1660 of July 24, 1972, to External (FAP), reports on the personal dynamics of the Canadian delegation.

78   The person in charge of the embassy when the ambassador is out of the country.

79   The restricted telegram 1660 of July 24, 1972, was addressed directly to Under Secretary Ritchie.

80   External Affairs restricted telegram PDM-120 of July 24, 1972.

81   He was referring to the CAHA and Kryczka among others.

82 A report on the broadcasting negotiations is contained in a memorandum to file by A.T Chernushenko of Information Division entitled "Canada-USSR Hockey Matches Report on television and radio transmission discussions," Moscow, July 19-29, 1972. See also Moscow restricted telegram 1678 of July 23, 1972, addressed to External (FAP) entitled "Soviet Hockey Series."

83 Unclassified memorandum of July 31, 1972, from Information Division/Chernushenko to Consular Division/Munro.

84 "Private and Confidential" letter of September 5, 1972, from Minister of Veteran Affairs Arthur Laing to External Affairs Minister Mitchell Sharp.

85 Ibid.

86 The Soviet Foreign Ministry at that time had a separate division for the US.

87 Contained in Moscow restricted telegram 1723 of August 1, 1972, to External (FAI), entitled "Hockey Matches Moscow."

88 Moscow restricted telegram 1848 of August 1, 1972, to External (FAP), entitled "Hockey Series."

89 Ibid. Includes report on this entire discussion.

90 EXTOTT telegram (FAP) 119/72 to Embassy Moscow entitled "Hockey."

91 Moscow restricted telegram 1870 of August 21, 1972, to External (FAP), entitled "Hockey Series–CDN Del."

92 Moscow restricted telegram 1869 of August 21, 1971, to External (FAP), entitled "Exchange of Coaches."

93 Vsevolod Kukushkin, who worked for TASS at the time of the Summit Series and has had a long career as a Russian sports journalist.

94 It was unclear who decided to keep the visit to under a week.

95 Report on meeting with Intourist August 24th (Len Knott, Gary Smith, John Alexander). Source: Library and Archives Canada/Department of External Affairs fonds/file-55-26-Hockey-1-USSR

96 The Intourist hotel was still a "vipers' nest" of black marketers and sex workers and their KGB handlers, but it was the most modern hotel at the time.

97 Contained in Moscow restricted telegram 1951 of August 28, 1972, to External (FAP), entitled "Hockey Series CDN Del."

98 Moscow restricted telegram 1976 of August 30, 1972, to External (FAP), entitled "CDN-Soviet Series-Hockey Equipment," and my letter to John Cooper dated August 30, 1972.

99 Moscow restricted telegram 1959 of August 29, 1972, to External (FAP).

100 Ibid.

101 Moscow confidential telegram 1995 of August 31, 1972, to External (FAP), entitled "CDA-Soviet Hockey Series-Business and Other VIPs."

102 Howe sat out the 1971–72 and 72–73 seasons before joining the Houston Aeros in the autumn of 1973.

103 Referred to by Alexander Kubyshkin in his article "Hot Ice during Cold War: Soviet Reflections on Summit Series 1972," contained in the book Coming Down the Mountain, Rethinking the 1972 Summit Series, edited by Brian Kennedy (Wolsack and Wynn, 2014). Kubyshkin says there is reference to this analytic chart in Vladimir Tretiak's book Hockeynaya Epopeya [The Hockey Epic] (Leonardo, 1993).

104 Ibid., p. 180.

105 Details of this discussion and action are contained in External Affairs documents: confidential memorandum from FLA (Legal Operations Division) to PDS of September 06/72, entitled "Equipe de Hockey Sovietique: Procedures Judiciaire"; GEP – Director General of European Affairs restricted memorandum to file of September 06/72, entitled "Dagenais Case: Conversation with the Soviet Ambassador"; and FLA memorandum for the minister of September 14/72, entitled "Quebec Provincial Court Action Involving the Government of the USSR." All three documents can be found in Library and Archives Canada file RG-25, Volume 10921, File 55-26-Hockey-1-USSR Pt 4.1.

106 Vsevolod Kukushkin, Big Time Hockey: The Beginning (Chelovek Publishing, 2017), p. 38.

107 Covering my travel costs and expenses while in Canada were easier to manage if I was listed as part of the Soviet team rather than a standalone participant. Hockey Canada covered the domestic costs of the USSR as per the Prague Agreement.

108 Extremely low by today's prices, which run into the hundreds of dollars for a quality seat. Season ticket-holders were able to purchase tickets at seven dollars per ticket.

109 *The Globe and Mail* account of August 1, 1972, by Rick Fraser, entitled "Ticket applications show Quebec fans least interested in Canada-Russia series."

110 "This Country in the Morning," September 2, 1972, CBC Radio Archives.

111 *Big Time Hockey*, p. 34.

112 Patrick White, "The Story of the Summit Series, as its never been told before," *The Globe and Mail*, September 15, 2012. This version just says "a communist..."

113 Related to the author in later years by Team Canada member Pat Stapleton.

114 "The Story of the Summit Series, as it has never been told before," *The Globe and Mail*, September 15, 2012.

115 The Soviet press coverage was monitored by the Canadian Embassy, and these articles were contained in letter number 575 of September 7, 1972, to External (FAP), entitled "Canadian Hockey in the Soviet Press (Part 1). Library and Archives Canada/Department of External Affairs fonds/ file-55-26-Hockey-1-USSR

116 Ibid.

117 Wikipedia records that Eagleson ran federally, in 1963, for a seat in the House of Commons in the riding of York West but was defeated by Toronto Maple Leafs hockey player Red Kelly of the Liberal Party. Later the same year, Eagleson won the newly created provincial riding of Lakeshore and served as a Progressive Conservative member of the Ontario legislature until 1967, when he was defeated by a representative of the New Democratic Party. He was a major fundraiser for the PC party in the late 1960s and 1970s and was president of the PC Party of Ontario from 1968 until 1976.

118 I was given two seats for the game.

119 Dating from 1967.

120 This was done in Sweden just prior to the arrival in Moscow.

121 Not too long afterwards, Dent was involved with Jean Chrétien, then Minister of Indian Affairs and Northern Development, in a program to send musk oxen to the USSR. We at the embassy named the first to arrive "Little Ivor." The herd is now said to number in the thousands.

122 Internal External Affairs memorandum of September 6, 1972, from L.A.D. Stephens (FAP) to John Halstead (PDH), entitled "Air Canada Brochure for Canadian Hockey Pilgrims."

123 Ibid.

124 This was a proposed addition to the brochure from Stephens. Halstead lamented, "It was too bad Air Canada went ahead with the printing of the brochure without getting the green light from us."

125 *Big Time Hockey*, p. 66.

126 Ibid.

127 In later years the Soviet players would blame Bobrov for this action, saying it would never have been permitted under the reign of Tarasov, the strict disciplinarian.

128 Referred to in *The Official 40th Anniversary Celebration of the Summit Series*, told by the Players with Andrew Podnieks (McClelland and Stewart, 2012), p. 69.

129 The first board advertising in the NHL occurred in 1979 in Minnesota.

130 Eddie Johnston was dressed as the backup goalie.

131 The Russian word *Rybiata* might also be translated into "guys" or "teammates."

132 Jean Beliveau and Chrys Goyens, *Jean Beliveau: My Life in Hockey* (Greystone Books, 2005), p. 114.

133 *Big Time Hockey*, p. 82.

134 Elaborated upon in Chapter Fourteen.

135 Ibid.

136 *Shayba*, in Russian, means the puck.

137 Sault St. Marie was the hometown of the Esposito brothers.

138 This was the first game in which the USSR outshot Team Canada (29–22).

139 As related directly to the author.

140 *Wild Colonial Boy*, p. 214.

141   Ibid., pp. 214–15.

142   Contained in Moscow confidential telegram 2194 of September 25, 1972, to External (GEA), entitled "Laing Call on Kosygin." Library and Archives Canada/Department of External Affairs fonds/file 55-26-Hockey-1-USSR.

143   No one readily admitted to being the culprit, and Esposito would later say it was all a made-up joke.

144   *Wild Colonial Boy*, p. 213.

145   *Coming Down the Mountain*, pp. 184–5.

146   Game Six was the other.

147   *Wild Colonial Boy*, p. 216.

148   Ibid., p. 147.

149   As related to the author by Peter Hancock.

150   The Plouffe affair is detailed in Moscow telegrams 2226, 2238 and 2248, of September 28 and 29, 1972, addressed to External (GEA) under the heading "Detention of Plouffe, Pierre."

151   This is my recollection of how this conversation went. Every word spoken may not be entirely as written, but the sentiment and thrust of the arguments presented are duly reflective of what transpired. Orr's last comment has clearly stuck with me for these almost fifty years.

152   Ambassador Ford was told this story by well-known Russian poet Andrei Voznesensky and forwarded it to External in numbered letter 672 of October 30, 1972, entitled "Tail-piece to the Hockey Epic."

153   *Wild Colonial Boy*, p. 217.

154   Ibid.

155   The *Time Canada* four-and-a-half-page photo-essay cover story of October 9, 1972, was entitled "What a Difference a Goal Makes." It was written in Montreal by associate editor Geoffrey James with considerable input from correspondent Bob Lewis, who was at the games in Canada and Moscow.

156   Neither were there any Team Canada players from Alberta, British Columbia nor the Northwest Territories.

157   Like Dick Beddoes of the *Globe and Mail*, Robertson ended up eating his own words in a "Crow Salad" with Russian dressing at a Montreal restaurant.

158   External (GEA) unclassified telegram 956 of September 29, 1972, to Embassy Moscow.

159   Contained in an unclassified telegram from Embassy Moscow on October 10, 1972. This was for the record only, as the original message from Kosygin was delivered via the Soviet embassy in Ottawa.

160   Confidential telegram to External (GEA) number 2281 of October 4, 1972, entitled "Hockey and Soviet-CDA Relations."

161   Ambassador Ford's restricted letter of October 20, 1972, to L.A.D. Stephens, Director General of Public Affairs.

162   A photograph of this letter was contained on p. 131 of *Power Play: The Memoirs of Hockey Czar Alan Eagleson* (McClelland and Stewart, 1991), by Eagleson, with Scott Young.

163   Conveyed to External (FAP) in a numbered letter as part of the embassy's ongoing coverage of "Canadian Hockey in the Soviet Press."

164   Translated by the embassy and sent to External (FAP) as part of the numbered letter series mentioned above.

165   Ibid.

166   Ibid.

167   Julia Cart, "Sometimes He's the Terror of Toronto Hockey: Even to His Own Team. Maple Leafs Owner Harold Ballard Is a Master Manipulator," *Los Angeles Times*, November 14, 1989.

168   Reported to External (FAP) in Moscow confidential telegram 2364 of October 13, 1972, entitled "NHL/USSR Hockey."

169   Ibid.

170   Embassy Moscow restricted letter number 28 of January 18, 1973, addressed to External Affairs (FAP) under heading "International Hockey: National Hockey League Proposals for 1973-74 Games with USSR."

171   Wikipedia, London Lions ice hockey.

172   While having a social orientation, RHOMA also has an educational and advocacy mandate for the profession of diplomacy. In 2020, the name was changed to AmbCanada (The Canadian Ambassador's Alumni Association).

173   At that point, President Putin had held the office from 1999 until 2008 and then been elected again in 2012 for a further six-year term. He was re-elected in 2018 for another six-year term. The Russian Constitution had limited office holders to a once-renewable six-year term, but that restraint has now been removed. During the period 2008–2012 he served as prime minister, not president, but in effect still controlled the Russian government.

174   It could also be translated as "Fair Russia" or "A Fair and Just Russia." It has been described as a "managed opposition" party as a result of its apparent foundation by the Kremlin.

175   *Big Time Hockey*, p. 10.

176   Ulf Sterner was the first European to play in the NHL, but it was only four games with the New York Rangers, in 1964–65. This was in an era in Europe when body-checking in the offensive zone was not permitted.

177   Other rooms (beyond the Tretiak room) expected to be named at the new official residence, highlighting positive elements in the bilateral relations, include: the "Murmansk Run" map room (for military cooperation during WWII); the "Glenn Gould" salon (for cultural cooperation honouring his precedent setting and highly successful eight piano concerts in Moscow and Leningrad in May 1957); the "Inuksuk" gathering room (highlighting arctic cooperation); the "Cosmos" room (highlighting space cooperation) and the "Robert and Theresa Ford" room (highlighting diplomatic relations).

NOTE: All the diplomatic documents referred to in the notes and in the text are held by Library and Archives Canada and are contained in the following archival files.

EXTERNAL AFFAIRS FONDS:
RG 25 Vols 9293/9294/9295 File 20-Cda-9-Trudeau Pts 3/4/6/7/8/9/13 re Trudeau visit to Moscow
RG 25 Vol 9302. File 20-USSR-9-Kosygin pt 4.3 K-3 re Kosygin visit to Canada
RG 25 Vol 10921 File 55-26-Hockey-2-1-USSR pts 2.2/3.0/3.1/3.2//4.0/4.1/6.0
RG 25 Vol 10922 File 55-26-Hockey-2-1-USSR pt 9

HOCKEY CANADA FONDS:
MG 28 I 263 Vol 04. 300-1 and 300-5

FRED SGAMBATI FONDS (PRIVATE COLLECTION):
MG 31 K17 Vol 2 File International Hockey

INDEX

Kukulowicz, Aggie, 49, 51–52, 88, 91, 93, 114, 122, 129, 156, 251, 255

Kukushkin, Vsevolod, 170, 197, 204, 208, 218, 232

Kulagin, Boris, 8, 124, 141, 148, 173, 179

Kur, John, 287

Kurri, Jari, 296–97

Kurtenbach, Orland, 86

Kuskin, Viktor, 150

Kutuzov, Mikhail, 44

Kutuzovsky Prospect, 44

Kuzkin, Victor, 165, 186, 209, 219, 221, 231

Labour/Work. See Trud

Laika (Soviet space dog), 49

Laing, Arthur, 10–11, 86, 133, 136, 194, 202, 215-16

Lang, Chris, 118

Langevin Block, 25, 29, 33

Lapointe, Guy, 165, 173, 186, 201, 209–10

Larionov, Igor, 296–98, 297

Larocque, Michel "Bunny," 118

Larsen, Frank, 4

Laxer, James, 238

le Carré, John. See Cornfield, David

Leacock, Stephen, xi

Leavitt, Val, 304

Lebedev, Yuri, 150, 179, 182, 200, 219

Lecavalier, Vincent, 282

LeClaire, Alison, 299–300

Lee, Gord, 4

Lefaive, Lou, 72, 104, 119–20, 122, 124–30, 145

Legends Park, 275–76, 283

Lenin Stadium, 125, 290

Lenin, Vladimir, vii, 43, 96, 169

Leningrad, 50, 61–62, 65, 76, 101, 135, 139, 214

Lennon, Frank, 303

Levine, Michael, 304

Levy, David, 126

Lewis, Bob, 226

Liapkin, Yuri, 175, 179, 200, 210–11, 234

Lidstrom, Nicklas, 296

Little Flame. See Ogonek

Loktev, Konstantin, 246–48

Lombardi, Vince, 230

London Lions, 256–57

Los Angeles Kings, 297

Lotte hotel, 274, 288

Lutchenko, Vladimir, 150, 163, 173, 186–87, 213, 230, 276

MacGregor, Roy, 190, 302, 304

Maclean, Donald, 48

Macleans, 108

Mahovlich, Frank, 117, 154, 165, 176, 186, 188, 209, 213, 217, 226, 257, 271, 277–78, 291–92, 302

Mahovlich, Peter, 154, 165, 168, 175–77, 179, 186, 197, 199, 201, 228, 232–34, 277–78, 289

"Main Coaches' Council," 149–50

Malkin, Evgeni, 284, 298

Maltsev, Alexander, 131, 150, 155, 167, 186–87, 276, 298

Manulife, 263

Maple Leaf Gardens, 17–18, 117, 139, 141, 173, 176, 250

Martin, Paul Sr., 86

Martin, Richard (Rick), 186, 200, 207, 285

Marx, Karl, 43, 169

Massey Ferguson, xi

Massey Harris, xi

Matryoshka dolls, 185, 227

Mayorov, Boris, 97

McLellan, Johnny, 139–41

McLeod, Jack, 108

McNamara, Gerry, 295

McQueen, Steve, 50

Meagher, Margaret, 5

Metropole Hotel, 125, 142, 235

Michigan Wolverines, 277

Middle East, 74

Mikhailov, Boris, 131, 150, 155, 166–67, 174, 186–88, 213, 220, 222–23, 227, 285, 294–95, 298

Mikita, Stan, 18, 154, 172, 176, 186

Minneapolis Millers, 51

Minnesota Vikings, 91

Miroshnichenko, Boris, 137

Mishakov, Evgeni, 150, 154–55, 174, 182, 186, 200, 209, 219, 232

Mitterrand, François, 260

Mogilny, Alexander, 297

Molson brewery, 53–54

Molson, John "David," 53, 91, 164

Montreal, 3, 9, 21, 40, 49, 53, 110–11, 131–32, 159–62, 171–76, 186–87, 198–99, 205, 252–53, 258

Montreal Canadiens, 1, 16, 53, 79, 86–87, 91, 106, 113, 118, 153, 158, 164–65, 207, 237–39, 296

Montreal Forum, 137, 163–67, 174, 176

Montreal Olympics, 145

Montreal Star, 126, 130, 168, 190, 238

Moore, Spencer, 127

Moores, Frank, 238

Morris, David, 271

Moscow International Tournament. See Izvestia Tournament

parents of, 15

personal contact with Russians, 64–65

recreational sports activities of, 50–55

return to Moscow, 269–92, 298–99

Russian language training, 36–38, 40

Russian literature studies, 39

school education of, 15–17, 20

Vice-Consul designation, 41

wedding of, 30

Ziegler's employment offer to, 253–54

"Snegovik" (The Snowman), 95

Sochi, 272–73, 277–78, 283

Soloduhkin, Vyacheslav, 150, 186

Solzhenitsyn, Alexandr, 39

South Vietnam, 74

Sovetsky Sport, 94, 198

Sovetsky Sport Tournament, 100, 104–5, 112, 139

Sovetsky Sports Club, 100

Soviet gulag prison system, 39

Soviet Ice Hockey Federation, 4, 88, 93, 96–97, 105, 126, 143, 185, 199, 208, 227, 249, 255–56, 282

Soviet Ice Hockey Hall of Fame, 181

"Soviet Man," development of, 9–10

Soviet militia, 6, 58, 62, 134, 195, 203, 207, 214, 223–25, 229, 233–35, 241

Soviet Post Office, 198

Soviet State Committee for Physical Culture and Sport, 10, 103–4, 121, 123, 128, 131, 136–37, 139, 141, 144–45, 148, 196, 209, 215, 227, 254

Sovintersport, 297

Spartak, 98, 101–2, 140, 149, 152, 255, 257, 286

Spassky, Boris, 146–47, 235

Sport Canada, 72, 119

Sports Games, 246

Sports Palace. *See* Palace of Sports

Stalin, Joseph, x, xii, 10, 37, 47, 64, 84, 283

"Stalinist Gothic," 283

Stanfield, Robert, 164, 173, 183

Stanley Cup, 3, 17–18, 51, 79, 92, 96–97, 153, 165, 190, 237, 251, 284, 294, 297–98

Stapleton, Jackie, 268, 293, 302

Stapleton, Pat, 18, 173, 175, 201, 203, 210, 221, 231–34, 257, 262–73, 275–88, 292–94

Starovoitov, Andrei, 4, 88, 97–100, 103, 105–6, 109, 111–15, 119, 121–25, 129, 131, 145, 148–49, 152, 162–64, 168, 175, 184, 208, 214, 226, 249–57, 282

Starshinov, Vyacheslav, 150

Stasi (East German intelligence), 63

State Automobile Authorities, 67

State Committee for Radio and Television, 126–27

Stoyles, Harold (Hal), 267, 301

Strathroy, 262, 268

Sundin, Mats, 296

"Super Series," 257–59

Suslov, Mikhail, 9–10

Sweden, 5, 71, 75, 89, 94, 100, 103, 106–7, 115, 119, 127, 130, 136, 196–98, 201, 229, 251, 258, 282, 294–95, 298

Tallon, Dave, 186, 271–72

Tamerlane, ix

Tampa Bay Lighting, 298

Tanchik, Granny, 36–37

Tarasov, Anatoli, 90–94, 97, 99–103, 105, 155–56, 297

TASS news agency, 52, 93, 100–101, 106–7, 243

Tatneft, 282

Tchaikovsky, 10, 39

Team Canada '72, 1–8, 12–13, 18, 68, 109, 117–19, 121, 123–24, 126–27, 129, 136, 138–41, 145, 148–50, 153–55, 158, 160–61, 164–69, 171–72, 174–78, 181–83, 185, 187–90, 192–93, 195–201, 203–15, 217, 219, 221, 223, 225, 227–35, 238–39, 246–47, 250, 253–55, 262–72, 265, 277–78, 283, 286, 288–89, 292–94, 302

Team Canada '74, 258

Team Canada Productions, 118

"Team Five," 120

Team Sweden, 5

"Team Ugly," 238

Teutonic Knights, ix

Thatcher, Margaret, 259

"Third Rome," x

Thompson, Wendy, 271

Tikhonov, Viktor, 297

Time Canada, 71, 99, 226, 237, 238, 257

Tolstoy, Leo, 39

Toronto, 2, 4, 9, 15, 17, 20, 22, 24, 28, 41, 93, 107, 117, 120–21, 127, 132, 134, 145, 151, 159, 161, 168, 171–72, 174, 178, 181, 198, 204, 232, 239, 252, 264, 267–68, 272, 286, 292–93, 295, 304

Toronto Argonauts, 19

Toronto Daily Star, 16, 126, 178

Toronto Maple Leafs, 16, 51, 53, 106, 117, 121, 139, 176, 215, 250, 295

Toronto Marlies, 18, 19

Toronto Telegram, 51

Trans-Siberian Railway, xi

Tremblay, J.C., 117, 160, 257